SMALL REVOLUTIONARIES

SMALL REVOLUTIONARIES

PARTICIPATION OF CHILDREN AND YOUTH IN THE VIETNAM WAR

MAI ANH NGUYEN

SOUTHEAST ASIA PROGRAM PUBLICATIONS
AN IMPRINT OF CORNELL UNIVERSITY PRESS
Ithaca and London

Southeast Asia Program Publications Editorial Board

Mahinder Kingra (ex officio)
Thak Chaloemtiarana
Chiara Formichi
Tamara Loos
Andrew Willford

Copyright © 2025 by Mai Anh Nguyen

All rights reserved. Except for brief quotations in a review, this book, or parts thereof, must not be reproduced in any form without permission in writing from the publisher. For information, address Cornell University Press, Sage House, 512 East State Street, Ithaca, New York 14850. Visit our website at cornellpress.cornell.edu.

First published 2025 by Cornell University Press

Librarians: A CIP catalog record for this book is available from the Library of Congress.

ISBN 9781501783951 (hardcover)
ISBN 9781501783968 (paperback)
ISBN 9781501783975 (pdf)
ISBN 9781501783982 (epub)

GPSR EU contact: Sam Thornton, Mare Nostrum Group B.V., Mauritskade 21D, 1091 GC, Amsterdam, NL, gpsr@mare-nostrum.co.uk.

To young people, everywhere

Contents

List of Abbreviations viii

Introduction — 1

1. Vietnam's Wars: A Timeline — 23
2. Vietnam in Historical and Social Context, 1955–1975 — 41
3. "You Would Do the Same": Mobilization and Recruitment of Small Revolutionaries — 68
4. "If Everyone Can Do It, I Can Do It Too": Serving in the War — 98
5. "My Country Is Still Poor, but I Will Persevere": The Return to Civilian Life — 129

Conclusion — 156

Acknowledgments 173
Notes 175
References 177
Index 203

Abbreviations

CPV Communist Party of Vietnam
DRV Democratic Republic of Vietnam
GVN Government of Vietnam
NLF National Liberation Front
PAVN People's Army of Vietnam
RVN Republic of Vietnam

SMALL REVOLUTIONARIES

Introduction

In summer 2016, on a warm and bustling morning in a central Vietnamese city, I jolted awake to the sound of my phone ringing at 7 a.m. It was one of my local contacts. "You have a visitor. She's waiting for you downstairs—for the interview," they explained. I had been staying in a modest hotel for fieldwork, and in a city like this, still being asleep at 7 a.m. was considered unacceptably late. I do not remember if I had time to properly wash my face or prepare tea for the visitor—my only thought was to rush downstairs. I could not keep her waiting.

This is how I met Hong. She had such a warm and welcoming personality that my anxieties about keeping her waiting disappeared quickly. As we sat at my hotel room table and drank tea, Hong told me that she was the first person in her province to volunteer to join the communist military struggle against the United States and their allies in Southern Vietnam. She was sixteen at the time. Her father didn't want to let her go but eventually agreed, on the condition that she did not desert and completed her mission without running away.

Her father's worries were well-grounded: work was hard and physically demanding. Prior to her official enlistment, when she was as young as twelve, Hong had already interacted with local guerrillas. She helped them by buying small tools such as knitting materials for warm clothes, delivering secret messages, sometimes assisting with cooking, and digging secret tunnels in her village. Joining the military operations was different, however. Hong and her comrades climbed mountains, carried items weighing as much as thirty kilograms, and nursed injured soldiers. Every morning, she tended to and cleaned their wounds, which were sometimes so rotten that maggots were crawling all over the place. Some people burned their bodies, face, eyes. The smell was unbearable. She and her unit were also very hungry: because of frequent bombing raids and the need to relocate (or sometimes not being able to set fires) to keep their locations secret, they did not have adequate access to food. She would go days without eating.

"And then," Hong continued, "There were B52 bombing raids." During one of these, she and her unit were playing cards in a stone cave. Heavy bombs rained down on the village where they were based. Everything "bounced all over the place, up and down. It was more like a circus; we weren't even humans anymore." She hit her head, blood spilling everywhere. Her comrades transported her to the hospital, where the doctor told them that if they had arrived only fifteen minutes later, she wouldn't be alive anymore. When she was conscious again, she found out that nothing in that village survived—no trees, no houses. The US-supported counterinsurgency forces aimed to flatten the village completely. A few people in her unit died. Had the unit not been in a stone cave, *everyone* would have faced the same fate.

Hong had many tragic stories to recount, all firsthand experiences with brutal counterinsurgency and the consequences of serving in wartorn locations. Yet she also laced these stories with a sense of empathy and humanity. For example, she admitted that tending to wounded fighters was so difficult that she probably wouldn't be able to do it in her normal life; what kept her going was compassion for the people who were enduring even more pain and hardship. She empathized with the wounded guerrillas so much that she cried.

She also liked singing and dancing. Whenever she could, she would sing to cheer up her unit. She liked playing and having fun with her comrades. Sometimes, they joked and played cards, and she recounted being particularly grumpy whenever she lost against stronger players. They kept a sense of optimism and love for each other; even during the hardest moments, she never felt lonely. In the end, she concluded: "My country is always in my heart."

I collected similar interviews across Vietnam. Forty people shared their stories with a generosity and richness that I will never be able to repay. These were stories of hardship and struggle, grief and loss; but they were also stories of courage, camaraderie, creativity, optimism, and perseverance. They are also echoed in many Vietnamese books and TV shows on the topic.

I came back to the United Kingdom, determined to do justice to these stories to the best of my ability. However, I was surprised to see that there was little material in Western scholarship in which I could ground my findings: seemingly, despite the interest in the Vietnam War, the stories of Vietnamese young recruits largely go unnoticed. Why had these stories been unacknowledged? What does this reveal about the differing perceptions of childhood and the experiences of children and youth?

And what stories remain to be told?

Participation of children and youth in military conflicts is not a new phenomenon. From young boys going through harsh preparation for military life in ancient Sparta (Campbell 2012), young recruits participating in the US Civil War (Singer 2006), to Soviet "sons of the regiment" during World War II (Merridale 2012), young people have performed a range of tasks and jobs, as messengers, soldiers, spies, and nurses. They have fought in wars, had legends written about their lives and deaths, and have been upheld as examples of bravery and courage. Some are still involved in wars today (e.g., in Congo, Colombia, and Myanmar).

Remarkably little, however, is known about why children and youth participate in armed conflicts, how they experience and interpret ongoing events, and how they navigate postwar life. This book joins a growing body of scholarly work that aims to foreground the personal testimonies of children and youth who served time in the armed forces, and to frame their experiences within an understanding of the intersection of sociocultural practices, wider political contexts, and their own understanding of wars. In building this argument, this book looks at the lives of young people who participated in the military conflict against the United States and South Vietnamese regime either as part of the Vietnamese National Liberation Front (NLF) guerrilla forces, People's Army of Vietnam (PAVN), or by supporting them from the rear (as part of the Youth Shock Brigades or simply running errands informally). While acknowledging their active participation, I also trace how their social environment—specifically the presence of Confucianism and communist ideology—intersected to shape the experiences of children and youth in twentieth-century Vietnam. These forces had an undeniable influence on the young people, and they cannot be ignored if we are to make sense of why and how they participated in the military struggle.

Drawing from veterans' own testimony, I give an account of youth associated with armed forces that goes beyond the tendency to dehumanize their experiences. On the contrary, I hope that this book provides a nuanced and empathetic reading of their lives, one that acknowledges the intelligence, creativity, and humanity with which they have always approached the reality of their participation in, and life after, the Vietnam War.

Children and Youth: Some Definitions

Children and youth associated with the armed forces have attracted much attention from the Western media, inundating popular news and media images (Denov 2012). However, the young people featured within such accounts are highly racialized and saturated with multiple presumptions and stereotypes (Berents 2009). On the one hand, they are portrayed as "sociopaths caught up in cycles of unrelenting and irrational cruelty," inherently ignorant, bloodthirsty, and barbaric (Denov and Maclure 2007, 244). On the other, they are portrayed as helpless, passive victims to whom events happen, rather than as subjects actively and intelligently navigating their surrounding environment. As Beier (2015) notes, young people often have to become victims for their actions to attract any kind of media attention—see the case of Malala Yousafzai, who gained recognition as an activist only after being shot by the Taliban, despite having been involved in activist work prior to this event.

Such representations of young people associated with armed conflicts can be traced back to uninterrogated assumptions about childhood and children. When imagining what constitutes the perfect childhood, a Western, white, middle-class, male child is often cast as a "global ideal" (Hopkins and Sriprakash 2015, 3). This child is understood as apolitical, innocent, transcending time, space, history, and culture; real children and young people, regardless of the political and geographical contexts in which they live, are expected to conform to this standard (Davis and Marsh 2022). Insofar as this deeply racialized and gendered, imaginary figure of childhood operates as a social fact, it is also unrepresentative of the lives of many actual young people. It is therefore not a coincidence that pictures of nonwhite children in distress are frequently mobilized to evoke an image of an infantilized "Other" from the Global South (Burman 1994); of communities that presumably failed to take care of their children and therefore are in need of a savior from the Global North. The presumption of the imaginary (white, innocent) child also results in a dichotomous view of young combatants as either victims or perpetrators—deviants, in either sense, from the ideal (Lee 2009). As Moynagh (2013, 658) then explains, in the case of the "child-soldier figure" participating in roles considered "adult" (e.g., combat), the child is seen as "having improperly lost his (or her) childhood innocence." In turn, such a perception of children who participate in armed conflict (and other children labeled "abnormal") translates into Global South–Global North relations, representing whole communities as incapable of keeping their children out of military conflict, and therefore backward, irrational, and embroiled in illegitimate struggles—thus also justifying international intervention (Macmillan 2009). Obscured in these portrayals are the complex social and political worlds in which young people are embedded.

Such malleability concerning what a "child" is also points to the malleability of age-related definitions of children. The United Nations Convention of the Rights of the Child, which gave root to the "universal" definition of childhood (Rosen 2007, 296), states that a child can be defined as "every human being below the age of eighteen years unless, under the law applicable to the child, majority is attained earlier" (*Convention on the Rights of the Child* 1989, 2). A closer look reveals much more uncertainty in such age-based ideas about when "childhood" ends and "adulthood" begins. For example, as Berents (2009, 3) points out, "the UN recognizes differences and overlaps in understandings of childhood, adolescence and adulthood; and although 'child' is the more frequently deployed definition, it also recognizes 'youth' as people aged fifteen to twenty-four and 'young people' as people aged ten to twenty-four." The term "child" as denoting someone under the age of eighteen (also known as the "straight-eighteen" position), however, continues to be the most prevalent definition influencing legal and humanitarian discourse (Rosen 2007).

The terms "childhood" and "youth," as used in Vietnamese, are flexible. Keeping this flexibility in mind, generally, in Vietnamese, there is a division between *nhi dong* (which roughly translates to "young children"), corresponding to approximately six to ten years old; *thieu nien*, about eleven to sixteen; and *chua thanh nien*, about sixteen to eighteen years. At the same time, broader categories include *tre em*, which can encompass children up to sixteen years old, and *thanh nien*, young people over eighteen. In some definitions, *chua thanh nien* also encompasses ages ten to nineteen. What is more, throughout my interviews, I frequently came across individuals who did not know their precise age, or openly talked about how their age "on paper" is different from the "real" one, and instead referred to their age in terms of different rites of passage as markers of time, such as marriage. Yet when discussing their experiences as members of the Vietnamese revolutionary forces,[1] there still was an acknowledgment of their young age, biological limitations, and an awareness of common traits frequently prescribed to those labeled as children, such as excitableness and mischievousness.

Despite how slippery the concept of youth and childhood seemed to be, my conversations with prospective interviewees make it clear that both the resistance armed forces and the Youth Shock Brigades (Thanh Nien Xung Phong)—an organization which provided various "key responsibilities in the rear echelons" (Guillemot 2009, 19)—generally deployed eighteen as an age of majority and frequently did not accept recruits under that age—or accepted them only after a series of tests (e.g., the recruits had to meet certain weight criteria). As a general or plural group, therefore, I will refer to my interviewees as "children and youth," "young people," or "young recruits" to acknowledge that many do not always identify with the "child" label. They would rather think of themselves as *thieu nien* or *thanh nien*, or simply as "grown/mature enough" (*du lon*) and capable of participating in the political life of their country and community. The need to share specific contexts and narrative situations throughout this book, however, may sometimes require a more nuanced use of terminology. At such times, if my interviewees were at the age where Vietnamese people would call them *nhi dong*, I will refer to them as "children." I make these distinctions with an aim of acknowledging the breadth of ages involved in the struggle involving the United States and its South Vietnamese allies, rather than conflating the two categories. One exception is when describing studies conducted by other scholars—if in the original works, they refer to "children" or "child soldiers,"[2] I will keep their terminology.

Taking this level of care with language is important for two reasons. The first is recognition of cultural specificity of the notion of childhood. The "straight-eighteen" position is loaded with assumptions about the role, capabilities, and "proper" place of young people in society; prior to the age of majority, children are still seen as "irrational incompetents in need of protection and separation from the adult world" (Berents 2009, 5). Academic research focused on children and youth in military conflicts has repeatedly questioned this representation and pointed out that simplified categorizations obscure voices of children and youth and the variety of their experiences (Tabak 2020; Hart 2006; Macmillan 2009; Rosen 2005). As Podder (2011, 143) has argued, while the biological immaturity of young people is "undeniable," the expectations and social perceptions of children and youth are culturally and geographically specific. To understand the lives of young people, this specificity needs to be taken seriously.

Second, using the terms "children and youth" or "young people" still acknowledges that regardless of whether my interviewees identified as children at the time, they still had to navigate a terrain where their actions were constrained by other people's (i.e., adults') perceptions of their capabilities. As Wyness (2006) explains, adults produce children as social and cultural subjects. In Vietnam, there was still a general societal sense of separation between who was perceived as a child/young person and as an adult. Inevitably, this perception influenced young recruits' experiences and constrained them within specific hierarchies and power relations. Although someone who was recruited at nine would have a very different experience from someone who was recruited at seventeen, they all shared feature of "young-ness," as Berents has put it (2009, 16). The childhood of many of my interviewees is a particular social construction of mid-twentieth-century wartime Vietnam. Being specific with my language, therefore, allows me to draw direct comparisons between the stories that my interviewees told me and the stereotypical image of the figure of the young combatant frequently adopted by the advocates of the "straight-eighteen" position. Moreover, using the term "children and young people" allows me to simultaneously acknowledge the malleability of these definitions and respect the self-perceptions of my interviewees. It is also particularly useful when talking about the experiences of recruits after they returned from the battlefield, as many of my interviewees were over eighteen by the time the war ended. In turn, it fits with definitions of childhood and youth as social constructions that are shaped by specific cultural and geographical environment.

Children and Youth as Social Actors

Informed by the awareness that young people (including those who are involved in military struggles) are important political actors in their own right and their experiences are shaped by culture and history, important research by academics, ethnographers, and childhood studies scholars demonstrates that young people's participation in armed conflict cannot be reduced to passive victimhood. Rather, there needs to be a sensitive reading of their experiences, intertwined with an acknowledgment of their agency, internal complex worlds, and the political and social processes in which they are embedded.

While children and youth can be seen as victims in war, "war victimizes everyone" (Podder 2011, 146). Similarly, D'Costa, Huynh, and Lee-Koo (2015, 34) confirm that "there is no escaping" the notion that children and youth are victims of conflict, like all civilians. Their experiences are complex and do not always fit the "perfect victim" label. Young people can be traumatized by violence, but they also display impressive amounts of resilience to hardship (Cortes and Buchanan 2007). They can be affected by ongoing wars, but they can also play an important role in affecting the wars' outcomes, often choosing to fight "with their eyes open" (Peters and Richards 1998, 183; also see Drumbl 2012). They can display empathy and care for each other, thus contradicting the common representation of children and youth associated with armed forces as "killing machines." Engaging with the phenomenon of children in wars also helps to dispel common myths about them. For example, Tynes (2018) addresses some of these: poverty is associated with armed conflict, but not necessarily the participation of children and youth in it; not all children who participate in armed groups are drugged; and, more important, they are a global (not just "African") phenomenon that shapes, and is shaped by, ongoing cultural constructs.

Berents (2009, n.p.) states that it is "obvious" that children "challenge the dominant discourse's understanding of children as passive, incomplete adults who are dependent, irrational beings." She describes child soldiers as "rationally and independently" looking to change their lives. Rosen (2005, 133) further confirms these sentiments, stating that "children, even young ones, are far more sophisticated, knowledgeable, rational, and skillful than is assumed." Instances such as the peace activism movement organized by Colombian children have shown that recognizing children's agency also can help in reintegration and peacebuilding processes (Watson 2008). As Berents (2009) pointed out: children engage with military conflict, both affecting and being affected by it. In other words, as D'Costa, Huynh, and Lee-Koo (2015, 2) state: "Increasingly, it is becoming apparent that children have much to teach us. They should thus be recognised as actors who contribute in positive, less than positive, sometimes unique and enlightening ways to conflict, peace and security. Like everyone else, they should not be silenced or ignored."

Empirically, academic research also confirms that young combatants are capable of engaging in politics meaningfully and actively. Cortes and Buchanan (2007) have indicated many areas where Colombian child soldiers maintain a sense of agency: even in highly restrictive circumstances, children in their study maintained a sense of hope for the future, actively fostered warm relationships with other children, and refused to dehumanize the enemy, thus maintaining respect for human life. Former Liberian child soldiers studied by Utas (2011) have shown a considerable ability to navigate the postwar environment, often using the "victim" image to improve access to educational and employment opportunities. Similarly, Denov and Buccitelli (2013, 193) have demonstrated that, contrary to "being passive or powerless, as is often assumed of former child soldiers, and despite significant structural barriers and challenges," the accounts of former Sierra Leonean child soldiers highlighted their "agency and social navigation in the aftermath of war."

These studies represent important work that humanizes children and youth who participate in the armed forces, acknowledging that their experience is more complex than that of passive victimhood. However, there is still considerable space to theorize and understand their experiences. In recent years, scholars have emphasized the prioritization of marginalized individuals' agency as the starting point of research rather than the end point (Thomas 2016). In doing so, Gleason (2016) argues, it becomes possible to see how children's agency is intertwined with and shaped by wider social, historical, and cultural forces. Acknowledgment of these forces is also important because it allows a reading of children's and youth's experiences that makes meaningful sense of their own context-specific decisions while still considering the impact of the unequal power relations, hierarchies, and constrained social worlds in which young people frequently find themselves.

Shepler (2014) has advocated for the importance of understanding child soldiering in a cultural context. In her study of children in Sierra Leone, she found that children's participation in military activities had a continuity with many practices already present in their lives. This is a country, she argues, where work is a part of being a child, models of child fosterage are common, and therefore separation from one's biological parents is not a unique or shocking phenomenon. Therefore, for the vast majority of child combatants in Sierra Leone, the duties they carried out remained within a familiar framework. Pauletto and Patel (2010) have similarly critiqued a lack of understanding of the cultural context within which child soldiering in the Congo has taken place, pointing out that childhood is often believed to be closely connected to witchcraft and magical abilities, which in turn leads many children to leave their homes and join armed groups. Coulter (2008), while acknowledging that girl soldiers in Sierra Leone made active choices, points out that these choices need to be seen as shaped by convention, religion, and other social relations in which these girls were embedded. Groups such as the Islamic State of Iraq and Syria (ISIS) employ complex methods of socializing children (from public events to "meet-and-greets"), as well as leveraging structural conditions such as poverty (Bloom 2019).

Further work has explored child soldiers in the Soviet Union (Kucherenko 2011), the Philippines (Özerdem, Podder, and Quitoriano 2010), and Sierra Leone (Zack-Williams 2001). While Kucherenko (2011) highlights how Soviet political indoctrination encouraged children to become patriots by surrendering their individuality for the larger revolutionary project, Özerdem, Podder, and Quitoriano (2010, 313) emphasize that child soldiers were driven not by economic motivations but by a sense of duty to family and community. All these studies acknowledge the intelligence and agency of children and youth, as well as their broader political and social contexts. Such an approach has theoretical and practical implications. Theoretically, as Gleason (2016) further argues, viewing agency as contextual and relational allows researchers to engage in a more nuanced exploration of how shifting cultural constructs and power dynamics shape children's lifeworlds. On a practical level, as Wessells (2019) emphasizes, to humanize children and youth associated with armed forces and provide adequate resources for their reintegration into society, there is a need to place their experiences in a complex historical and cultural context.

While multiple ways out of the agency trap are being proposed, perhaps the most common framework is the relational one. Within this framework, agency and structure (the objective environment where young people are located) are seen as mutually co-constitutive of each other. The literature that I align with contests the idea of young people as passive victims, but it also questions the notion of them being completely autonomous, rational agents. Instead, they are neither: like all social actors, they are simultaneously constrained by and are capable of transforming structures around them. Acknowledging these constraints does not automatically label young people as victims—there are still many "in-betweens." It is thus more fruitful to address the experiences of children and youth as interactions among different agents, environmental factors, and complex internalized attitudes. I build further on these studies next, with the help of a Bourdieusian analytical framework.

A Relational Approach

In line with recent critical research, I have employed a relational approach as my conceptual framework. From this perspective, decisions to participate in armed conflict are theorized as a product of history and the societal context within which violence takes place. Within this ontology, agency becomes more than a property that "breathes life" into passive objects (Emirbayer 1997, 294), as is often the case with young people. Rather, Emirbayer sees it as inseparable from concrete situations—agency is conceptualized as an engagement *toward* something—events, places, or people. This perspective helps to frame actions not as "good" or "bad" because they are not presumed or given; rather, actions are evaluated as consequences of actors' engagement with one another, often in uncertain and difficult circumstances (Emirbayer 1997, 309).

In mobilizing the relational approach to understanding participation of children and youth in the Vietnamese military conflict, I rely on Bourdieu's (1990, 13) notion of habitus as "a system of acquired dispositions" (thoughts, beliefs, and values), influenced by conditions such as social class or cultural trajectory, which organize and predispose individuals to action. Bourdieu (1998, viii) also opposed the idea that actors are simple "epiphenomena of structure." For him, people may not always be rational, but they are *reasonable*. He makes space for factors that go beyond rational calculations, such as desires (sometimes subconscious) or a collective sense of what is simply "done," yet hardly articulated. This sort of reasoning, he argues, is possible *precisely because* actors have internalized objective conditions and learned to navigate them subconsciously. Bourdieu (2000) compares this process to that of a composer constrained by the keys available on the keyboard; yet he does not question the creativity and the autonomy of the composer.

The formation of habitus is a lifelong process (Bourdieu 1990, 86), a product of childhood experience and socialization, which is why habitus can also be described as "a complex interplay between past and present" (Reay 2004, 434). Socialization, education, and other social forces shape individuals' habitus and with time, actors internalize ways of understanding the world, patterns, and principles of social contexts that surround them, to the point where they intuitively understand the constraints of (or opportunities to adapt to) the social, cultural, and material conditions—"intentionality without intention, the knowledge without cognitive intent, the prereflective, infraconscious mastery that agents acquire of their social world by way of durable immersion within it" (Bourdieu and Wacquant 1992, 19). Through habitus, past experiences constantly affect present social practices, regulating them into a constancy stronger than explicit rules and norms (Bourdieu 1992, 54).

Habitus is durable but always changing through its continuous dialogue with the *field*: social space in which actors and their relations are positioned. Bourdieu uses the analogy of a football field to describe actors' "feel for the game" (Bourdieu and Wacquant 1992, 223). Players understand the rules very well and can, without being aware of it, predict possible outcomes or consequences of their actions. In his study of youth entering gangs, Baird (2011, 254) quotes one interview subject: "You don't dream of packing biscuits in a factory," which reflects the constraints of the fields in which the youth grew up. Given its influence on actions, understanding the field (e.g., the field of war) is vital to understanding the courses of action that people take. Within the field, actors are struggling for capital. Bourdieu (1986) differentiates between economic capital (material assets), symbolic capital (honor and prestige), and social capital (affiliations and networks, family, religious and cultural heritage).

Influenced by Bourdieu's thinking, the relational approach that I take in this book allows me to demonstrate that actions, while partially shaped by rationality and autonomous choice, are also constructed by social environment and historical dispositions (Csernatoni 2012, 212). The thoughts and actions of children and youth are influenced by their social environment but are not entirely predetermined by them.

Young People Associated with Vietnamese Liberation Forces

The Vietnamese military struggle involving the United States and its allies presents fruitful empirical grounds for investigating the phenomenon of children and youth engaging in military struggles. Depending on the source, the conflict can be conceptualized as lasting for almost two decades,[3] inevitably transforming social contexts in villages and cities. The extent to which the war shaped the everyday experiences of various Vietnamese communities has already been explored extensively. For example, Jamieson (1995) presents a thorough investigation of the transformation of Vietnamese society in both rural and urban settings as it encountered the West, colonialism, and communism. Pham (1999) traces changes in the Vietnamese family resulting from the country's history with war and guerrilla warfare. These works make it clear that the conflict presented a complicated interweaving of various social forces, including colonialism, the impact of the Cold War, communism, and religion. Yet even these detailed studies make almost no mention of how Vietnamese military conflicts affected children and youth, how young people responded to the ongoing events around them, and how the war shaped their choices and courses of action.

It is important to note that in Vietnam, children's and youth's participation in the revolutionary struggle was not rare. Within Vietnamese society, their role in the conflict is widely recognized to this day. Multiple books and memoirs, written by people who served as children and as teenagers, have been published in Vietnamese. For example, the book *Đội Thiếu Niên Du Kích Đình Bảng* (Children's Guerrilla Team of Dinh Bang), written by Xuan Sach (2012) in 1966, is particularly well known. It was also adapted into a TV show funded by a local People's Committee. *Tuổi Thơ Dữ Dội* (Violent Childhood), written by Phung Quan (2018) and published in 1988, is similarly a well-known book about children's work as spies and recons during the Vietnamese struggle against the French. Both books are based on real people and events. Indeed, many people formerly associated with what they perceived as the revolution are proud of having participated in and contributed to it at such a young age. For example, in the documentary *Truong Son Mot Thoi Con Gai* (Truong Son—a Time of Girlhood), produced by Quoc Phong TV (a Vietnamese channel exclusively dedicated to issues of national security, defense, and politics), several women cheerfully report that they were "not of age," but nevertheless volunteered to join the military struggle at fifteen or sixteen years old. In general, the history of these young fighters is known and openly discussed in Vietnamese society—notably, documentaries about them have been produced and approved by national television, which also indicates the lack of stigma accompanying young people's revolutionary activities. The limited focus on children and youth associated with Vietnamese armed conflicts in Western academic literature, however, does not reflect the empirical significance and commonly accepted knowledge in Vietnam of their participation.

This is not to say that there has been *no* acknowledgment of young people participating in the Vietnam War in Western academic literature. Children and youth sometimes appear in dedicated chapters within books that focus on women—for example, Taylor's (1999) chapter "Youth at War" in *Vietnamese Women at War*, and Stur's (2011) analysis of weaponizing the child as a propaganda tool in *Beyond Combat: Women and Gender in the Vietnam War Era*. Taylor's work is enlightening with regard to the specific tasks that young people carried out and highlights that participating in the military struggle with guerrillas quite often went beyond combat duties. In Taylor's chapter, she notes that young girls performed essential tasks behind the lines: carrying heavy loads containing food and weapons or gathering information on the location of the enemy (espionage, she notes, is one area in which children particularly excelled).

More recently, several scholars have offered theoretically nuanced conceptualizations of children's and youth's participation in Vietnamese military conflicts. Hynd (2020), for example, adopts a generational lens. Similar to many scholars mentioned previously, she argues that the recruitment of children and youth should not automatically be presumed to be a consequence of the evil of adults; rather, it should be understood in the context of "wider mobilization of youth and the generational hierarchies that shaped independence struggles" (Hynd 2020, 685). She demonstrates that children and youth are a legitimate category of analysis, with their own grievances, motivations, and set of experiences. Guillemot (2009) offers an important and comprehensive overview of the Youth Shock Brigades. Tracing the history and context of this organization's establishment, he argues that these youths were neither heroes nor exploited victims, but simply "individuals absorbed by an inhuman human task" (Guillemot 2009, 30). The third approach, proposed by Huynh (2015), emphasizes the importance of engaging with cultural factors that predisposed children and youth to volunteer and support guerrilla forces. Investigating the life of a former Viet Minh child soldier, Huynh finds that stories were a particularly important cultural element shaping his decisions. Citing that "Vietnam is and always has been one of the most intensely literary civilizations on the face of the planet," he focuses his analysis on stories and legends about past fighters and martyrs, which are an inseparable part of Vietnamese culture (Huynh 2015, 144). These stories were especially powerful because, as Huynh (2015, 156) argues, "they encase in cultural amber a sense of national innocence and pride that is threatened by foreign aggression and protected by the sacrifices—violent if need be—of youth."

Vietnamese childhood was also shaped by two social forces: communism and Confucianism. Certain Confucian social practices, such as filial piety and the notion of duty, shaped cultural expectations for Vietnamese children and youth and became an essential part of their everyday lives. In addition, revolutionary armed forces strategically launched an "all-people" mobilization campaign in Vietnam, and their recruitment tactics shaped and transformed everyday social practices. It is important to highlight that the guerrillas and political cadres did not specifically target children and youth under eighteen years old to join the struggle. In fact, there were many institutional barriers that potential young recruits had to overcome—some of my interviewees were initially denied participation due to their age. However, the intensity and reach of the revolutionary campaigns, coupled with deep-seated grievances against the US-backed regime and the ongoing militarization of childhood, led many Vietnamese children and youth to feel compelled to support the struggle. In the messaging of the recruitment and ideological campaigns, the guerrillas and political cadres used concepts familiar to Vietnamese peasants, such as "good Confucian man," "filial piety," "honor," and "duty," to recruit more people. The notion of the "ideal" childhood was altered by the presence of guerrillas, cadres, and their mobilization and message-spreading tactics (which in turn were inspired by a specific political ideology, communism) and was further shaped and changed once children and youth entered—and exited—the military struggle. These messages were internalized in young people's habitus to the point of common sense, something that was simply "done," although not without challenge and complex internal deliberations and negotiations. Placing children's and youth's courses of action within their historical and social contexts has implications beyond the case of the Vietnam War. It demonstrates that youth participation in armed conflict is a gradual process—an intertwining, complex web of multiple forces over time.

Methodology

For this research, I collected life-history interviews, asking participants to recount their lives (including early childhood prior to joining the military struggle) in their own words. Focusing on past as well as present events can help uncover the ways that a person's identity was shaped during childhood and adolescence, and thus provides insights into the development of specific courses of actions and beliefs. It also allows me to trace how important events or fundamental life changes altered a person's sense of self and relationships (Denov and Maclure 2007). For relational researchers, the life history method has been a valuable means to investigate the context in which decisions such as joining an armed group are made. It is also crucial to locate an individual's personal stories within a broader social history—local contexts and structures, as well as cultural circumstances (Caplan 1997).

The interviews took place across various cities and villages in northern, central, and southern Vietnam. I conducted interviews with thirty-two people (nineteen men, thirteen women). I have also been able to talk with eight people who participated in the guerrilla movement in the earlier war of independence with France (members of the Viet Minh). The information that they provided has helped me gain a deeper understanding of the social context preceding the Vietnam War and better understand and frame the later association of children and youth with the revolutionary armed forces. Some of their responses to my questions will be referenced in footnotes. All my interviewees were veterans who performed a diverse range of tasks and jobs, including combat, nursing, message delivery, camp maintenance, reconnaissance, and spreading information about the communist movement.

My interviewees were recruited to this study via word of mouth, snowball sampling, and a targeted approach in specialized forums and associations, as well as through social media. The interviews ranged from about one to two hours. Before each interview, the interviewee was debriefed about the study's aims and could withdraw at any point. The interview questions focused on the interviewees' tasks and jobs throughout the war, as well as their reasons for participating in the struggle. They were free to disclose any information that they felt was appropriate. I conducted all the interviews in Vietnamese and then recorded, transcribed, and translated the responses into English. I then analyzed the interviews and identified the most prominent recurring themes related to interviewees' recruitment and combat experiences. As required by ethical guidelines,[4] the names of my interviewees have been changed to protect their identities.

The life-history interviews that I conducted were retrospective—at the time they took place, my interviewees were adults in their sixties and seventies. I was aware that the findings derived from such a method may not be entirely reliable and accurate. As Sturken (1997, 7) points out, remembering goes "in tandem" with forgetting. Nevertheless, the aim of this study was not to produce an account of historically accurate facts, but to understand the experiences and perceptions of former young recruits themselves. The main goal is not to evaluate the memories based on their accuracy, but to approach them as "forms of action," to be evaluated on their own terms. In this vein, Atkinson and Coffey (2003, 118) claim that memory is not just an individual act; it is also a collective one—it is shaped, and therefore it can illuminate "what is thinkable and what is not, what is counted as appropriate, what is valued, what is noteworthy." What my interviewees chose to tell me, along with what they omitted, is indicative of specific cultural perceptions surrounding childhood and war. In the end, then, whether or not memory is objectively true, it will not obstruct understanding the experiences of former young recruits, but it can add to the stories by revealing how these events were responded to and perceived, both on an individual and a collective level. To further help me navigate what was left unsaid, I employed a "thick description" of the responses of my interviewees (i.e., the context within which their actions took place and their interpretation of it).

Bourdieu's framework, moreover, helped me ensure the rigor of my work in the process of approaching, collecting, and interpreting interviews. His approach encourages the researcher to "listen beyond, between, and underneath participants' words" to understand social conditions and internal logic that shape their responses—their gender, culture, or social class (Power 2004, 858). To do so requires grasping the details of participants' circumstances and background and putting oneself in the position of the interviewee to the extent that the respondent's world vision becomes "self-evident, necessary, taken for granted" (Bourdieu 1996, 33). The researchers should be able to understand that if they were in the "shoes" of the participant, it would be "doubtless" that they would think just like them (Bourdieu 1996, 34). Instead of pursuing hard truths, Power (2004) states, such methods offer "the satisfaction of understanding" (858): "A truth of understanding is a contextualized truth, with no claim to certainty, that, nevertheless, holds the potential to illuminate both the logic of the interview process and the rich, complex social logic of human life" (864).

To achieve this "truth of understanding," I needed to mitigate potential inaccuracies, misrepresentations, and biases. Therefore, the trends in my data were further cross-checked for accuracy in the wider literature on Vietnamese military conflicts; most were consistent and in line with the records of the wider social context and the impact of communism and Confucianism. I further ensured internal consistency by asking clarifying questions and comparing the responses of each interviewee with the general patterns of all the other interviews. Where differences and contradictions were identified, they were analyzed further to establish the reasons why they occurred. For example, one interviewee noted that he was conscripted, while another said that there was no conscription. This contradiction was explained by the different years in which the two were recruited, which in turn reflected the course of the Vietnam War and the need of the NLF for new recruits (confirmed by wider literature on the conflict, such as Donnell 1967 and Rottman 2007).

No study is without limitations, and I would like to highlight some caveats in light of which my findings should be considered. The first is the limited sample of my interviewees. The issue of access presented itself early in my research. While I have set out to gain an understanding of what it meant to be a young revolutionary in the Vietnam War, all my interviewees grew up as children from Vietnam's ethnic Kinh majority. However, many other populations are known to have participated in the war from a young age, such as ethnic minorities. I have not been able to record these experiences. Yet their accounts are likely to be different from those whom I interviewed: for example, young people from ethnic minorities had experienced the additional difficulty of surmounting language and cultural barriers when they joined the struggle. In addition, I only interviewed people who volunteered and stayed in the resistance movement; however, as interviews conducted by Leites (1969) or Carrier and Thomson (1966) point out, there were some instances of desertion. For people who experienced this, working with guerrillas was likely to be a much more difficult experience. Yet, in Vietnam, the issue of deserting is considered to be shameful, thus making many people reluctant to speak about it. There were also young people who chose not to participate in the armed struggle and most likely interpreted the ongoing social and political events differently. Their stories, too, remain to be told. While this book, then, provides an account of an understudied case of children and youth being associated with the armed forces, there are still layers to young people's lives, even within Vietnam itself, which I could not access.

Outline of the Book

The data and analysis presented in this book aim to critically engage with the experiences of young people associated with the armed struggle against the United States and Government of Vietnam (GVN) forces. I will analyze children's and youth's lives before, during, and after their participation in military conflict to trace the motivations, experiences, and postconflict reintegration of young people formerly associated with the NLF, main armed forces, and Youth Shock Brigades. In collecting the empirical data, I paid particular attention to the following questions:

- Why did children and youth join the military struggle?
- What experiences did they have once they joined the struggle, and how did they understand them?
- How did they reintegrate into civilian life after the military conflicts?

This book is concerned with understanding how deep structural factors, derived from the integration of political context and social practices, affected children's and youth's motivations and courses of action. Therefore, I have framed my data collection and analysis through posing the following theoretical questions:

- How do the politics of military conflict shape the social context within which young people operate?
- What role does ideology play in shaping the sociocultural practices of children and youth participating in military struggles?

These questions have helped me navigate and understand the phenomenon of Vietnamese youth participating in military conflict. Moreover, my analysis cannot be divorced from the fact that young people, like adults, are complicated and diverse beings. They consciously and unconsciously navigate and affect their social and political environments; they have their own personal histories and rich internal worlds. All these factors need to be taken into account to gain a deeper understanding of, in the case of Vietnam, why some young people decided to join the military struggle, how they interpreted their experience during war, and how this experience affected their lives after war.

It should be noted here that communist ideology and Confucianism were not the sole causal factors that predisposed children and youth to support the revolution or shaped their subsequent participation in the war. As with adults, young people's participation in military struggles can be influenced by economic needs, coercion, or a desire to escape abusive households. But the impact of dominant social ideologies and organizing frameworks need not stand in competition with alternative explanations—rather, it is possible to understand these forces as working together, shaping and transforming each other. Conceptualizing young people's military participation in this way also opens a line of inquiry into how certain aspects of their social and political environments (such as ideology and filial piety) intertwined with others.

Insofar as Confucianism and communist ideology were two major themes emerging in my primary and secondary research, however, this book will focus largely on the influence of these social forces in the lives of Vietnamese children and youth who fought in the Vietnam War. Chapters 1 and 2 discuss the cultural and political backdrop against which the Vietnamese revolutionary movement began recruiting their fighters. Chapter 1 focuses on the basic outline of the wars in Vietnam in the twentieth century. Chapter 2 explains how communist ideology gradually merged with one of the main social forces guiding the behavior of peasants and elites alike—Confucianism. While Confucianism arrived as a consequence of Chinese colonization, it gradually became appropriated by Vietnamese rulers and spread to the masses. The chapter elaborates on the messaging about Confucianism's core virtues, which one must understand to interpret subsequent actions by my interviewees, such as the notions of filial piety, ties to one's village, and collectivism. The Vietnamese guerrillas and cadres took these core societal values and transformed them to echo revolutionary sentiments, thus bringing the struggle close to the Vietnamese peasants. The chapter then elaborates on what it was like to be born and grow up in mid-twentieth-century Vietnam, examining, in particular, how the intersection of Confucianism with the ongoing war and communist ideology shaped the notion of what constituted a "good" Vietnamese peasant childhood at the time.

The next chapters of the book present analyses of my empirical data. Chapter 3 starts by exploring young people's lives prior to joining the military movement. It focuses not only on the personal motivations that my interviewees identified as their primary driver toward joining the struggle but also the societal and political factors that enabled taking up arms to become a conceivable option for children and youth. To understand children's and youth's motivations, it is necessary to understand the importance of cultural and social practices, such as labor and filial piety. While many of my interviewees insisted that their motivations were nonpolitical, their evocations of issues of justice and equality imply that politics were at play. Even if they did not articulate their motivations in terms of "high politics," they were still embedded in the political landscape surrounding them. Building on the backdrop that I described in chapters 1 and 2, the chapter explores how this political environment became a "structure" that was internalized by youth's habitus, to the point that practices such as participating in agricultural production to contribute to the revolution became common sense.

Chapter 4 discusses the experiences of my interviewees as they worked alongside their respective groups (guerrillas, Youth Shock Brigades, etc.). When childhood intersected with military group structures and the Confucian social hierarchy, this wider political and cultural framework affected young people's work, duties, and identity formation. Young recruits quickly adapted to their situation and learned to appropriate many new rules and norms associated with revolutionary life, displaying proactiveness and creativity despite very limiting circumstances.

In other words, they learned to navigate the new field of military hierarchy and gained the "feel for the game," in Bourdieu's words. Nevertheless, even with some space for creativity and independence, children and youth were still beholden to the expectations of Confucianism, and therefore they were never completely free, autonomous agents. This is particularly relevant to girls, who had to endure an additional layer of structural violence in military conflicts. Young people were constantly navigating the tension between strict hierarchy and power relations, as well as finding some space to exercise creativity and independent problem-solving.

Chapter 5 analyzes the lives of my interviewees once the wars ended. For many young people who worked for the revolutionary forces, reintegration into their civilian lives was a fairly seamless, almost mundane process. Much of this is due to the nature of their participation in guerrilla warfare in Vietnam, which did not require many to leave their homes and villages. Even the recruits who had to leave their home villages were never completely isolated from wider society—by the nature of the "people's war" that the revolutionary forces were carrying out, most fighters were tightly integrated with the lives of other villagers and peasants. Nevertheless, life in postwar Vietnam was still characterized by many hardships and disappointments, as the country was left in ruins and had to rebuild its political and economic life.

My interviewees, as former members of the revolutionary forces, however, still had many advantages in adapting to these hardships due to their earlier socialization with guerrillas and political cadres. For example, they were already familiar with communist policies due to the intense political lessons that they were exposed to while working for the revolutionary movement; they cultivated formal and informal networks to help each other financially and psychologically; and they further received some priority in access to employment and education. Altogether, then, this made the reintegration of young people who worked for the NLF, armed forces, or Youth Shock Brigades much easier than for their counterparts (veterans who had served the GVN).

In the conclusion, I present two main takeaways with regard to my findings. Empirically, my case study uncovers the experiences of children and youth associated with armed forces in a setting (Vietnam in the mid-twentieth century) where the experiences of young combatants have been understudied. I demonstrate that within this specific context, Confucianism became intertwined with communism and the ongoing militarization of everyday life. This combination affected the meaning of a "good" childhood, manifesting also in the motivations and modes through which children and youth chose to express their dissatisfaction with the American-backed regime. Conceptually, I contribute to an understanding of children's and youth's participation in military struggles as a socially conditioned phenomenon. We need to understand the experiences of young people who participate in military conflicts as being shaped by context-specific sociocultural frameworks and political ideologies in order to grasp the "making" and subsequently, the "unmaking" (to borrow phrasing from Denov and Maclure 2007) of their place within the armed forces.

CHAPTER 1

Vietnam's Wars
A Timeline

In line with this book's commitment to be socially and historically grounded, chapters 1 and 2 provide the necessary background to understand the environment that my interviewees navigated. This chapter focuses on the general timeline, while chapter 2 focuses more deeply on the social and cultural practices prevalent at the time.

Although the focus of the book is the Vietnam War, I start with the Vietnamese colonization by France. Doing so serves two purposes. First, it points to the American involvement in Vietnam long before 1955, tracing it back to the US support for French colonial efforts. Such an approach follows the evolution of what began as a local anticolonial struggle into a conflict that pulled in global superpowers. Second, it allows for a deeper historization of the revolutionary forces, particularly the National Liberation Front (NLF) and its close ties to Hanoi. Many (although not all) of my interviewees worked alongside the guerrillas; those who supported them from the rear were still affected by the NLF's presence in local communities, social structures, and daily life. The NLF's history is tightly intertwined with the Viet Minh, the guerrilla group that led the anticolonial struggle against France. The NLF inherited many of the former Viet Minh revolutionaries and retained the organizational structure and ideological commitments. Further, the revolution against the French set the environment in which my interviewees grew up. Indeed, a few of them were already closely familiar with guerrilla life and duties due to witnessing the fighting against the French. Any comprehensive understanding of the Vietnam War, particularly the guerrilla struggles during it, therefore must begin with an examination of the earlier anticolonial struggle against the French.

It is important to acknowledge that both the Vietnam War and the Vietnamese revolution for independence against France were long, complex struggles. In this chapter, I do not attempt to encompass all the major events within these conflicts. Much debate has also taken place over how to conceptualize the Vietnam War; for example, whether it was a national liberation struggle or the result of communist aggression; whether the fighters against the United States and its South Vietnamese allies were brainwashed or genuinely dedicated to the cause of what they perceived to be national liberation; what role political figures such as Ngo Dinh Diem had to play; among many others (e.g., Miller 2024; Nguyen 2024; Vu 2009; Hess 2015).

These are not the questions I will be addressing in this chapter. In doing so, I do not mean to dismiss the rich and critical debates on the Vietnam War, much of which have informed my own understanding of the period. Rather, I am particularly interested in the perspective of the NLF guerrillas and other revolutionaries, particularly young people, in this context. Many of my interviewees were exposed to the NLF or North Vietnamese teachings about the war. They also had firsthand experience and genuine grievances about the brutal counterinsurgency methods, particularly the destruction and bombing of villages. As such, many fighters, including my interviewees, viewed the conflict as a war of liberation and unification of North and South Vietnam rather than a civil war. For them, the perspective of the US involvement in Vietnam as a neocolonial conquest was formative. A similar tendency of how the NLF recruits viewed the war was noted in earlier observations about the motivations of guerrillas (e.g., Donnell, Pauker, and Zasloff 1965). It also remains pervasive in accounts of the war in current Vietnamese sources—as Miller (2024, 8) confirms, "Communist Party historians depict the conflict as a Vietnamese war of national liberation, fought against US imperialism." Donnell, Pauker, and Zasloff's observation that many guerrillas saw the Vietnam War as a continuation of the previous anticolonial struggle against France similarly rang true in the case of my interviewees. Therefore, rather than attempting a critical and comprehensive account of mid-twentieth-century Vietnam, I aim to provide a focused overview that highlights only *some* specific developments relevant for understanding the broader context in which my interviewees operated.

French Colonization and Establishment of the Viet Minh

Wiest and McNab (2016, 8) refer to Vietnamese history as dominated by "wars of resistance against foreign powers": China, the kingdom of Champa, Mongolia, and others. France, as SarDesai points out (2019), has had a longstanding presence in Vietnam (since at least the early 1600s). Its efforts to establish control started to occur in the late nineteenth century, and by the turn of the century, France seized control of Cochinchina, Annam, and Tonkin; the three regions that made up Vietnam (Wiest and McNab 2016, 8; SarDesai 2019). Like many colonial conquests, it was framed as a "civilizing mission" (Garrett 1967, 308). In practice, it involved exploiting the region's resources for profit under the rule characterized by Schulzinger (1997, 4) as "often incompetent, usually inconsistent, and regularly harsh." Asselin (2018, 21) echoes this sentiment, stating that "exploitation, suffering, and misery characterized French rule in Vietnam." Violence inflicted on the local population is well described by Rydstrom (2015), who observed frequent beatings, dehumanization, and torture. The French government established monopolies on salt, opium, and alcohol, and yet the "pursuit of revenue enacted colonial domination among ordinary Vietnamese subjects, associating state monopoly control with unjust exploitation" (Lentz 2017, 887). As for land ownership, Karnow (1994, 128) records that the French systematically "dispossessed" many Vietnamese peasants of their own land; by the 1930s, as Asselin (2018, 22) further observes, the majority of peasants were "landless." Despite Indochina transforming into one of the largest rice exporters, the peasantry continued to live in economic hardship (Karnow 1994).

It is therefore no surprise that the poor economic conditions and humiliation of the local population led to revolts (Asselin 2018). Many groups resisted the colonization; however, the group that is particularly relevant to this book, which laid the foundations for the NLF, is the Viet Minh (Viet Nam Doc Lap Dong Minh, translated as "Vietnam Independence League"). It was established in 1941 and led by Nguyen Ai Quoc, known later as Ho Chi Minh (Katz 1980). The group first positioned itself as fighting for national liberation; their main goal was to unite people from diverse backgrounds (workers, peasants, landlords, and elites, among others) in the fight against the French and later, the Japanese (Bradley 2010; Asselin 2018). Its process of achieving power was gradual, and a significant turning point came on March 9, 1945. As Huynh (1971) and Asselin (2018) recount, the Japanese quickly and unexpectedly disarmed most of the French armed forces and imprisoned the French military leaders. They installed Bao Dai, who is described by Tønnesson (2024, 106) as a "French puppet" to subsequently "declare an independent" Vietnam. The regime lacked either popular or military strength; this, however, created a power vacuum that the Viet Minh were able to exploit (Bradley 2010). On August 14, after the US bombing of Hiroshima and Nagasaki during World War II, Japan surrendered to the Allies (Corfield 2008). The "ensuing power void," Jennings (2024, 85) argues, "rendered the August 1945 Revolution—and the rise of Hồ Chí Minh and his Việt Minh movement—possible."

After the proclamation of independence of the north of Vietnam and the establishment of the Democratic Republic of Vietnam (DRV), the Viet Minh were also working alongside the Communist Party and the Vietnamese army (Marr 2004). As Marr (2004, 46) further describes, the Viet Minh took on various state tasks, such as political campaigning, labor mobilization, and standing guard. The group recognized the importance of garnering popular support (Asselin 2018). There were many opportunities to gain popularity, given the harsh French takeovers and bombardments of North Vietnam. Some examples include Hanoi residents being forced to flee to the countryside in 1947; and bombings of Hai Phong in 1946, which similarly displaced most of the population (Goscha 2013). As Goscha points out, in addition to displacement, these attacks contributed to "a sea of hate which the Viet Minh easily exploited" (Goscha 2013, 228). By contrast, the Viet Minh established itself as an effective and helpful force. As observed by Bradley (2010): in the winter of 1944–1945, a famine occurred in north-central Vietnam. While other political actors, including both colonial powers and Vietnamese political groups, ignored the famine, "the Viet Minh jumped in to help ... these efforts won them the allegiance of many desperate peasants" (Bradley 2010, 102).

Nevertheless, France and their allies (which included Britain and, later, the United States), were determined to restore their colonial regime. Thus, the First Indochina War began and continued until 1954 (Pham and Tran 2024). China and the Soviet Union sent support to the Viet Minh, which included training, military equipment and advisors, and food (Li 2020; Ghosh 1975; Asselin 2018). The United States similarly aided the French, "eventually absorbing much of the cost of the war"

(Ghosh 1975, 19). For example, when the French formally requested US help, President Harry Truman's administration gave them $15 million (Corfield 2008). Over time, then, what seemed like a local conflict drew in international powers and had consequences beyond Vietnam. As Goscha (2010) points out, however, despite the international support gathered by the Viet Minh, it would be a mistake to represent the conflict as having even levels of strength. He continues: "The internationalization of the war might have allowed the DRV to produce an army and deploy artillery, mortars and machine-gun fire, but it also put their men at the mercy of some of the deadliest weapons produced during the first half of the twentieth century" (Goscha 2010, 213). The war, which Vu and Sharrock (2014, 192) labeled as "war without frontiers," also subjected the Vietnamese civilian population to constant threats, including carpet bombings, poverty, and hunger, giving them a "desperately hard life."

Despite their military superiority, the assumption that the better-resourced French army would "crush" the Viet Minh was mistaken (Ruane 1998, 20). This was due to the Viet Minh's guerrilla tactics, as well as their efforts to mobilize the general population, which allowed them to effectively blend in, gather intelligence, and conduct ambushes (Trager 1966; Jamieson 1995; Bradley 2010). The French were often unaware of the Viet Minh's presence until they were under attack: they would find themselves under sudden strikes that caused damage and quickly disappeared before the French could respond (Ruane 1998). Here, we already see some mentions of youngsters blending in with the civilian population but still participating in the revolution. See, for example, Goscha's description of "surveillance boys": "because of their young age, scruffy appearance, and menial jobs—they tended to go unnoticed by the French security services" (2013, 233).

The Viet Minh, then, were much better organized and resilient than the French anticipated (Ruane 1998). Throughout the course of the war, the group managed to increase their strength, with about 250,000 recruits by 1948; liberate some villages; and by the following year, build rifles and mortars (Vu and Sharrock 2014). In 1954, the French were defeated at the Battle of Dien Bien Phu. They underestimated the enemy's ability to bring artillery and heavy anti-aircraft guns and organize the supporting logistical system (Goscha 2024). Contrary to expectations, the Viet Minh and their supporters managed to surround and besiege the French forces by manually carrying heavy field guns up the hills and using them to "cut off French supply routes and batter the French garrison on the plain below" (Vu and Sharrock 2014, 199). The battle ended with the Viet

Minh's victory, but it came at great human cost—Goscha (2010) cites that according to French statistics, the Vietnamese lost about 20,000 men, while DRV estimates stand at 13,930 casualties. Despite this, it was still a "humiliating" defeat for the French, who lost 15,000 soldiers (Corfield 2008, 54).

Following the French defeat at Dien Bien Phu, the Geneva Accords were signed in 1954. They resulted in the temporary division of Vietnam into two zones—the DRV in the north and what would become the Republic of Vietnam (RVN) in the south (Landon 1966). There were planned elections to reunify the two, promised to be held by 1956 (Pham and Tran 2024). Although temporary, the division still had a significant impact on the experience, recruitment methods, and participation of many individuals I interviewed, reflecting the differences in regimes and governance.

Cold War as a Context

As Herring (2004, 18) states, "the Cold War and the American war in Vietnam cannot be disentangled." What seemed to be a small struggle, related only to France and their colonies, was enabled and significantly shaped by two features of the post–World War II period: decolonization and the Cold War (Lawrence 2010; Herring 2004). Taking advantage of the weakening European powers, Vietnam, like many other colonies, sought to destroy the colonial system. However, the anticolonial movement in Vietnam was led by communists—Vu (2017, 104–5), for example, recounts that in a biweekly journal, they asserted as one of their goals "to show fellow Indochinese a basic truth: that there was only one way to achieve freedom, peace, and happiness for mankind, for every nation, and for the working class. This way was through implementation [*thuc hien triet de*] of Marxism." The Viet Minh's positioning, as well as their relations with and support from China and the Soviet Union, contributed to framing the conflict in terms of the Cold War (Herring 2004).

From the US perspective, preventing communism from spreading in Vietnam was a matter of ideological and national interest, "part of a larger effort to contain the spread of communism in Asia and around the world" (Asselin 2018, 6). In the first instance, the domino theory posited that if South Vietnam became communist, "the floodgates would be open for Communism to sweep across the peninsula to Malaysia, the Philippines and the rest of South Asia to the south, and through Cambodia, Thailand, Burma and other newly-independent countries to the west"; that is, to the rest of the world (General Jesus Vargas, as cited in Girling 1967, 61). In the second instance, losing Vietnam would also mean losing a sphere of influence—a threatening possibility in the context where the Soviet Union had already gained control of Eastern Europe and China (Herring 2004). As such, the "dominant US attitude to communism was one of containment" (Wiest and McNab 2016, 25). The involvement of the United States in Vietnam also drew in China and the Soviet Union, thereby further internationalizing the conflict. Both major powers recognized Vietnam as a strategically vital ally, not only because of its geographical location but also its abundant natural resources (Lawrence 2010). In words of Chapman (2014, 105): "Each of those Cold War superpowers perceived at one time or another that the success of their domestic and international programs hinged on their support for Vietnamese allies."

As mentioned in the previous section, the country was split into North Vietnam and South Vietnam in 1954. Each part aligned with the global power blocs of the Cold War era. The north received support from the Soviet Union and China, thus becoming part of the communist bloc, while the south was backed by the United States, reflecting the anti-communist alliance (Wiest and McNab 2016). This division mirrored the ideological confrontations of the Cold War, but this is not to say that Vietnamese leaders in the communist movement were mere pawns in the global superpower struggle. They were "no stooges of Moscow and Beijing" (Vu 2017, 9); Vu further recounts that they were genuinely disappointed by the Soviet Union and China for not challenging what they perceived to be imperialist ambitions displayed by the United States. The communist leaders were motivated by a deep and consistent commitment to communist revolution (Miller and Vu 2009). The importance of ideology is further highlighted in Vu's (2017, 116) claim that while the interpretations of communism by the Vietnamese revolutionaries could have been correct or incorrect—either way, they served as important lenses through which the communist leaders "interpreted world events," interacted with foreign powers, developed their strategies, and, perhaps more important, *sustained* their vision.

I find that this sentiment echoes the general tendency that I found with my interviewees. The context of the Cold War has undoubtedly affected the dedication of some of my interviewees to communism (intertwined with nationalism), and their subsequent understanding of the state's postwar policies. In this context, they displayed genuine dedication to this ideology and a particular vision of the revolution.

The Vietnam War Timeline

From when the Geneva Accords were signed until 1960, Vietnam was characterized by escalating conflict and political instability (Short 2013). After the withdrawal of the French, the southern region faced an unstable political landscape and a weak economy (Bradley 2021). With support from the United States, Ngo Dinh Diem emerged as a leader of the RVN (Lawrence 2010). He described Vietnam as looking like "France at the time of Joan of Arc," acknowledging that the country was "falling apart" at the time he took the position of president (Shaplen 1965, 113).

As Chapman (2013, 6) further observes, Diem's regime can be described as authoritarian and oppressive of all opposition; it therefore "inspired widespread opposition within a short matter of years." For example, he introduced Public Law 10/59, according to which military courts could sentence to death those who commit or attempt to commit "crimes with the aim of sabotage" or otherwise threaten "the security of the State" (cited in Asselin 2018, 116). There was no right to appeal. As Kahin (1986, 98) argues, this law could be used "against anyone who annoyed the regime or whom it suspected of disloyalty," making communist supporters a particularly easy target (Asselin 2018 similarly mentions this law specifically in the context of eradicating the communist presence). These opponents could be jailed, persecuted, or sent to reeducation centers (Ngo 1989; Bradley 2021). Such surveillance and oppression relied on help from the United States, including Michigan State University–trained secret police, which similarly silenced opponents through torture and imprisonment (SarDesai 2019). By 1962, Shaplen (1965, 157) concludes, there were "some thirty thousand prisoners in about fifty jails throughout the country, about two-thirds of whom were political prisoners." This intolerance of dissent alienated many, both rural people and members of the urban middle class (Pike 1966; also Miller 2013).

This period saw the rise of an armed insurgency against the Diem regime in South Vietnam. Corfield (2008) records that as early as 1957, communists based in South Vietnam were instructed to organize armed groups, although he simultaneously observed that Ho Chi Minh urged the guerrillas to lay low as late as 1959. By late 1959, however, discontent among the communist forces in Vietnam over the lack of progress in the south led to calls for a full-scale, armed insurrection (Moyar 2006). For example, the Ben Tre uprising was launched in January 1960 with an aim of establishing a permanent "liberated area" (Moyar 2006, 88). While this goal ultimately was not achieved, the uprising did revitalize the communist movement in the region, and throughout 1960, communist forces carried out a series of attacks and ambushes against the South Vietnamese army (Moyar 2006). These deliberate escalations of the insurgency were aimed to disrupt the South Vietnamese government's control in rural areas (Bradley 2021). The communist insurgency had steadily grown their armed troops and exerted influence over portions of the countryside (Olson and Roberts 2011; Tanham 2006).

This internal pressure, combined with the escalating US military aid to South Vietnam, set the stage for the increase in US involvement and the deployment of American combat troops. As South Vietnam was perceived by the United States as a key ally to stop the spillover of communism, the United States continued to provide significant financial assistance from the outset of Diem's rule in 1955 (Asselin 2018). As Taylor (1961, 244) observed, South Vietnam depended on American aid significantly, receiving $13.7 per capita in 1960 compared to Korea's $8.6, India's $9, and Thailand's $12.2. Asselin (2018, 6) further elaborates that "US policymakers spent a staggering $200 billion—more than one trillion in today's money" on aid to South Vietnam.

While initially hesitant to commit ground troops, the United States increased their number of military advisers and authorized covert operations against North Vietnam (Bradley 2021). At the beginning of the 1960s, the United States focused on strengthening the armed forces of South Vietnam, but did not get involved in direct fighting in combat (Ruane 1998; Nguyen 2012). As part of this effort, they also committed to training and restructuring South Vietnam's army: as of 1961, there were over 3,200 military advisors in South Vietnam; this number reached 11,000 in the next two years (Olson and Roberts 2011). By the late 1960s, the number of American troops reached 500,000 (Westheider 2011).

The United States also supported the strategic hamlet program, "which would eventually become the centerpiece of the regime's counterinsurgency and nation-building efforts" (Taylor 2013; Miller 2013, 222). The program included a deployment of special self-defense forces and security perimeters around contested areas (Asselin 2018). According to initial plans, the hamlets would promote active participation of local residents in self-defense and communal solidarity (Nguyen-Marshall 2024). However, it ended up alienating peasants further: due to its coercive nature, many of them were forcibly removed from their homes and confined to poorly constructed hamlets (Olson and Roberts 2011; Nguyen-Marshall 2024). As Nguyen-Marshall (2024, 340) further highlights, the requirement to participate in labor and security patrols exacerbated general "resentment" even further. In the words of Immerman (2010, 137), "the hamlets became prisons rather than sanctuaries," and "became breeding grounds for the NLF and PLAF."

President John F. Kennedy's administration grappled with these complexities and contradicting viewpoints on how to proceed—as Olson and Roberts (2011) note, some advisors urged for withdrawal while others advocated more aggressive escalation. Ultimately, the United States opted for "incremental escalations, hoping that each new installment would finally do the trick and allow South Vietnam to survive" (Olson and Roberts 2011, 92). Yet Diem's increasing authoritarianism, brutal crackdown on Buddhist protests, and resistance to the US recommendations on how to more effectively appeal to the broader population led to growing criticism among his own allies in the United States (Karnow 1994; Immerman 2010). In 1963, he and his brother were assassinated in a coup (Wiest and McNab 2016).

Following Diem's assassination, South Vietnam experienced a period of political turmoil, with another series of short-lived governments and coups (Corfield 2008; Dror 2018). The instability in South Vietnam continued, and the war "was progressing badly," as Corfield (2008, 73) put it. The 1964 Gulf of Tonkin incident, in which US destroyers allegedly came under attack by North Vietnamese torpedo boats was a turning point (Taylor 2013). The incident, although its veracity is disputed, provided President Lyndon B. Johnson with the pretext to secure congressional authorization for expanded military action in Vietnam (Bradley 2021; Daddis 2015). A number of operations escalated the military struggle further, such as Operation Rolling Thunder, which aimed to isolate the South Vietnamese communist insurgents from support from North Vietnam (Daddis 2015). By the end of 1965, as Bradley (2021, 78) observes, "southern and much of central Vietnam was engulfed in a military struggle the Vietnamese would come to call the 'American war' (chien tranh My)."

The destruction that faced Vietnam cannot be understated. For example, Operation Rolling Thunder initially meant to strike at North Vietnam's military installations and infiltrate the Ho Chi Minh Trail, with an aim to disrupt the supply of soldiers and equipment to South Vietnam (Emerson 2018). The bombings, however, are described as "indiscriminate" by Kocher, Pepinsky, and Kalyvas (2011, 205): as they further point out, "it could not target individual VC [Viet Cong] supporters while sparing government supporters or the uncommitted, even when intelligence was good." While there were attempts not to target civilians in counterinsurgency methods, as Sheehan (1971) importantly observes:

> No one was fooling himself when he marked off those "free-fire zones," and ordered those "preplanned airstrikes" and that "harassing and interdiction fire" by the artillery. People and their homes were dehumanized into grid coordinates on a targeting map. Those other formalities, like obtaining clearance from the Vietnamese province chief before you bombed a hamlet, were stratagems to avoid responsibility, because he almost never refused permission.

Certain provinces, such as Quang Tri, were "basically bombed flat" as a consequence—Miguel and Roland (2011, 2) state that only 11 of 3,500 Quang Tri villages were unbombed. As Asselin (2018, 128) further notes, regardless of the punitive nature of the bombing, northerners "saw them as something they had to endure for no sensible reason. Fear turning to anger stirred patriotic fervor." The intensity of the bombing is summed up by Miguel and Roland's (2011, 2; further statistics are provided by Asselin 2018) further statement: "Vietnam War bombing thus represented at least three times as much (by weight) as both European and Pacific theater World War 2 bombing combined, and about fifteen times total tonnage in the Korean War. Given the prewar Vietnamese population of approximately 32 million, U.S. bombing translates into hundreds of kilograms of explosives per capita during the conflict."

The bombings did end up disrupting the infrastructure on the local level: Clodfelter (1995, 134; also Lawrence 2010) records the destruction of "65 percent of the North's oil storage capacity, 59 percent of its power plants, [and] 55 percent of its major bridges," while Miguel and Roland (2011) note the displacement of population, potential reduction of economic activity, and schooling. The operation also ended in a massive number of civilian casualties, with Pape (1990) calculating that 52,000 civilians died—about 0.3 percent of North Vietnam's 1965 population (see also Lawrence 2010). However, the morale in the north did not decrease, the insurgency in South Vietnam persisted, and the goals of guerrillas remained largely the same (Milne 2007). As one of the villagers reported (cited in Lawrence 2010, 102), this only fueled hatred toward the enemies and "turned their hatred into activity."

The bombing was not the only operation to cause large-scale destruction in Vietnam. Another campaign that caused devastation, still particularly prominent in Vietnamese historical retellings of the war, is the use of Agent Orange and other herbicides. These chemicals, with "lethal doses of dioxins," were sprayed throughout many villages—"approximately 12% of the land area of Vietnam" (Frey 2013, 3). Despite reassurances that the herbicide is safe for humans, Agent Orange had destructive consequences on the health and ecosystem of local populations (Than and Bui 2022; Asselin 2018). Weaver (2010, xi) further details "repetitive occurrences" of sexual acts of violence committed by American GIs against Vietnamese women. In another example, the My Lai massacre, where five hundred civilians were killed, was described by a Vietnam War veteran, Charles McDuff, as being "eclipsed by other similar American actions across the country" (cited in Turse 2013, 1). In general, the commitment to drain communists and destroy their forces by superior firepower has had a "devastating impact on the rural population" (Brigham 2010, 324). It is in this context, in 1966, that Ho Chi Minh appealed to civilians via radio, in a speech titled: "Nothing is more precious than independence and freedom." In the speech, he specifically referred to the US policy of "burning everything, killing everyone, destroying everything" (*dot sach, giet sach, pha sach*), and continued that "they used napalm bombs, poison gas, and toxic chemicals to kill our people and destroy our villages" (cited in Tran et al. 2011, 130).

Despite the massive US military deployment, by the late 1960s, the war still had not reached a decisive end. The North Vietnamese leadership, recognizing the stalemate in the conflict and the growing antiwar sentiment in the United States, saw an opportunity to strike. They therefore launched the Tet Offensive on January 30, 1968. As Lawrence (2010, 122) recounts: "within hours, communist forces had struck five or six major cities, thirty-six or forty-four provincial capitals, and sixty-four district capitals." The attacks came as a surprise to the United States. In the end, the communist forces were defeated; however, the Tet Offensive had a profound psychological impact. The fact that the communist forces had managed to attack and penetrate supposedly secure areas pointed to the South Vietnamese government's inability to control and protect its citizens (Tucker-Jones 2014). It further set the stage for deliberations to scale back American involvement in the conflict (Gardner 2010; Lawrence 2010).

The next years saw the "Vietnamization" of the conflict, as the US administration aimed to gradually withdraw American troops while strengthening the South Vietnamese army to fight independently (Lawrence 2010). Even then, however, the United States continued to support and aid South Vietnam, and it recognized the Government of Vietnam (GVN) as its sole legitimate government (Lewy 1980, 203). In the words of Lawrence (2010, 144), the American aid program "gradually transformed the ARVN into one of the largest and best-equipped militaries in the world." Despite this, Lawrence (2010, 148–49) continues, South Vietnam "remained fragile," many peasants were alienated from the government, and ARVN "continued to suffer from corruption, desertion, and poor leadership."

In 1973, a peace agreement was signed in Paris, which stated that the United States would withdraw its troops from South Vietnam within sixty days and "will not continue its military involvement or intervene in the internal affairs of South Viet-Nam" (United Nations 1973, 7). However, fighting between North and South Vietnam continued. By 1974, with the United States making significant cuts to their military aid, the army of South Vietnam faced critical shortages in ammunition, fuel, and supplies, leading to declining morale (Taylor 2013; Lawrence 2010). The South Vietnamese cities were left to deal with unemployment and rising inflation, while many peasants continued to associate "corruption and brutality" with the GVN officials (Lawrence 2010, 165). The South Vietnamese regime therefore struggled to repel the North Vietnamese. The revolutionary forces, in turn, seized the opportunity and launched a final offensive in 1975. After days of intense combat, on April 30, a North Vietnamese tank broke through the gates of Dinh Doc Lap, the presidential residence in South Vietnam (Han, Tran, and Nguyen 2005). The year 1975 marked the definitive end of the Vietnam War.

The National Liberation Front: History, Establishment, and Ideology

Establishment and Structure

While Ngo Dinh Diem was consolidating his power, the remnants of the Viet Minh were reorganizing themselves. As observed by Carver (1966, 357), about 50,000 Viet Minh troops and 25,000 adherents regrouped and moved north. However, the move was not total—the guerrillas still left behind a network of cadres (approximately 85,000) and caches of weapons to use when needed (Asselin 2018). These regroupees were meant to "blend into the scenery" (i.e., lay low while Hanoi assessed their next steps), according to Carver (1966, 357). Short (2013) and Asselin (2018) similarly identify the initial hesitation of the north to start another armed struggle. Initially, the North Vietnamese government hoped to unify North and South Vietnam through the Geneva Accords that had been signed earlier and reiterated to international and domestic audiences "that the plan of action for the South remained political, not armed, struggle" (Asselin 2013). They also expected that Ho Chi Minh's regime would win the elections to unify Vietnam due to be held in 1956 (Tanham 2006); similar perceptions seemed to be shared by the US officials (Wiest and McNab 2016).

As 1956 approached, it became clear that the South Vietnamese government under Ngo Dinh Diem was not going to collapse or allow elections (Bernal 1968; Tanham 2006). By the late 1950s, Hanoi was dissatisfied with the political situation in the south and opted for armed resistance (Lacouture and Cunneen 1965; Immerman 2010). Le Duan, a high-ranking member of the Vietnamese Workers' Party, went to South Vietnam in December 1958 to assess the situation (Taylor 2013). Upon his return, he recommended the creation of what became the NLF, as well as a "liberation army" to overthrow the South Vietnamese government and pave the way for reunification under Hanoi's control (Tanham 2006).

The NLF was then established in 1960, although there were already reports of insurgent activity and recruitment in the mid- and late-1950s (Bernal 1968; Asselin 2013). It enabled support from diverse backgrounds, whether people were motivated by dissatisfaction with Diem's regime or by nationalism (Carver 1966; Brigham 2024). During the early years of their insurgency, the NLF primarily focused on organizing disgruntled elements of the population, levying local grievances, and simultaneously showcasing their understanding of peasants' lives (Tanham 2006). The exact amount of support garnered by the guerrillas is unclear. Pike (1966) estimates that in 1960 (shortly after its formal founding) until 1961, the membership in the NLF doubled, doubled again in late 1961, and redoubled yet again by early 1962. By 1966, according to Pike, there were 300,000 recruits in the NLF. Short (2013, 262) cites Vietnamese numbers, which similarly place the membership at about 300,000 people, "with a passive following of more than a million." Lawrence (2010, 103) estimates that communist forces numbers made up "perhaps half a million by 1967."

Either way, the military and political situation in early 1960s was volatile and turbulent (Miller 2013). Some sources estimate, however, that by 1963–1964, the group's military strength and control increased significantly—as Tanham (2006, 94) recounts, "conservative estimates gave the NLF control over at least half the population and perhaps two-thirds the area of South Vietnam." While not mentioning specific numbers, Lawrence (2010) confirms that during the early years after its establishment, the communist forces increased in strength and expanded their military apparatus and support despite Diem's efforts to weaken them. Such a turn of events put considerable pressure on the South Vietnamese government and their morale.

In terms of structure, the NLF military apparatus was structured similarly to the Viet Minh of the First Indochina War, with a hierarchical system encompassing full-time soldiers, regional troops, and local guerrillas (Tanham 2006). The ties between the Party and the NLF were carefully concealed (Brigham 2024). Yet, as Dror (2018, 8–9) clarifies, "The Front existed under the aegis of the DRV government, receiving directives and supplies from Hanoi. Moreover, it was constantly expanded and reinforced by people from the North, both those who regrouped to the North after 1954, were retrained there and sent back, and by northerners." As Brigham (2024) concludes, then, the NLF was *both* a South Vietnamese phenomenon while also being under the direction of the Party.

Indeed, at the heart of the NLF's governing system was the principle of party supremacy (Pike 1966). The hierarchical structure ensured that directives from the top (leadership of North Vietnam), including administrative functions, were disseminated and implemented effectively, and the NLF remained under Hanoi's control. The tight relationship is described as follows by Carver (1966, 369):

> Village directing committees have village platoons under their control; district committees, district companies; provincial committees, provincial battalions. Regional committees have forces of regimental and multi-regimental size at their disposal, and the whole Viet Cong military establishment is subject to the direction of the P.R.P.'s Central Committee. . . . There is no such thing as a Viet Cong military unit of any size independent of the Party's political apparatus or free from tight political control.

This structure enabled the group to maintain a cohesive movement and align all aspects of their operations with the strategic goals dictated by Hanoi. In addition, the NLF created numerous affiliated organizations purportedly representing various social and political groups, such as the Liberation Peasants' Association, Women's Association, Youth Association, and others. These aimed to broaden their appeal and involve a larger segment of the population (Carver 1966).

NLF Ideology

The NLF's operations depended heavily on their location, their resources, and the availability of guerrillas; as Asselin (2013) further points out, its membership had a diverse range of personal and ideological motives. As a result, I do not aim for this section to be a comprehensive overview of the NLF. For this book, I outline some ideological features to better understand how they engaged with and changed Vietnamese sociocultural practices. Since guerrillas' influence and operations arguably began as early as the 1940s, when the Viet Minh was established, this section therefore includes the Viet Minh's history as well.

Nationalism was a prominent feature of both the NLF's and the Viet Minh's messaging (Asselin 2018). Much of these groups' rhetoric was infused with statements about the unity of the people, patriotism, and expelling foreign invaders. For example, Ho Chi Minh's speech in 1945 (as cited in Van 2023) directly refers to "our country's oneness" and being prevented from being "united" by the "French imperialists." In the military struggle against the United States, he once again made the call to fight for "our country," referring to the US troops as "*chung*" (a degrading form of "they"). Other materials distributed by the guerrillas, as translated by Srichampa (2007, 91), framed the fight against the United States as a war for national independence, referring explicitly to "our" (Vietnamese) clouds and sky and calling to youngsters to "construct and protect the nation of Vietnam." The role of nationalism in the guerrilla groups' ideology cannot be ignored; as Weiner (1967, 505; emphasis added) says, "Logic dictates that if we are fighting only a military enemy, the war would have been over long ago. But something, some tenacious force—namely, Vietnamese communism allied with *not a little Vietnamese nationalism*—is tying down an estimated 400,000 American troops." Similarly, Donnell (1967) and Bergerud (2010) reported that the NLF successfully capitalized on nationalism by drawing on the long Vietnamese history of expelling foreigners. The calls were "designed to appeal to the widest possible audience in Vietnam" (Bergerud 2010, 265). Asselin (2018) further notes that the Front "intended to harness Vietnamese patriotism and nationalism."

Another prominent theme was Marxist principles, which shaped the ideological foundation of the group. Below is an example of the "Marxian message" (Huynh 1976, 461):

> You are poor and you are exploited, and you are going to be poor and to be exploited because of the existing economic and political conditions; because of the French, the notables and the landlords.... Those who rule over you and keep you poor and miserable will be overthrown. By the revolution you can eliminate once and for all the exploitation of man by man; you can enter into a socialist society, in which you can be your own master.

Hunt (2008) indicates that this message of ending poverty, along with promised policies such as land redistribution and ending unemployment, made the group attractive to peasants; in villages like My Tho, two-thirds of the peasants supported the NLF enthusiastically (Hunt 2008). For Vietnamese peasants, who were used to poverty and hunger, "communism" (*cong san*) meant simply common property, sharing and "dividing them [properties] equally among everyone" (Huynh 1976, 103). The villagers in Hunt's study frequently refer to liking the campaign for class struggle, identifying with the NLF's hatred of landowners and the rich, who oppressed the poor. Similarly, one of the former NLF members in Zasloff (1968) remembered that he joined the group precisely because they advocated against exploitation and for bettering the welfare of the people. The leadership in the North itself mixed "an obsession with national liberation and reunification under communist authority" and genuinely believed in their duty "to contribute to . . . the final triumph of communism" (Asselin 2018, 110–12).

Another notable feature of the NLF operations was the extent to which they relied on peasants in the war effort. Potential fighters were recruited through extensive message-spreading campaigns, and the group made a conscious effort to include those participating in noncombat activities such as agricultural production, digging tunnels, giving assistance at the rear (carrying equipment, wounded guerrillas, or nursing), and spreading the group's messaging. Peasants and villagers also provided the guerrillas with food and shelter. This support needs to be put in the context of the revolutionary leadership deriving inspiration from principles of mass mobilization (Conley 1968; Asselin 2018). The notion of "people's war" was one of the "key pillars of the Vietnamese revolutionary doctrine" (Short 2013, 33). Echoing Mao Zedong's statements that "peasants to guerrillas are like water to fish," Ho Chi Minh (as cited in Mach 2019) declared: "The people possess great strength. Mass mobilization is very important. Poor mass mobilization leads to poor performance in everything. Good mass mobilization leads to success in everything."

To achieve this support, the guerrillas needed to be in tune with the expectations of their local communities. The NLF was notable for their sensitivity to Vietnamese traditions, particularly those of the villages, and their ability to build on the values of the already existing social order to mobilize the masses (Lanning and Cragg 2008; Halberstam 2007). In addition, they worked hard to establish friendly and intimate relations with the communities within which they were embedded (Bergerud 2010). The group found what Opper (2019, 216) called "high levels of compliance, low levels of coercion," further observing that throughout the insurgency, rural peasants were the movement's "most reliable allies," even during times when the insurgents' influence was "at a low point" and collaborating with them carried a particularly high risk. In chapter 2, I will look closer at how the ideology of the revolutionary movement intertwined with existing social practices.

CHAPTER 2

Vietnam in Historical and Social Context, 1955–1975

The Vietnam War, as Malarney (2002a, xiii) astutely observed, "did not occur in a vacuum"; it "had to cope with a broad range of local values and attitudes"—"cultural worlds," as he terms them. In turn, these forces structured the environment that shaped young people's habitus and became internalized to the point of "common sense," in the words of Bourdieu and Wacquant (1992); children and youth mastered their social world by being immersed in it. This habitus provided a framework for young people's intuitive knowledge of the ongoing war and influenced their understanding of how a good young person should act in the case of military conflict.

This decision-making process was not uniform for all children and youth; even in the sample of my interviewees, there were differences in geographical location and gender (among other factors) which greatly shaped responses I received. I therefore make no claims that *all* children in Vietnam internalized the cultural and political messaging and reacted to it in the same way (Dror [2018] further examines the diversity of cultural and political messaging to children in Vietnam in the 1965–1975 period and points out that it was particularly diverse and fragmented in South Vietnam). Nevertheless, this initial sketch of social context, as well as its internalization by young people, provide a useful framework for understanding the patterns in responses that I encountered throughout my fieldwork, particularly showing—in the words of Shohet (2021, 20)—how "despite differences, participants engage in similar practices with similar results, whether with shared, different, or contradictory motives."

To be clear, in examining cultural practices or history (those involving Confucianism or communism, most explicitly), it is not my intention to claim that they necessarily lead to young people joining the military struggle. I do not attempt to draw direct causal conclusions, nor do I aim to justify the practice of recruiting youth into armed groups. Rather, the aim of this chapter is to contextualize the responses, decisions, and courses of action of children and youth, conveying their understanding of what constituted an ideal childhood, what participation in the military struggle meant to them, and how they constituted themselves as "good" children in light of multiple social and cultural relations. In the words of Shepler (2014, 21), such prior contextualization and examination of local models of childhood represent "an effort to understand historical continuities and cultural practices and meanings surrounding children and youth that make the participation of children in conflict somehow legible." These historical continuities, in turn, shaped the boundaries of what was thinkable and desirable for children and youth at a time of ongoing war. Similarly, as Coulter (2008) points out, the decisions of young combatants are frequently circumscribed by religion, relations, and the many webs of hierarchy in which they find themselves. As I describe the historical conditions that restricted and shaped my interviewees' actions, I also trace the origins of the specific, unequal, and sometimes contradictory power relations that they had to navigate and that influenced their experiences prior to, during, and after they joined the struggle.

The approach to culture in this study, which I prefer to frame as cultural practices, draws heavily on the works of Sewell (2004) and Wedeen (2002), in addition to my earlier theoretical, Bourdieu-inspired framework. Sewell (2004, 49) describes culture as having a "thin coherence," operating with a distinct logic that allows individuals within a "semiotic community" to engage in "mutually meaningful symbolic actions." This perspective aligns with Bourdieu's writings, which emphasize how internalized ways of understanding and interacting with the world shape actors' perceptions of what is "common sense." Yet cultural systems are not rigid structures that fully determine individual actions. They are dynamic and fluid (Sewell 2004). Therefore, Confucianism, as explored in this study, is not a static doctrine. The particular Confucian values and practices that I explore here were altered by an ongoing war, the presence of guerrillas and political cadres, nationalist and communist messaging, and rural settings. In other words, cultural practices were situated at the encounter of unique and specific political, economic, and historical forces. Berezin, Sandusky, and Davidson (2020, 105) demonstrated similar complexities by discussing how political institutions shape culture (what they call "culture in politics") and how political practices intertwined with cultural practices ("politics in culture"). Wedeen (2002, 714) further captures this idea succinctly: "In an empirically grounded, practice-oriented approach to culture, meanings are understood to exist within historical processes that are always intertwined with changing power relations."

Culture as analyzed in my study was reproduced, but it was also appropriated, contested, and adapted by young people. It has led to significant political repercussions, such as their desire to participate in military struggle. Wedeen's (2002, 720) concept of culture as a process of meaning-making through practice—understood as "repeated actions or behaviors over time"—provides a helpful lens for analyzing how individuals navigate cultural contexts. This perspective portrays actors not just as strategic individuals but also as participants in collective practices (Wedeen 2002). I consider this insight in the context of Bourdieu's assertion that while actors are not always strictly rational, they are guided by a sense of reasonableness shaped by their field; social practices, in this sense, are a product of *both* wider, internalized cultural messaging and individual agency. Wedeen's (2002) emphasis on meaning-making as a social process—where people collectively reproduce the conditions that make their world intelligible—adds a layer of critical framework for this study, as I analyze and contextualize the motivations and courses of action of my interviewees.

Confucianism in Vietnam: A Brief History

Social practices in Vietnam were influenced by multiple forces—throughout its history, many faiths, religions, and customs (including folk, Buddhism, Taoism, and Confucianism) coexisted, influencing societal organization in combination, rather than in competition, with each other. Indeed, as noted by McLeod and Nguyen (2001, 43), by the nineteenth century, Vietnam presented a "diverse mosaic: its peoples followed many traditions and did not see them as contradictory." Nguyen and Kendall (2003, 35) have further observed, "In Vietnam, we can easily imagine a state official who in the morning places offerings on his ancestors' altar at home, who attempts to uphold Confucian values of respect and hierarchy in dealing with both his family and his office staff, who seeks out a diviner to determine the propitious date for a new venture." That being said, one observation stands out in Nguyen and Kendall's remark: namely, that Confucian values specifically shape the everyday interactions of individuals with their communities. Similar observations are noted by Smith (1971, 20)—"the Sphere of Confucianism was the external order of society," with other religions occupying a less prominent position in guiding social order. Similarly, Phan (2015, 201; my translation) notes the outsized influence of Confucianism, remarking, "There is no element in Vietnamese culture that does not bear a Confucian character, whether it is in literature, politics, tradition, rituals, arts, or faith. There is also no Vietnamese person, even among those opposing Confucius, who isn't under some influence of Confucianism." Confucianism thus remains one of the prominent forces in Vietnam (although not the only one by far) and therefore is the main focus of this book.

Confucianism is a secular social doctrine originating in China, first and foremost concerned with achieving a harmonious society (King and Bond 1985). It is not a religion concerned with spirituality, karma, or death (Cheng 1990); rather, its teachings are utilitarian, covering politics, ethics, and society. It is thus often described as "extremely rationalistic" and "bereft of any form of metaphysics" (Max Weber, as cited in Nakamura 1964, 16). Its core virtues include benevolence (*ren*), ritual propriety (*li*), righteousness (*yi*), loyalty (*zhong*), and filial piety (*xiao*). All of these are oriented toward maintaining human relations and upholding the role of individuals within their families and the community.

In ancient Vietnam, Confucianism spread through contact with the Han culture, from c. 111 BC (Nguyen 1998). At first, it was part of the assimilation strategy instituted by the Chinese ruling and feudal systems because Confucian core ideas about maintaining social order and respect for authority were useful for cultivating obedient subjects and thus were beneficial to nation-building (Nguyen 1998). It was further institutionalized through the system of choosing government officials, who had to pass the Confucian national examination to be able to work. Although Buddhism and Taoism were also introduced during the Chinese domination of Vietnam, the centrality of Confucianism persisted in both social and moral codes; Buddhism and Taoism, by contrast, primarily affected the spiritual realm.

The religions and social doctrine, therefore, were able to coexist: many Buddhist and Taoist monks, "being open-minded and learned men," taught Confucianist philosophy to those who wanted to become civil servants along with practicing their own religion (Nguyen 1998). While the first generation of Vietnamese Confucianists included Buddhist monks, the second generation could spread Confucianism independently, without the help of Buddhists, thus keeping the practices alive in villages. Confucian dissemination was further aided by the fact that Vietnamese rulers would exert Confucian influence and conduct themselves according to the Confucian code even if they were Buddhist (Nguyen 1998, 93). And because Confucianism was also used in state examinations, the elite were heavily influenced by its doctrines. As a result of persistent dissemination policies, Confucianism slowly "pushed aside" Buddhism and Taoism and infiltrated all levels of Vietnamese society, including the ruling class, government officials, scholars, and villagers (McHale 2004, 87). By the tenth century, Confucianism was well rooted in Vietnam as the dominant social guiding force (Nguyen 1998). This continued through to the nineteenth century, with the Nguyen dynasty (1802–1945) acknowledging the presence of other religious systems such as Buddhism and Taoism (and also using them for political purposes), but still ensuring that "Confucianism always [came] first" (Pham 2021, 2409). Confucianism was also propagated through the educational system to reach all people, from elites to students (Pham 2005). Core Confucian virtues such as ancestor worship and filial piety became prominent in Vietnamese peasant life in particular, although the culture still exhibited some features of indigenous Vietnamese practices.

Despite its imposition on them by the Chinese, the Vietnamese did not see Confucianism merely as a colonizer's social doctrine (Kelley 2006). It was the dominant doctrine regardless of whether Chinese or Vietnamese rulers were in power (Jamieson 1995). Some of the leaders of rebellions against the Chinese were Confucianist: for example, Nguyen Trai, after gaining victory against the Ming dynasty, began the proclamation of independence (Binh Ngo Dai Cao) with a reference to Confucian philosophical principles of benevolence (*nhan*, the Vietnamese translation of the Chinese *ren*, or humanity—*jen*, in Whitmore's translation and transliteration) and righteousness—*nghia*, the translation of the Chinese *yi* (Whitmore 1977). In the fifteenth century, the Vietnamese Le dynasty made Confucianism the national religion (Nguyen 2016). It then published a deeply Confucian code of morality and law and circulated books on Confucian values to distribute in villages (Pham 2005). The dynasty enjoyed much prestige and a long reign, thus, in words of Nguyen (1998), successfully modeling Vietnamese society according to

Confucianist rules. Further, Vietnamese people did not blindly copy Confucian concepts. The Confucian texts were consulted by Vietnamese rulers largely because they already had proved effective in China; however, Vietnamese officials tended to ignore the Chinese historical framework that gave rise to the texts (Kelley 2006). As a result, they were interpreted with a much more practical intent—Vietnamese rulers extracted only select tenets relevant to problems experienced by their people (Hoang and Hoang 2020).

Confucianism did not concern itself with questions of spirituality and metaphysics; Hanoi's intellectuals today such as Nguyen Khac Vien (as cited in Tonnesson 1993) thus claim that by the fifteenth century, Vietnam had been effectively secularized. On the other hand, Woodside (1984) argues that Confucianism was a religion in the sense that its codes were presented as the ultimate truth. Confucian rules of social behavior were considered the rules of the universe. Within both interpretations, historical evidence suggests that in Vietnam, Confucian scholars were regarded with respect and often acted as advisors on both governmental and village levels. This influence was particularly prominent during the Nguyen dynasty, when Confucianism reached the height of its powers. As the Vietnamese historian Dao Duy Anh put it: "For more than two thousand years . . . in Vietnamese society, one breathed a Confucian atmosphere, fed on the milk of Confucianism, ate Confucianism, and even died with Confucian rites. . . . [N]othing escaped the control of Confucian philosophy and ritual teaching" (cited in McHale 2002, 422).

From the nineteenth century onward, the French influence over Vietnam increased and Confucianism ceased to be an official state doctrine. This led to competing reconceptualizations of social and cultural practices; however, regardless of the collapse of Confucian institutions and the disappearance of Confucian teachers, the Confucian morality and approach to social conduct were retained (Dam 1999). Indeed, Smith (1971, 30) observed that a "complete transformation of a whole population was out of [the] question; and in any case, with an exception of a tiny minority, the Vietnamese themselves did not want to become Westerners." From the time it was introduced by Chinese rule then, Confucianism entrenched itself and remained the main guiding framework within which practices with regard to society, community, village, and family unfolded. It was never a static social framework, transformed through its encounter with other religions, French domination, and social engineering conducted by communist guerrillas who carried out the struggle against the French. There were moments of contradiction and contestation which, by the time the revolutionary movement emerged in the mid-twentieth-century, generated a complicated terrain that many of my interviewees encountered and navigated as youths.

Manifestations of Confucianism in Vietnamese Social Practices

As Confucianism was disseminated, it inevitably interacted and coexisted with pre-Confucian Vietnamese social customs. Some Indigenous traditions, such as matriarchal families, were completely replaced by the Confucian patriarchal order (Nguyen 1998). Other Confucian ideas were echoed and strengthened by already-existing practices—for example, the Vietnamese culture of wet-rice cultivation had encouraged a tradition of hard work and tight social bonds in villages and communities (Pham 2005). Tran (2003) further points out that Confucianism, with its emphasis on practicality, fitted and blended well with Indigenous Vietnamese people's pragmatic approach to solving problems. I turn now to some principles of Confucianism-influenced social practices that are particularly relevant to understanding responses by my interviewees.

The Individual as Part of the Community

Vietnamese society is often characterized as collectivist, whereby an individual is perceived not as a free-floating molecule but as deeply constrained by social bonds (Schafer 2000). At birth, everyone is a member of not only a family, but a village and a country. Collectivism was already present in Vietnam prior to Confucianism due to the country's dependence on agriculture, as common efforts were needed to cultivate crops (Pham 2005). Confucianism, with its emphasis on relationships, has strengthened this collectivism; as Park and Chesla (2007, 301) highlighted, some of its core virtues, such as ritual propriety (*li*) and benevolence (*ren*), exist "only in the context of relationships and social structures." Within a Confucian society, the individual does not exist alone and thus, by definition, cannot be detached from their relationships (Yao 2000). All actions are seen as a form of interaction between person and person (King and Bond 1985). As a result of this perception, Confucianism has an elaborate code of conduct, with clear guidance on rules and duties in various social contexts. Social harmony in general, and the individual's self-cultivation in particular, are achieved through interacting with others and fulfilling one's prescribed duties, such as filial piety (in father-child relationships), brotherliness (in brother-brother relationships), and loyalty (in servant-ruler relationships). External opinions, shame, and social pressures are powerful factors that regulate people's behavior (Phan 2017).

As such, Confucianism stresses duty-based morality, as opposed to rights-based morality, and tends to encourage its followers to be more socially dependent beings. Maintenance of the social order is essential: "Let the ruler be ruler, the father be father, the son be son" (Cheng 1990, 513). Multiple loyalties (to family, community, and state) are not in conflict with but rather complementary to one another; these relations shape the individual. The importance of these bonds is additionally reflected in the Vietnamese language: relational terms are used as personal pronouns and every first-person pronoun changes depending on one's relationship with the addressee. An equivalent of the English "I" (a neutral first-person pronoun that does not reflect the social relations of the speakers), and even the word "individual," are relatively recent phenomena in the Vietnamese language, appearing only in the early twentieth century (Marr 2000). Moreover, in times of difficulty in Confucian cultures, collective interests are valued above individual rights. One's successes and failures are not one's own; rather, they are experienced by those around them—the closer the relationship, the more intense the feeling (Hwang and Han 2012). These codes have maintained social order powerfully, to the extent that Confucian societies have also been known as "no-law societies." Collective scrutiny underpinned by Confucian values has acted as a disciplinary force, thus decreasing the importance of legal institutions (Pham 2005).

Linked to this close awareness of social relations is the concept of "loss of face." Borton (2000, 24) noted that "loss of face is painful in any society, but unbearable in Vietnam." The Vietnamese notion of "face" or "honor" is not seen as an individual matter, but something that affects an individual's whole family (and sometimes the whole village) and future generations. This is illustrated by a common saying: "After death, a tiger leaves behind its skin, a person leaves behind one's name and reputation" (Rydstrom 2006, 333). The community and family (including future generations and ancestors) can experience the honor achieved by an individual; but they can also take the blame or experience shame in response to an individual's misconduct or failure (Pham 1999). Unlike Western experiences of individualized blame or shaming, "in Vietnam, one's transgressions have both a horizontal and a vertical dimension," affecting those around them as well as the generations to come (Slote

1998, 325). Slote (1998) also observes that this threat of "loss of face" is an important factor that holds society together.

Although powerful, collectivism was far from uniform across history and social classes: for example, after French colonization, Vietnamese collectivism did experience some swings toward individualism (Marr 2000). However, that turn was particularly prominent among the Western-educated elite. Some Vietnamese intellectuals attempted to articulate the novel concept of individual conscience—"a court of law that sits in your own heart," one that did not concern itself with reputation and "face," but with an internal sense of right and wrong (Jamieson 1995, 81). Yet these ideas of individualism never went beyond an urban minority (Marr 2000). Within Western-educated circles, there were observations that in Vietnamese society the individual was nothing, French influence notwithstanding (Marr 2000).

Collectivism was further strengthened in the wake of the First Indochina and the Vietnam wars. Notions of individualism were criticized for threatening group solidarity, which lay grounds for spreading socialist ideas (Schafer 2000). Vietnamese Confucianism, like the Chinese version, prioritized loyalty to one's in-group and family. However, the Chinese notion of loyalty primarily consisted of loyalty to the ruling dynasty, master, or monarch; Vo (2016) observes a similar interpretation of Confucianist loyalty in the Japanese samurai code. In Vietnam, on the other hand, this notion was considered too narrow. Le Quy Don, a Vietnamese poet and government official, for example, argued that loyalty should also manifest in devotion to one's country and its people rather than to a particular monarch (as cited in Hoang and Hoang 2020). This broadening of the concept is often linked to frequent Vietnamese rebellions against invaders. Given the country's political instability, with almost one hundred independence-related revolts and numerous changes in political leadership "from the third century BC . . . for the past 22 centuries," it was difficult to practice loyalty to one dynasty—once lost, Vietnamese feudal dynasties ceased to exist (Hoang and Hoang 2020, 49). As such, the Confucian notion of loyalty expanded beyond loyalty to the ruling dynasty to include one's country and fellow countrypeople.

Righteousness and Duty

Scholars have argued that the Confucian virtue of righteousness (Chinese *yi*, Vietnamese *nghia*) is most pronounced in Vietnam. Doan (2009) observed that while all Confucian-heritage societies strongly exhibit the key virtues, if only one "keyword" were chosen to describe each, China would be characterized by filial piety, South Korea by ritual propriety, Japan by loyalty, and Vietnam by righteousness. "Righteousness" refers to the fulfillment of one's obligations, and thus is sometimes translated as "duty" in English. Indeed, a strong sense of duty—"often laced with no small amount of guilt"—is a prominent feature of Vietnamese society (Jamieson 1995, 19). In the traditional Confucian interpretation, *yi* referred to the fulfillment of obligations in set relationships (son to father, servant to king); in Vietnamese, this notion extended to include a duty toward people who have been wronged in general (Doan 2009). The Vietnamese idea of righteousness was somewhat diluted by French rule and the new norms that the colonizers attempted to introduce—for example, the French-influenced education manual *Ethics in Primary Education*, published in 1914, explained the novel idea of "duty to oneself" (Jamieson 1995, 81). The extent to which this idea replaced older notions of duty is unclear, however. In recent writings about Confucianism, the idea of duty toward other people is still strongly articulated by Vietnamese scholars: "Many researchers often criticize Confucianism, stating that this doctrine only emphasizes carrying out personal duties and responsibilities in their relationships, and not addressing the desire for personal happiness. This perspective is not entirely correct, because everyone feels happy when fulfilling their obligations and duties towards family and society. In fulfilling their responsibilities towards other people, every person will be able to find their own happiness" (Hoang 2017, 12; my translation).

Filial Piety

Many Vietnamese concepts of obligation and social duty—including *nhan* (benevolence) and *le* (propriety)—are first and foremost directed toward family. Principles of family structure and the centrality of filial piety from Confucian philosophy were incorporated; however, Vietnamese Confucianism also retained some of the flexibility that was characteristic of Southeast Asian societies (Hirschman and Vu 1996). For example, Phan (2015) observes that while Vietnamese families are patriarchal (due to Confucian influence), with the father associated with authority and discipline, a Vietnamese father is not like a Chinese father, whose authority was similar to that of a king. Traditionally, Vietnamese families have preferred boys, which echoes patriarchal Confucian family values. However, even in the past, daughters were not completely isolated from society and restricted to their homes; they shared many legal rights with sons, such as the right to inheritance (Yu 1994). Therefore, many Vietnamese families reflect the impact of the nuclear family (like that of Confucian families) but at the same time, they rely more strongly on kinship networks for social and emotional support, echoing the structure of Southeast Asian families. This has been particularly evident in rural areas. A common thread in both these value systems is the centrality of family networks in people's lives.

In the Confucian understanding of the origin of human lives, there is no conception of a common creator as with Christianity; rather, each individual's life is recognized to be a continuation of the parents (Han 2016). Thus, the principle of filial piety was not optional since children were indebted to their parents for creating and rearing them. For example, we can observe the historically important role of the family in Vietnam in the Le dynasty's legal code. It was influential through the dynasty's reign (1428–1788), which extended into the eighteenth century. The code noted that two of the "ten great crimes" (*thap ac*) were specifically related to family. One was, "killing or murdering parents, grandparents, uncles and aunts, [or] in-laws," but another was related to displaying specific unfilial behaviors, "denouncing/accusing, cursing parents and grandparents, [or] disobeying teachings of parents," lying about parents' death, marrying someone, or "having fun"/dressing inappropriately during parents' funeral, failing to organize a funeral for parents (as cited in Binh Phuoc 2018; my translation). Disobeying parents could result in military service, while insulting them could be punishable by being beaten, wearing chains, or being sent to labor in other provinces (Phan 2008). Later, the Gia Long law code, issued by the Nguyen dynasty in the early nineteenth century, similarly expressed the sentiment that "of all evils, no evil is greater than being unfilial" (Le 2013; my translation).

This principle has persisted despite French attempts to introduce individual responsibility in some areas (Phan 2006; Pham 1999), and the presence of the United States in the mid-twentieth-century. As one scholar has put it: "Filial piety is one of the basic virtues; a standard and a ruler for a person's personality" (Hoang 2014, 70; my translation). A child or young person is expected to respect and obey their parents when young and take care of them in their elder years once they have grown up. Filial piety also continues beyond death (Ngo and Hoang 2018), with children required to bury and worship their parents according to proper rituals. Pham (1999) traces such unity and allegiance to family to the harsh environmental conditions and climate. Pham further argues that in Vietnam, there is "no individual in the Western sense, and certainly no free individual," precisely because the person is never completely free of the family, and continues, "While the raison d'être of the Western family may be to produce and support the individual, whose maturity will signal the attainment of its objective, in the Vietnamese family the raison d'être of each individual member [is] to continue, maintain, and serve the family" (Pham 1999, 18).

As Phan (2006) similarly observed, family and kin relations have undergone few changes throughout Vietnamese history, remaining a source of harmony and energy for other societal roles. Political, economic, and societal structures may change, but Vietnamese family life persevered (Phan 2006). Notably, within Confucian societies, this principle is also translated into other organizations, such as work teams or voluntary organizations. These become families as such, and thus the relationships within them are defined by interdependence and loyalty. As Madsen (2012) observes, in the West, family often becomes a voluntary association whose members have the ability to affiliate or not as they please. But for Confucian societies, even voluntary associations, like learned societies or guilds, should be like families—"their members should be bound by loyalties that make exit difficult" (Madsen 2012, 202). This in turn has implications for a person's individual freedom and agency. In Confucian society, freedom means not the ability to join and leave a family or organization at will, but rather to creatively use and negotiate the commitments assigned to them, striving to deeply understand the meaning of one's roles and obligations and to shape one's relationships to the best of their ability (Madsen 2012).

Villages as Units of Society

Confucianism has strongly affected Vietnamese social life, including contexts in which children and youth joined the liberation forces. However, the social context within which my interviewees took up arms also needs to include an important part of their everyday environment: life in rural villages. Since my interviewees (including those who were not part of the NLF) came from a peasant background, the influence of villages cannot be ignored.

Multiple Vietnamese authors have stressed that in Vietnam, villages are the main unit of society, rather than cities. For example, Phan (2015) and Mai (2009) go so far as to say that Vietnamese cities and towns, including Hanoi, were extensions of villages; without villages, there would be no Vietnam. The village is an important point of allegiance for its inhabitants, coming only after family (Pham 1999; Phan 2006); *lang*, the Vietnamese word for "village," itself is commonly translated as "village community." Mai (2009) further asserts that every Vietnamese person, no matter where they are in the world, is a "village person" (*nguoi lang*). The tight links among individuals, families, and villages have manifested in several cultural practices. For example, "Where is your home-village?" is one of the first and most common small-talk questions in Vietnam. Village is the beginning and ending of one's life—as Phan (2015) states, Vietnamese people do not dream of going to heaven, but rather of being buried in their home village.

This is a divergence from the Chinese tradition—the Chinese built their social organization around extended family clans, while the Vietnamese did so with villages (Brigham 2010; Khuat 2009). Further, unlike loosely structured villages in Cambodia, Laos, and especially Thailand, where the members of different kin do not have rigid responsibilities for one another, the Vietnamese village is a tightly cohesive community (Phan 2006; Kleinen 1999). During peacetime, villages gained so much autonomy and cohesion that "the king's word is weaker than law of the village" (Phan 2006, 16).

Phan (2015) also states that unlike villages in Thailand and some other Southeast Asian countries, the social structures of Vietnamese villages have been an outcome of the natural environment rather than a creation of colonialist or nationalist policies. The harsh monsoon climate, with rain, heat, and humidity, has contributed to irrigation-based agriculture and the establishment of close-knit, almost autonomous villages. If a family wants to manage their rice fields, they have to manage the water intake. This means that water has to flow through their fellow villagers' rice fields, sometimes damaging them. Thus, villagers have to cooperate, with village life encouraging mutual solidarity. Every family and individual has to constantly work hard to maintain their relationship with the neighborhood and the rest of the village. As Phan (2006, 20; my translation) further put it: "Due to the multiple relations that merge into each other, the collective spirit of villages is very tight and strong. In the village, the place of the individual is very small."

Common Vietnamese sayings reflect this collective spirit: "Once it floods, the whole village will drown" (warning villagers not to be nonchalant about environmental dangers because they will affect everyone), and "Collective foolishness is better than being selfishly cunning." Moreover, one's success or failure would reflect on the whole village-community, with individuals assuming many obligations and constraints. This is strongly articulated in Phan's (2015) assertion that even if an individual were unhappy with their obligations to the village, they still would need to accept it in the same way that they would accept weather conditions such as rain or sunshine. Some villages even codified the importance of loyalty and collectivity. For example, Phan (2006) records regulations that were used to govern one village in central Vietnam for four centuries (from the seventeenth to the twentieth centuries), which includes not only orders to live harmoniously with each other, but also that people from the same village should help each other in their faraway travels; if they selfishly leave their friends behind, they need to be punished.

Village loyalty, then, is strongly influenced by indigenous Vietnamese sociocultural practices. At the same time, village codes of conduct have not remained static, evolving to reflect the wider changing political and social contexts. It is no surprise, therefore, that life in Vietnamese villages has gradually been influenced by Confucianism at the time of its dissemination. Confucianist scholars were generally well respected and often acted as influential advisors who provided guidance on various occasions (Nguyen 1998). As the Vietnamese historian Dao Duy Anh (as cited in McHale 2004, 88) argued, villagers were more Confucianist than educated scholars: "It is said that we venerate Confucianism, but one has to enter the peasantry to see clearly what the feeling of filial piety and loyalty truly is." By the time the First Indochina War broke out in the 1940s, village consciousness, founded on collectivity and strong Confucian principles, was deeply embedded in everyday life. It was strengthened even more during French colonization. As colonial policies drove many people into poverty, families had to look for ways to survive, which included relying on institutions outside of the family—that is, neighborhoods and villages (Jamieson 1995). As such, colonial and economic changes only made village and kin relations closer. Indeed, life in villages continued to deepen and to change with the arrival of the guerrillas and communist political cadres.

Transformation of Societal Practices in the Mid-Twentieth-Century

Rebel groups reproduce and rely on cultural and political practices that already exist in society, even if their goal is to overthrow the dominant social order. In doing so, they create and align the group's legitimacy with the population's expectations (Podder 2017). The NLF was no exception.

It influenced not just social practices, but also transportation, civil service, and administration; this is particularly well documented by Goscha (2022). As noted in chapter 1, the NLF inherited many features, including close relations with peasants, from the Viet Minh; as such, I now begin to trace their engagement with civilians from this group.

Viet Minh

Throughout their struggle with the French, the Viet Minh guerrillas engaged with Vietnamese social norms actively, transforming some but perpetuating others, in line with Hoffman's (2015, 158) observation that "rebel rule is always embedded in historically contingent values, norms, beliefs and forms of governance." They readily adopted common values from Vietnamese society, particularly those rooted in Confucianism, and reinterpreted them to align with the narrative of the liberation movement. Much of the Viet Minh's skillful use of these concepts, as well as their understanding of peasant consciousness, stemmed from the fact that the leadership, including Ho Chi Minh and Vo Nguyen Giap, came from rural families of Confucian scholars. Ho Chi Minh, for example, studied Confucianism for ten years before departing to the West, reaching the knowledge level of a bachelor's degree (Bui 2013). However, Confucianism itself, especially its tenets on family, was often criticized by the group for being out of date, feudal, or simply not fit for the new realities of Vietnamese life (Brigham 2010). However, unlike the French, who strived to abolish the sense of collectivity, solidarity, and mutual support that underpinned life in Vietnam, the Viet Minh did not contest the cultural importance of Confucianism. On the contrary, they built on familiar values and traditions for mass mobilization, making their consequent victory "predetermined," as Brigham (2010, 318) speculates.

The same principles of benevolence and righteousness already familiar to the public (with the same Vietnamese terms, *nhan* and *nghia*), and indeed already used in earlier liberation movements against China, were reevaluated in light of the revolution. As the Viet Minh saw it, benevolence consisted of loving one's comrades and compatriots, and thus not hesitating to wage the struggle against those who would harm one's people. Righteousness included fulfilling one's obligations toward the revolutionary leadership (or, later, the established government)—any tasks assigned to peasants, large or small, were to be carried out conscientiously (Bui 2013). In addition to adherence to the five key Confucian relationships, a core sixth relationship was emphasized: that between a person and a society (Vu 2009), or self-cultivation as serving one's people. This framing justified joining the struggle for liberation in order to fulfill duties toward one's people who lived under exploitative conditions.

Derived from Confucian teachings, other virtues were given a revolutionary bent. An honorable individual would exhibit diligence (*can*), thriftiness (*kiem*), integrity (*liem*), and honesty (*chinh*). "Integrity" emphasized the importance of not being corrupt ("not stealing even one grain of rice from the people of the country"), and always showing empathy toward the hardships of the people (Van 2019). "Diligence" referred to working hard to fulfill labor production goals, while "thriftiness" referred to saving money—whether it be the money of the people, the party, or one's own family (Nguyen 2009). Someone who was striving to be a revolutionary, then, did not have to go against their familiar understanding of what constituted a good person—despite their denials of Confucianism as an ideology, many of the Viet Minh's desirable characteristics already had "a strong Confucian flavor" (Duiker 2018, 27). The group used their core ideological principles—the power of the collective, the unity of the Vietnamese people, and the importance of labor—to engage with familiar Confucianist sociocultural practices.

The Viet Minh themselves presented behavior that was in line with these values. They knew that Confucianism required rulers to show exemplary behavior; for Vietnamese villagers, leaders who conducted themselves with arrogance and cruelty lost legitimacy. Ho Chi Minh's public persona, for instance, projected qualities of the Confucian gentleman such as righteousness, modesty, and sincerity (Bradley 2010). Moreover, the Viet Minh recruits emphasized the failure of the colonial rulers to exhibit the same exemplary characteristics, which they then used as an argument for engaging in the struggle against the French regime (Tonnesson 1993). Significantly, the virtue of filial piety was the one that perhaps was both utilized the most and transformed the most significantly by the Viet Minh. On the one hand, the revolutionary leadership insisted that there was no need to continue maintaining family as one of the central units of Vietnamese society, particularly once they established agricultural cooperatives to regulate production (Khuat 2009). They also criticized the patriarchal order of traditional Vietnamese families (Pham 2005). Instead, they sought to introduce a new concept of being emancipated from one's family to serve the greater revolution (Jamieson 1995). Recruits were encouraged to leave their family worries behind once they joined the struggle—a good comrade was one who instead focused their mind on serving the people. Historical records sometimes note that recruits, after coming home, exhibited little care for family matters—their thoughts were with the Front (Leites 1969).

At the same time, the Viet Minh transformed the same principles of family loyalty and filial piety into fuel for the revolution. First, they articulated the concept of "loyal to country, filial to people" (*trung voi nuoc, hieu voi dan*)—a revision of the older Confucian principles of loyalty and piety, which usually implied piety to parents (Luong 2007). When the recruits left their families to join the guerillas, then, they were not liberated in an individual sense—after all, individualism had no place in the insurgency's value system (Jamieson 1995). Rather, their loyalty shifted from family to the task of serving the revolution, which would achieve the greater liberation of the people, including one's parents. The revolutionaries perceived this act as the ultimate embodiment of filial piety, where failure to fulfill this duty signified a betrayal of one's own parents as well as the collective (Nguyen and Nguyen 2012).

This ideological stance served as a justification for recruits to leave their families when, according to Confucian perspectives, departing from one's home while their parents were still alive constituted a grave violation of filial piety. The compatibility of filial piety with revolutionary participation is transcribed in the following Viet Minh interrogation, in which cadres asked a soldier whether he told his parents about his decision to join their forces. After learning that he had not, they replied: "Comrade, your words show that you are a fine son filled with filial piety and we admire that very much, but you have to choose between filial duty and duty to your country. In this war the people are your family too, and you have to suffer. If you do your duty toward your parents—tell them of your decision—then you fail your country. But if you fulfill your duty toward your country, then by the same act you will have completed your duty toward your family, because they will be free and no longer exploited" (Halberstam 2007, 92).

As Pham and Eipper (2009) have observed, the development of "national" mothers and fathers—with Ho Chi Minh elevated to the status of "national father"—echoes anxieties about the success and destiny of the Vietnamese nation. But as the Viet Minh's influence demonstrates, although familial and filial piety have been evoked frequently as values steeped in thousand-year-old traditions, these concepts have constantly shifted and changed in response to broader social transformations.

The revolutionary forces in the Vietnam War built on the same strategies of mass mobilization of the Viet Minh, with many overlaps: the same notions of filial piety, loyalty to one's country, thriftiness, and honesty were portrayed as desirable. Vietnamese Marxist cadres who grew up with Confucianist principles continued to incorporate these ideas into their revolutionary lives (Nguyen 2018). Confucianist and communist doctrines converged in a number of ways: for example, the placement of collective before individual interests; the active role of the state (or a ruler) in serving the people; and the prioritization of practical issues over questions of spirituality and death (Tonnesson 1993).

Family loyalty and subordination continued to be an important part of attracting new recruits. Throughout continuous attempts to shift loyalties from family to the wider revolutionary cause, the revolutionary forces also expediently made the family and social ties crucial components for building the nationalist spirit and the liberation movement. For example, NLF cadres tried to make sure that at least one family member from each Vietnamese household became a member of their group (Davidson 1968). They also often persuaded young men, their wives, and their parents to join the guerillas at the same time; if they needed to send letters of persuasion (e.g., in contested areas), they would do so via relatives of potential recruits. Many people who participated in the revolution were following in the footsteps of family members (Tovy 2010). The leadership also used family background to judge an individual—it was recorded in an official document that went back three generations (Barbieri and Belanger 2009). Again, then, one's reputation and future could depend on family and kin history, further subordinating individuals to their families. New Vietnamese recruits were also told that desertion would result in shame or "lost face" for their families—a frequent and highly persuasive argument for many of these recruits (Leites 1969).

Encouraging participation in the military struggle, the movement relied on the Vietnamese familial model to make participation seem less alien. An individual would be "liberated" from their old family, with their new comrades acting as a surrogate family (Nguyen 2023, 22). The group leaders presented themselves as fathers of the Vietnamese nation, while younger recruits were regarded as their children, with those in higher positions expecting loyalty and respect from the recruits (Tovy 2010). Alternatively, some commanders became "older brothers" to their men (often referred as *anh em mot nha*—meaning "brothers from the same family"), which is also indicative of their close ties and affection—they were expected to give each other the same loyalty and support that is expected of blood-related siblings (Lanning and Cragg 2008; Ho Chi Minh, cited in Pham 2018). The replacement of kinship with communist brotherhood was thus not difficult to get used to—"parent-child" and "brother-brother" are two of the five key Confucian relationships.

Life in villages was also transformed with the presence of the revolutionary forces. Villages have been common agents for "social change and development" (Kleinen 1999, 3) and were the first source of protection and safety during the French and American wars. During the 1945–1975 period, this was recognized by the guerilla group, centralized communist leadership, and foreign policymakers: both sides concluded that gaining control of the villages was crucial (Tovy 2010). Everyday life was inevitably affected by this goal, as villages became targets of both insurgent and counterinsurgent groups. The success of either side of the war depended on how well they understood village norms and grievances.

In liberated North Vietnam, after the communists established their socialist government, they attempted to change the position of the villages in society. The principle of collectivity was applied to include not only one's village, but the entire nation. The villages were no longer largely autonomous, with the state's power becoming inferior once it reached the village gates. Instead, villages were recast as part of a national agro-industrial collective (Tonnesson 1993). The villagers therefore worked not only to provide for themselves, but also for the people in other provinces, for soldiers who were marching from the north to the south, and other people who were outside their immediate communities. The extent to which these efforts undermined loyalty toward the village and shifted it toward the socialist state remains contested; nevertheless, the messaging was that "collectivity" now encompassed people beyond one's own village (Tonnesson 1993).

Everyday life in villages in the south further changed as the struggle between the guerrillas and the United States and Government of Vietnam (GVN) continued. Routine checks were conducted by US soldiers to find any potential guerillas residing in villages. Despite the fact that the targets were specifically guerillas, the missions could turn into raids and massacres; the US and GVN officials were often instructed to approach an entire village as an enemy target (Man 2018). It was not rare for the United States and GVN to burn entire villages that were suspected of shielding guerillas, aiming to achieve two goals: deprive the NLF of a source of support and demonstrate their own strength (Man 2018). This meant, in turn, that civilians could be forced to flee their ancestral villages at any time (Wiest 2009). Moreover, as observed by Opper (2019, 213), prior to 1965, the South Vietnamese forces had no presence in some rural areas at all with which to counter the guerrilla influence: "No evidence could be found in Dinh Tuong [Province] . . . that the South Vietnamese Government offered any systematic opposition to the [NLF] at village level or that it offered any workable alternatives to the villager." Although this changed as the war evolved, the US-Saigon plan to control the guerillas thus ultimately had limited success. Although recognizing the importance of villages in managing the insurgency, the reliance on frequent raids, village sweeps, and bombings strained relations between Vietnamese villagers and US and South Vietnamese forces. This is particularly highlighted by a 1964 *New York Times* article: "The reason is that they have suffered too often from destructive expeditions by Government forces. Whenever a skirmish occurs, the Saigon air force intervenes and whole villages are burnt down. How can one expect the countryside not to rally to the insurgents in such circumstances?"

Inspired by Maoist techniques, the guerrillas and local cadres also placed great importance on changing villagers' attitudes. As Mao himself said, "The Red Army fights not merely for the sake of fighting but in order to conduct propaganda among the masses, organize them, arm them and help them establish revolutionary political power" (as cited in Atkinson 1973, 61). The methods were diverse: recruitment and message-spreading campaigns, personality cults, study sessions, land reforms . . . all spread by "tens of thousands" of trained political cadres (Goscha 2012, 147).

The messaging and recruitment campaigns were targeted and specific, and appealed to the villagers' hardships, interests, and needs. Sometimes the methods would be subtle (e.g., spreading gossip); other times, they were more blatant (e.g., setting up public meetings, delivering speeches about the liberation movement, and posting bulletins). Further, campaigns and face-to-face meetings often occurred repeatedly. Brigades spreading messages about the liberation (consisting of about thirty people) often visited villagers, sometimes accompanied by entertainment teams that performed theater, dancing, and singing about patriotism or previous revolutions. In Hunt's (2008) and Davidson's (1968) account, some villagers would go to meetings primarily because of the performances.

Like the Viet Minh, the NLF and North Vietnamese local cadres knew that the villagers expected authorities to behave properly, in line with the Confucian code of a leader having to fulfill obligations toward his subjects. As such, their behavior while in villages was reported to be "gentle, affable, and friendly," always using correct language and avoiding rudeness (Lanning and Cragg 2008, 99). The NLF's conduct with civilians, for example, was based on the "three togethers": eating, living, and working together. They treated members of the lowest social class as equals, which was well received by the masses (Davidson 1968). Bergerud (2010, 264–65) further confirmed that although serving "as physical embodiments of the party's virtue especially in contrast to officials working for Saigon" was an ideal, "it was one that NLF cadres took very seriously." The NLF, therefore, could earn the trust and friendship of many villagers as a consequence of living nearby, dressing similarly, acting courteously, sharing a similar background, and assisting with agricultural work. Further, they drew from and reinforced already-existing societal and village values to communicate their messaging.

Childhood in Vietnam During the Vietnam War

Growing up in mid-twentieth-century Vietnam meant encountering different ideas about what it meant to be a good child or a young person. However, despite the influences of French, American, and socialist forces, the dominant notion of goodness remained embedded in Confucian practice and its values of collectivism, duty, and saving face. These features of the social environment would be incorporated into children's and youth's habitus—their internalized and embodied practices, norms, and values—which shaped their worldview and guided their actions when it came to their decision to take part in the military struggle.

In line with Confucianist philosophy, Vietnamese childhood is based less on rights and more on obligations. Children are considered "little human beings" and invited to participate in daily social life as small members of their community (Rydstrom 2003). As such, fulfilling their responsibilities toward family (e.g., doing household tasks, taking care of their parents or siblings when sick) is essential (Phan 2006). The practices surrounding collectivism also mean that the goodness of a child or a young person is defined by the extent to which they are willing to suppress their individual needs to serve the greater collective good (Burr 2014). Being so integrated into society, they also need to understand and navigate their own social position in the web of relations, exhibiting an "extraordinarily fine-tuned awareness" of who is their superior and who is their equal (Fung and Mai 2019, 285). Much of this is already ingrained in the Vietnamese language; thus, while learning to speak, children and young people are taught that they exist "only in relation to others" (Pham 1999, 23). They learn to respect hierarchy early, by age five or six. Even if young people never received any formal Confucianist education, growing up in twentieth-century Vietnam was consistent with Confucian ethics.

On the village level, much of what has already been described in this discussion of the importance of allegiance to one's village also applies to children and young people. It should be noted, however, that there has been much less emphasis on villagers' and communities' role in child-rearing in Vietnam than in societies in sub-Saharan Africa, for example, where it is commonly believed that it takes a village to raise a child (Mugadza et al. 2019). In Confucian societies, the responsibility for child-rearing has largely belonged to a child's parents. Consequently, children's loyalty to their Vietnam War–era village is less due to it directly "raising" them and more to the idea that every Vietnamese person belongs to a native village, regardless of their position and location. One of the first lessons that young people learn is that harmonious village life is important and communal standards should guide their behavior. From an early age, everyone is trained to consider the opinions of people around them, to realize the extent to which their personal desires conflict with what is best for their community, and to discipline themselves accordingly. Otherwise, they will be subjected to social disgrace (Pham 1999).

On the family level, the significance of the nuclear family remained strong throughout the seventeenth and eighteenth centuries, particularly during the Le dynasty. During this time, the bond between parents and children was notably close and endured throughout one's life (Yu 1994; Phan 2006). Parents had an important role to play—they were the ones who taught children filial piety and family loyalty and punished children if they disobeyed. Thus, young people would be cautious to behave appropriately, in a way that protects their family's honor and does not result in their parents losing face in the community (King and Bond 1985). The notions of filial piety similarly were very important, with children and youth learning at an early age from their school, parents, and peers that "filial respect and gratitude are considered the highest moral virtues" (Pham and Eipper 2009, 49). Children had to bear an unpayable debt to their parents for their birth, child-rearing, and education. From early childhood, the Vietnamese child would be taught to "readily forget himself for the sake of his family welfare" (Le 2018, 172); if someone were believed to not care about their family, they were simply viewed as a bad person or subjected to criticism (Yu 1994; Malarney 2002a). Children's primary loyalties and obligations lay with their families, even if this priority sometimes conflicted with a wider morality as imposed by the state—a struggle that can be seen today in

Vietnamese children and youth who engage in work while underage, which is against the law, but in doing so, they fulfill their obligations toward family (Burr 2014).

Much of these findings about the importance of duty, collectivity, and filial piety were still prominent in mid-twentieth-century Vietnam, as illustrated in an intriguing study conducted by Leichty (1963). In a study comparing American and Southern Vietnamese children, Leichty asked participants to complete the sentence "I like my mother, but . . ." American children tended to add something they did not like about their mother (e.g., "sometimes she gets angry with me"). On the other hand, a large majority of Vietnamese children tended to end the sentence with a statement such as "but I am still young and cannot repay my debt to her." American children tended to fear external factors, such as the dark and animals; Vietnamese children expressed fearing personal inadequacy and violating societal norms. In their hopes for the future, half of the Vietnamese children spoke about wanting to do something good for someone else (usually their families); none of the US children proffered a similar response, usually wanting things for themselves (like a swimming pool). This confirmed Jamieson's (1995) and Liechty's (1963) contention that although the value of filial piety was transformed by the militarized realities shaping mid-twentieth-century Vietnam, familial loyalty and a strong community ethic still existed in Vietnamese children.

It is important to highlight that while Vietnamese social practices required children and youth to be respectful and obedient to authority, this does not mean that they entirely lacked agency. Research on children shows that in the process of growing up and learning about their position in the hierarchy of social relations, children and youth actively engage with the rules through role-playing, teasing, observing other young people, and independently coaching younger siblings in the rules of proper conduct. Fung and Mai (2019, 300) note that, over time, "they come to understand and appreciate the intertwining nature of good morality and affection in interaction and communication with people in a hierarchical structure." This was also the case with many children and youth who grew up in wartime Vietnam.

Such tendencies are more in line with the Confucian idea of "freedom"—freedom, for these young people, may not be manifested in challenging their status in society, but rather in creatively navigating and striving to understand the roles assigned to them. The belief that the highest virtue was serving the family did not contradict the parents' noninterference in their children's life choices, allowing them relative independence (Yu 1994).

Militarization of Vietnamese Childhood

Like other domains of Vietnamese peasant life, childhood was also reconstructed to reflect militarized realities. The presence of the revolutionary forces shaped the Vietnamese "good" childhood in various ways, drawing on some existing concepts and changing others. For example, what follows are widely cited teachings of Ho Chi Minh (written by him in a letter to children in 1961, although below I cite the 1964–1965 version; both are cited in Nguyen Phong 2023), that would be encountered by children and youth at schools or magazines:

1. Love your Fatherland, love your people
2. Study well. Labor well
3. Good discipline, good unity
4. Maintain good hygiene
5. Modesty, honesty, and courage

Several connotations are notable in these principles. First, "Love your Fatherland, love your people" is the primary principle, thus indicating that within this framework, the nation as a whole should be the main object of a child or youth's love. Family and village are not mentioned, representing an attempt at shifting loyalties to the nation and its people. Second, "Labor well" is presented alongside "Study well." This reflects a specific view of what constitutes a good child or a young person: one who not only engages in studying but also participates in production and the economic life of family and community. Combined with a strong sense of duty and collectivity, this might manifest as a choice to work, despite being young, to support families and siblings. This idea of a good child or youth is not rare among the countries in the Global South—for many young people in Southeast Asian societies, childhood is not only a time to grow, learn, and play but also to work (Huijsmans 2008). It is also normalized in Vietnamese society—Nguyen (2000, 94) observed that children and youth were expected to help with household tasks from as young as two years old, and "their task performance made a significant contribution to the household." Even during the American presence in the country, schools accommodated the expectation that children and youth would help their families and work in the fields, scheduling vacations around harvest times. Third, the "good unity" virtue further draws attention to the idea that young people did not exist as free-floating molecules; they existed in a society and needed to cultivate good relationships with people around them.

The revolutionary movement also began to frame the "good" Vietnamese childhood as inseparable from supporting the revolution. As villages became epicenters of the military struggles, the everyday lives of children and youth were further militarized: they were now involved in building bomb shelters, had to bring first aid kits to school, or wore straw hats to protect themselves from flying debris. Neither the NLF and political cadres, revolutionary leadership, nor the Viet Minh specifically targeted children and youth over adults in their campaigns; however, many young people were exposed to calls to the revolution due to the mass mobilization movement. Ho Chi Minh himself urged all Vietnamese people to work for the revolution, regardless of age, sex, or religion (Taylor 1999). Again, this did not mean that he called young people to take up arms—"supporting the revolution" in this context meant that even mundane activities, such as studying well or helping one's family, were also framed as contributions to the revolution. Along with mass associations such as the Women's Association, Farmers' Association, and Buddhist Association, the Youth Association was established. The role of these organizations was to "involve every member of society in supporting the Front" and "promote revolution, inculcate national pride, combat the natural passivity of the peasantry, and overcome the dread of fighting a technologically superior enemy" (Taylor 1999, 13). Dror (2018, 29) further notes that schools in the north were militarized, seeking to "combine academic teaching with practical contribution to the country's ongoing efforts." Consequently, young people became more exposed to calls for patriotism and liberation, and already would be familiar with some activities supporting the revolution.

Notably, there were still acknowledgments that children were young; however, in the eyes of the resistance leadership, childhood was not seen as a barrier to supporting the liberation struggles. Their young age was sometimes presented as an asset, as highlighted in Ho Chi Minh's words when encouraging the youth to participate: "Your age is still small. But small tasks turn into big successes" (cited in Tam 2020). Young people, in general, were recorded to be particularly enthusiastic about supporting the struggle, and their motivations often echoed concern about honoring family and collectivity (Hunt 2008, 39–40).

The narratives around children and youth's role in the revolution were often embedded in the wider norms around young people's work. Ho Chi Minh (cited in Tam 2020) stressed that along with putting their efforts into studying, children and youth should contribute to agricultural production and helping with any activities that could be useful to the revolution. To facilitate this, the revolutionary leadership organized a branch of the Youth Pioneer Organization (originally named the "Children's Society to Save the Nation"). Its specific role was to distribute leaflets, deliver letters, and perform other war-related tasks to help political cadres. A common slogan was frequently used to address the children: "Young/Small people do small things, according to their capabilities—to participate in the revolution, to keep the peace" (Ho Chi Minh 1952, as cited in Tam 2020). Ho Chi Minh's letter to young people in 1951 further demonstrates the idea that children and youth were not seen as apolitical. His address did not make any references to childhood innocence or the need to protect children's "ideal" world. On the other hand, they were encouraged to get involved in politics on an emotional level, even if that meant that they needed to engage with negative emotions such as hatred:

> You must hate, detest the French colonialists, the American meddlers, the Vietnamese puppets. Because of them, we suffer. You must love, love the country, love the people, love labor. The children must try and help the wounded and the soldiers' families, try to keep hygiene and keep discipline, try to study. You must unite and unite among Vietnamese children, unite between children of Vietnam and children of China, the Soviet Union, other countries and children in the world (Ho, as cited in Thanh 2013).

In this context, then, "good" children and youth were those who actively joined the war effort. For example, Quynh (2019) recounts instances of young people gathering leaves and branches to camouflage fighters, or students from Bac Ninh tending cows and chickens to sell to cooperatives. These activities were encouraged and praised, with presents and personalized letters frequently sent to young people who particularly excelled in their tasks. A good young person was one who did not simply act to support the revolution but also felt the ideology on an emotional level—from intense hatred of the French and Americans to love of their country and people.

By the time the Vietnam War began, and the revolutionary actors began engaging the masses in political struggle, social practices such as duty, face-saving, and loyalty to the collective had long been prominent in Vietnamese peasant life. But life in Vietnamese villages was very dynamic and continuously transformed in response to social and military changes. Concepts such as patriotism were rearticulated as the cadres and guerrillas embedded new ideologies and practices within language already familiar to Vietnamese peasants, much of which can be traced to Confucianism. The peasants did not, however, accept all the changes passively (also recorded in works such as Malarney 2002a); while the revolutionary forces tried to shift family loyalties toward the country, filial piety and loyalty to one's village remained strong. Still, due to their influence and ongoing war, childhood in Vietnam became politicized and militarized. The notion of a "good" child was one who carried out their prescribed duties faithfully, exhibited filial piety, and participated in the revolution even through simple, indirect means like helping parents with work in the fields or studying well.

Chapter 3

"You Would Do the Same"
Mobilization and Recruitment of Small Revolutionaries

This chapter analyzes the processes through which children and youth formerly associated with the military struggle were recruited to join their respective organizations, as well as their primary motivations for joining.[1] The decisions of children and youth are best understood in consideration with their personal histories and social environments, which shaped their habitus and thus provide a useful framework to understand why they took up arms. Drawing on Bourdieu's (1990) arguments that socialization affects habitus and the possible repertoire of actions that are thinkable for individuals, I analyze the social context within which these decisions took place. Family, personal histories, and social norms became a part of young people's habitus, shaping their attitudes and subsequent actions. For my interviewees, the decision to join the struggle made sense in the context of their own militarized everyday lives and political predisposal by their families. They were also influenced by the flexibility of norms surrounding Vietnamese childhood, which at the time was not separated from performing labor and contributing to one's community. My interviewees also expressed significant concern about political issues from a young age; even as children, their lives could not be separated from politics. Young recruits were also not completely passive receptors of their circumstances—they negotiated the same social norms that prompted them to volunteer to bypass recruitment rules. Understanding the social norms that surrounded children's and youth's actions and how they creatively navigated them allows us to see young people's agency at work.

Recruitment Processes

Recruitment and mobilization processes experienced by my interviewees varied depending on the year, stage of the war (e.g., early or late), the organization they joined, and geographical location. The communist recruitment tactics followed Mao's notion of the people's war and stressed the importance of mobilization of all citizens in all aspects of the political struggle: fighting, agricultural production, and jobs at the rear of the battlefield, among other activities.

On the one hand, the political and military leadership of the revolutionary movement preferred encouraging potential recruits to join rather than threatening or forcing them (Donnell 1967). They built on tactics such as appeals to patriotism, peasants' hardships, and previous victories over France and China (Hunt 2008). For guerrillas, the most common recruitment tactic was coming to villages, studying the local social and economic structures, and approaching peasants to talk to them about joining the military struggle. Sometimes they would visit a single village as many as a dozen times (Denton 1968). The guerrillas and political cadres also held frequent meetings featuring speeches about nationalism and patriotism. As Hunt (2008, 38) further observes: although these meetings can be perceived as "indoctrination sessions," such wording "cannot do justice to assemblies charged with a revelatory fervor."

The cadres would then either ask attendees to volunteer to join the struggle or singled out those who responded most enthusiastically to the performances or meetings for separate visits, often preceded by gathering information about these possible recruits (Donnell 1967). Moreover, the guerrillas and political cadres were known to be quite selective when choosing recruits, even during the height of the Vietnam War (Donnell 1967). They employed multiple checks to ensure the support and reliability of potential recruits, seeking to foster a sense of trust and cooperation among their members.[2] Passing these tests and becoming a young recruit served as a source of pride and sense of achievement for my interviewees. In addition, the resistance forces had an age and weight requirement that potential recruits had to pass. Indeed, one of my interviewees, Quyen, was denied participation with the armed group because he was underage and eventually had to look for other ways to participate in the revolution (detailed below).

None of my interviewees referred to being forcibly recruited or witnessing forcible recruitment. Only one of the interviewees, Cuong, mentioned a conscription experience called "borrowing age" (Nguyen 2023, 7). Having joined the military struggle at seventeen, he explained that every village was expected to contribute a certain number of men to the front—however, if that village did not have enough men, they would "borrow age" (i.e., families sent their oldest son, even if he was under eighteen). His family had two sons, both underage. Upon deliberating, his mother asked Cuong to go instead of his brother because he was smarter and quicker, and thus had a better chance of survival. He said that he obeyed his mother "happily."

Quyen's and Cuong's recruitment experiences were very different: one was denied entry for not satisfying the age criteria, while another was conscripted despite being younger than the official age of enlistment. The two different experiences of recruitment could be explained by the specific timeline of Quyen's and Cuong's enlistment. Quyen volunteered in the early 1960s, when the resistance forces could still afford to be selective with their recruits (as observed by Donnell 1967). They could be more selective especially in the north, which is where Quyen was based, because the liberated areas experienced fewer bombings and less intense battles (Harrison 1993 details statistics on bombings in North and South Vietnam), and thus the need for personnel was lower. It made rejection more probable, although most of my interviewees also volunteered to join during the same time period and were accepted.

The recruitment efforts continued to intensify as the war progressed. In the late stages of the war, when Cuong was conscripted, the "recruits all but dried up," leading to more aggressive recruitment techniques (Rottman 2007, 12). Quyen's and Cuong's cases, however, seem to be outliers in the general pattern of my interviewees' recruitment processes. In a more frequent occurrence, my interviewees were neither conscripted nor actively sought out to join the struggle, but they also were not actively forbidden from participating. The general pattern that arises from these interviews is that theoretically, my interviewees had to face strict age, weight, and political background requirements. In practice, however, it was not uncommon to mobilize recruits who expressed a willingness to contribute to the revolution and proved to be smart and quick enough to do so. As a result, many youths were recruited despite not strictly meeting the formal requirements, so long as they demonstrated a desire to join.

The recruitment process also varied according to geographical and political factors. In the north, the recruitment groups had more opportunities to spread their message via meetings, radio, and posters. Children and youth from the north were thus more exposed to the revolutionary spirit than those farther south, and many of my interviewees directly cited meetings with political cadres and their supporters as where they heard of the opportunity to join the struggle. They described the process as being quite straightforward—potential recruits only needed to find where the cadres were located and fill out an application form. In such instances, there were likely to be no dangers associated specifically with the process of identifying oneself as a part of the revolutionary forces or their sympathizers. In other words, the participants would not be individually targeted or persecuted as they would have in the south, where the US-backed Government of Vietnam (GVN) regime controlled most of the territory.

Southern villages, by contrast, were tightly monitored for communist sympathizers and potential guerrilla meetings. An interviewee from Cu Chi, a district in Saigon and the location of some of the biggest counterinsurgency operations, remembered that there were always GVN soldiers patrolling, keeping guard, and watching for guerrilla activity. Abnormalities in families—like a young man suddenly disappearing—would raise questions from officials concerned about NLF recruitment. Thus, in the south, the communist operations were more informal and underground. This had two consequences for prospective guerrilla sympathizers: first, there were fewer opportunities for meetings or recruitment groups to spread their ideological messaging via radio, loudspeakers, or posters. Thus, it was more difficult to achieve the same glorification of the revolution that was present, on a large scale, in North Vietnam. Second, those who did join the revolutionary movement did so in secret; they often did not know whether their friends or even families supported the guerrillas. Some of my interviewees reported working for the GVN, running errands and doing small tasks for the local military bases, befriending the American soldiers, while at the same time supporting the revolutionary forces (e.g., providing guerrillas with intelligence and stealing American food and weapons). Given this repression, the process of joining the revolutionary forces was more complicated and had to be planned in advance. Duc, who grew up in Cu Chi, witnessed this firsthand:

> In the South, they controlled the population tightly. You know, it wasn't easy to join the fighting, like in the North.... You had to leave your family to go to Saigon to do little jobs, like selling some things, doing factory labor or working at a bakery. They [the GVN] would come to your family and ask where your children are. Your family would say you went to work and they don't know where you are. If there's a reason for your absence, they wouldn't ask anything else.... And you'd often work for the government officials for a few months. They'd ask and we would give proof that we worked for the government, like a piece of paper. And then next month—turn around, join the revolution. But you couldn't just pack up your belongings and go, otherwise they would hunt your family down.

The differences in geography, then, meant that joining the fighting in South Vietnam required more elaborate planning due to the possibility of being persecuted for associating with communists. In the north, parents might have opposed their child's decision to join, but they would not be personally harmed. By contrast, the Southern Vietnamese interviewees had to weigh and consider their actions carefully, as accidentally revealing that they were supporting the guerrillas (whether by participating directly or from the rear) could lead to harassment of not only themselves but their families. But whether recruitment was open or underground, and whether or not the young people's families were at risk of being persecuted, the circumstances surrounding the recruitment process shaped my interviewees' specific motivations for joining the resistance forces.

Motivations to Join: Common Themes

The first of the two most common motivations to join was a reaction to immediate (often dangerous) circumstances. An emphasis on motivations derived from living in a dangerous social environment was most evident in the South Vietnamese interviewees. This, again, aligns with the fact that the United States and their GVN allies conducted most counterinsurgency operations in South Vietnam. When the US and GVN soldiers did conduct raids, they lasted for several days and involved substantial firepower and use of air cavalry, ending in significant destruction of villages (Starry 2002; Joes 2001). It is not surprising, then, that for South Vietnamese interviewees, the primary motivation for joining the resistance movement was the desire to escape and stop the violence. Even my interviewees located farther from the fighting, in the north, would be exposed to bombings and poverty; one of them recalled that one of his earliest memories prior to joining the military struggle was witnessing hungry people who begged for rice. Another specifically noted that "bombs shot like rain," and the same village could be burned two or three times, not just once.

When asked about his reasons for helping the guerrillas with small errands, Hung stated: "Of course I was afraid, but there was no other way. The enemy was here, I was so frustrated.... If your home was suddenly disturbed, you would do the same." He specifically remembered how American forces entered his village and burned and destroyed "our homes." In that context, he continued, anyone who had the ability to participate would do so. Similarly, Nhung, who assisted with many different tasks, including administrative errands, *tuyen truyen* (spreading and publicizing a particular message), and nursing, articulated an intense hatred for the American forces and desire to change the regime, which she had felt from a very young age: "I thought how they were constantly killing civilians—I hated them, I thought I would kill them. Because my uncles and aunts all died. There were only a few people in my family who survived. I was ready to volunteer to do anything. They were carrying the strategy to burn everything, kill everyone, and destroy everything [Ho Chi Minh's appeal, cited in chapter 1].... I was only ten or eleven back then. You know, they came in and shot everyone. Rice fields—everything burnt. There was nothing left."

One of my interviewees, Loan, also witnessed the brutal treatment inflicted by the GVN and American soldiers on communist guerrillas. Her father, a supporter of communism, was discovered and targeted. One night, GVN soldiers stormed their home, arrested her father, and dragged him to a nearby well. There, they beat him, mixing tobacco, soap, and pepper to intensify his pain. "He [my father] was screaming so much," she remembered. The soldiers then locked her—a young child at the time who had not yet joined the guerrillas—along with her mother and a newborn sibling inside their home. After a few days, when they were allowed to leave, she recalled seeing blood all over the yard. Their house, now branded as a "communist house," was confiscated, and she and her family were evicted. Her father was imprisoned and suffered more abuse at the hands of the regime. She saw the consequence of this abuse when she and her mother went to visit him. She did not recognize her father. Instead, she saw a dirty, smelly man in ragged clothes. When he reached out to hug her, she burst into tears and screamed: "You are not my father."

The motivations of my interviewees were in many ways enabled by a constellation of social norms and expectations, as well as communist ideological messages. However, these social and cultural ideas would not have resonated without being grounded in the material realities of my interviewees—the destruction, the violence on the human body, the raids and sweeps, the loss of life, and the economic exploitation (I detail one of these stories later in this section). A similar argument is made by Race (2010), who observed that the resistance forces effectively linked abstract concepts like nationalism to the tangible, material concerns of peasants, such as land ownership. In turn, this cultivated loyalty to local communes, which often included communist leadership, thereby weaving local issues and loyalties into the broader idea of the "national." Although beyond the scope of this book, Dant's (1999, 2) arguments that the social and the material are tightly intertwined are applicable here: "Just as the individual cannot be understood independently of society, so society cannot be grasped independently of its material stuff." Therefore, while the phenomenon of children and youth supporting and participating in armed struggle is enabled by the specific historical and social context (as well as their own deliberations), many of my interviewees had firsthand experiences and grievances linked to material hardship and physical violence, which played no small role in compelling them to consider joining in the first place.

The second common narrative, more prominent among the North Vietnamese interviewees who participated in the Vietnam War, was the influence of *tuyen truyen* distributed by political cadres. The Vietnamese term *tuyen truyen* is often translated into English as "propaganda," but, as Hurle (2014, 3) points out: "the English word has quite a negative connotation and is often interpreted as 'official lying'. The Vietnamese term, particularly during the 1940s and 1950s, did not have that same implication." I therefore follow Hurle's suggestion to use the Vietnamese term instead.

Since the most intense battles occurred in the south, many of my North Vietnamese interviewees were mobilized to march to the south and assist with large-scale battles there. To encourage the North Vietnamese youth to leave their homes and assist in the political struggle, the recruiters employed a carefully curated *tuyen truyen* strategy, which emphasized patriotic duty and honor associated with supporting the liberation cause. An observation by Thai Bao (2020; my translation) described the *tuyen truyen* activities as lively and diverse, including "political activities, opening educational classes, compiling documents, messaging outlines, disseminating oral messaging to all classes of people in liberated areas . . . through the press, publishing, cultural activities, arts, visual materials." The content focused on broadcasting achievements of brave NLF fighters and encouraging listeners to emulate them, portraying the American forces in a negative light and spreading revolutionary ideology via songs and music (Chanh 2015; Hoffer 1973; Ó Briain 2021). Perhaps more important, these activities took place "regularly and continuously," as Thai Bao (2020) recounts.

For Quan, who joined the military struggle at sixteen years old, the honor and glory invested in the political struggle became his primary motivation: "You know, at the time, the whole country went to war. Everyone volunteered to join the army. . . . Everyone was excited to join, the battlefield was something honorable and glorious, it was beautiful. Everyone was oriented towards it. So going to the battlefield was like an ambition, a longing, among youth back then" (Nguyen 2022, 37). In addition, the conflict was presented as a struggle for justice, the right thing: by joining the revolutionary struggle, recruits would be rescuing their southern compatriots from the exploitation of American imperialists.

Alongside these motifs of glory, the political messaging also presented the war as exciting and fun. Tien, who ran away from home to join the Youth Shock Brigades at fifteen, described the atmosphere as festive, even suggesting: "Why wouldn't you join? The more, the merrier!" In both North and South Vietnam, some provinces held rallies, which featured entertaining performances and gatherings, designed to bolster the morale of villagers and encourage their active participation on the front lines. Frequently led by teenagers, these performances featured music, dance, and theatrical acts portraying significant events from Vietnamese history (Davidson 1968). Hunt's (2008, 38–39) informants recalled that if they were notified two hours in advance, as many as 3,000 to 4,000 people could join the meetings, and sometimes villagers would stay afterwards to further discuss that "they could no longer endure to Ngo Dinh Diem's regime's oppression." Overall, there was a sense of festivity and excitement recorded by Hunt (2008) and echoed by my interviewees. Many sessions would feature poems written by Ho

Chi Minh, which were specifically aimed "to inspire confidence in the revolutionary cause of all classes of people" (Chanh 2015; my translation). The tone of the following poem, "Happy New Year of the Ox" in 1961, for example, is enthusiastic and positive. It starts with wishing the reader, "Happy New Year, Happy new Spring," and continues that "The road to happiness is wide, the five-year plan is more exciting." It then addresses the wish for reunification with South Vietnam to move forward and finally, victory for socialism (republished by the *Vietnam Communist Party Newspaper* in 2022; my translation).

In addition, much of the *tuyen truyen* highlighted multiple movements with catchy slogans to encourage a collective but still festive atmosphere of competition among villagers and guerrillas: *Thi dua giet giac lap cong* (Competition to kill invaders and establish achievements); *Tat ca cho tien tuyen, tat ca de danh thang giac My xam luoc* (All for the front line, all for defeating the American invaders); *Moi nguoi lam viec bang hai vi mien Nam ruot thit* (Each person working the equivalent of two for the Southern brothers); *Thoc khong thieu mot can, quan khong thieu mot nguoi* (Rice will not be short of a kilogram, army will not be short of a person); *Tay cay, tay sung* (A plow in one hand, a gun in another); and *Tieng hat at tieng bom* (Singing over the sound of bombs), among many others. Many of my interviewees from the north described these slogans, particularly "Singing over the sound of bombs," as having a very prominent presence throughout their childhood (and later, military) lives. Regardless of region, then, and whether driven by survival and community protection in the south or excitement and the normalization of youth participation in the north, young people's decisions to enlist were shaped by their communities.

A Politicized Childhood

As young people, my interviewees made decisions within a context in which their everyday lives were politicized. However, many interviewees referred to their motivations for joining the revolution as nonpolitical, where *chinh tri* (politics), as they saw it, referred to an understanding of communism or revolutionary consciousness, often also including notions of loyalty to the state and patriotism. For example, Minh, without my prompting, explained that he did not understand what either communism or the revolution was when he first volunteered to join the armed forces at seventeen. His understanding of communism formed only while already serving in the political struggle. Many other interviewees echoed the same sentiments, frequently denying any "political" motivations and instead suggesting that they were guided either by a survival instinct or by the glorified image of the battlefield, as discussed in the previous section. It is also noteworthy that the instances of my interviewees (such as Minh) denying their ideological motivations as children and youth did not clash with their acknowledgment of their current support for communism as adults.

On the surface, these sentiments may appear to confirm that young people are apolitical by nature and therefore cannot be meaningfully involved in politics. However, at the same time, my interviewees spoke of perceived injustice and wanting to address it at a young age—feelings that could be described as political. This was most prominently articulated by Hung, who began helping the guerrillas with small errands when he was seven or eight years old. Growing up in the south, where bombings and raids were common, he remembered: "It starts with your dissatisfaction, with your frustration. It was a natural instinct. Suddenly there's someone disturbing your home, burning it. And you are very angry. There's nothing about patriotism—you wouldn't know anything at that age. And there was no education in the majority of houses.... No one knew what communism is. Only knew that America came. So whoever was frustrated and could do it, they wanted to stop them" (Nguyen 2023, 16).

His statement reveals two issues that highlight the role of politics in children's and youth's lives. First, he equates politics with formal ideology—communism or patriotism. This is generally in line with the prevalent definition of politics, which was used by the revolutionary forces to articulate their political struggle as connected to the state (e.g., protecting Vietnam from foreign invaders, or unifying North and South Vietnam). The "political" was seen as encompassing the state-level and formal governmental procedures, rather than being a matter of personal experiences. For those who subsequently joined the military conflict as young recruits, the association of politics with ideologies was even further reinforced by educational sessions labeled "political education," to which they were exposed when they became part of their respective group (elaborated further in chapter 4). These sessions included meetings, speeches, and classes on both patriotism and communism. Consequently, it is understandable that the children and youth did not have much knowledge about communism prior to joining the struggle, and they would perceive their initial motivations as apolitical after being exposed to the formal study sessions.

Second, an in-depth examination of Hung's motivations reveals significant allusions to matters of injustice, exploitation, and a heightened awareness of the US presence. These elements suggest that the impetus driving young people's involvement in the war was firmly rooted in political issues. Corroborative accounts from other interviewees further underscore the political nature of the children's and youth's motivations, though the process of comprehending and assimilating these politics was an ongoing and gradual journey. For instance, Quyen's narrative vividly exemplifies the subtle infiltration of politics into young people's lives from an early age and his gradual evolution toward understanding it. Before his voluntary enlistment, he recollected gathering with his friends around a loudspeaker, where communist cadres disseminated news. Even in the absence of radios in his village during that time, he engaged in discussions with his teachers and classmates about recent guerrilla victories. His recollection portrays a captivating image of weaponry, soldiers, and battlefields, which were all portrayed as beautiful, noble, and desirable. "Some people now say that we were indoctrinated [to volunteer], but it isn't true," he insisted. "They just talked about examples of bravery [martyrs], and it touched us. Who would tell a class of primary school children what to do?" (Nguyen 2022, 37).

Nevertheless, Quyen came to realize that even though he was not explicitly acquainted with formal ideologies at the time, notions of exploitation, social justice, and patriotism had already taken firm root in his thinking. A comprehensive understanding of "formal" politics only materialized later, owing to his active participation in the war: "The orientation toward the war was very clear. When they were shooting in Quang Ngai . . . our spirit really boiled. All we wanted to do was go there [the war]. We wanted to overthrow Diem's regime. . . . And then in Hanoi, there were already big protests. The speeches by the leaders really touched me; they gave me a really strong emotion. Thinking about it now, that's when my patriotism was awakened. But at the time, I didn't think like that. All I knew was that I really wanted to go to the battlefield; the spirit was bright."

Sang experienced a similar journey—joining the Youth Shock Brigades at fifteen, he denied having any patriotic feelings or communist sympathies prior to his involvement in the military struggle. However, he explicitly acknowledges the importance of the guidance and education he received from the revolutionary leadership once he joined. He makes a distinction between "informal" politics (i.e., his personal perception of injustice) and the knowledge and skills that he developed as a result of the leadership influence:

> We just saw how other people were exploited, so we were frustrated. But we were so small and didn't have the capability to do anything. But behind us were the [communist] leaders. They didn't directly do much, only instructed how to organize everything. So, you see, there was no revolutionary thinking. We saw the injustices and were frustrated, and then the leadership said—it doesn't have to be like that. Why are they exploiting you? What should the youngsters do? That's how the unity was formed among the youngsters, under the guidance. The older generation guided the younger. So eventually, it formed an organized movement.... But without their guidance, we wouldn't dare to do anything.

Some young recruits, however, were much more aware of their political rationale for joining the revolutionary movement. The most prominent example of this among my interviewees is Tam, who volunteered at fifteen. Growing up in Saigon (South Vietnam), she was already working at a factory by the time she turned thirteen and found the regime too exploitative, remembering that "they gave us two shirts but no trousers," and she reported having almost no food while the factory owners would eat well. In her story, the language of social justice and revolution is strongly present. As she and other factory workers could not stand the exploitation, they organized a protest, asking to have their rights acknowledged. The problem, however, was not solved—rather, the factory owners oppressed the workers even more, killing and injuring the protesters. She then remembered that in the end, "those who were able to, went to fight, and those who couldn't, quit working. Girls directly asked me to participate in the revolution, to fight for our rights.... At the time, I was just over fifteen but I already was 'enlightened'" [*giac ngo*, a term used to mean that the participants knew what revolution was]. She further recounted that in the beginning of her work transporting weapons for the NLF, she deliberately left three grenades in the yard of the factory owner "as a warning: if she continues to live like this, there will be a day when she dies."

Despite seeming apolitical on the surface, my interviewees' reasons for deciding to join the military struggle were underpinned by issues of social justice, foreign presence, and exploitation. Young people were aware of these issues and had a strong desire to participate in addressing them. However, there remain questions about the extent to which many children's and youth's participation in the struggle was voluntary.

Voluntary Participation

Alongside asserting that their participation was "nonpolitical," my interviewees continuously stated that they made independent, autonomous choices to participate in the conflict voluntarily. However, at the same time, they often referred to notions of duty and responsibility. One possible explanation for this contradiction is the communist and Confucian context within which the war was taking place. As Voicu and Voicu (2009) observed, volunteering in communist countries rarely involved agency and was instead a label for doing unpaid work on the state's orders. In the case of Romania, for example, many movements and organizations labeled as "voluntary"—even sports clubs—had compulsory membership and were fully under authoritarian control (Voicu and Voicu 2009). Similarly, Chinese soldiers during the Korean War in the 1950s were presented by the Chinese government as volunteers, "so apparently incensed by the wrong being done to their Korean friends that they come of their own volition to aid them" (Farrar-Hockley 1984, 293). In reality, they conformed to orders and were often not even aware that they had "volunteered." This may also have been the case for some of my interviewees—as we have seen in chapter 2, the revolutionary movement made an effort to appeal to the notion of "duty" toward the people.

However, institutional orders alone cannot explain the many cases when children and youth were stopped from participating by their families or by the revolutionary cadres due to their young age, or—in the case of my South Vietnamese interviewees—because there were not many outlets enabling participation in the first place. The fact that families and cadres sometimes had to deny them entry shows that the children and youth had some measure of volition. They wanted to join, even when it entailed work to find out where and how, and even when doing so was a high-risk effort. Furthermore, the perception by some interviewees that their participation was voluntary (i.e., not forced) was so prevalent that many reported it directly affecting how they behaved on the battlefields. As one interviewee put it, they were more disciplined because "we knew that no one forced us to be there." *They* perceived their own actions as voluntary. This, then, requires us to look at other factors that predisposed young people to volunteer.

The ambiguity of volunteering in communist countries has been explored in Audin's (2017, 48) study of retired neighborhood activists in China, where volunteering is described as "somewhere between imposition and moral responsibility." Similar to the cases cited by Voicu and Voicu (2009), calls for volunteers to keep the neighborhood safe came from local governing bodies. Potential activists still had an option to refuse; the reason why they couldn't, however, was connected to their sense of duty. The calls emphasized mutual belonging to the neighborhood and stressed that relationships developed with neighbors also created obligations toward them. Potential volunteers would be embarrassed to refuse an offer to keep the neighborhood safe, as that would mean that they were refusing to help someone they already knew. Furthermore, the decision to volunteer was also deeply influenced by "the norm governing the use of free time for the common good against idleness," meaning that the calls to volunteer relied on the fact that the pensioners were already feeling anxious over having free time (Audin 2017, 53). The ambiguity of their volunteering, then, lay more within social norms than with institutional calls. For Wu et al. (2018, 1203), this confirms Bourdieu's notion that "networks, norms, and social trust can transform contingent relations into relationships with durable obligations." It is through these relationships that collective action comes into being.

Paralleling the case of these Chinese neighborhood activists, the mass mobilization of the communist forces, with their aims to involve everyone in the revolutionary struggle—and subsequent tactics of *tuyen truyen* as a result—was likely to be only one factor that influenced the decision of the children and youth to enlist. The concept of volunteering could thus be approached as a social structure in itself: my interviewees were guided by notions that were socially prescribed, both by the communist framework and by Confucian expectations, that each individual fulfills their prescribed duties. This is particularly relevant in Vietnamese society, with its strong emphasis on collectivism.

Factors Influencing Decisions to Enlist

As we saw in the previous chapter, family loyalty, social scrutiny, and group dedication were powerful tools of behavioral control used by the guerrillas and political cadres. Without denying that children and youth exercise agency in their decision-making, there still needs to be an acknowledgment that their choices were embedded within an environment that shaped and predisposed their actions. I turn now to factors that played the most significant role in shaping their decisions.

"Revolutionary Family" and the Role of Tradition

In the interviews that I conducted, family influence featured prominently as a key factor influencing children's and youth's decision to join the military struggle. In line with claims made in chapter 2, the political orientation of family members had a deep influence on my interviewees in several ways. For example, My grew up in a *gia dinh khang chien* ("revolutionary family"), or a family in which at least one member supported the political struggle against the French or Americans and their GVN supporters. For her, family did not constitute an apolitical space, but rather brought politics into her everyday life. When My was a child, her father often brought her to guerrilla gatherings, where she met different political cadres: "It's not like I was determined to participate in the revolution, but . . . there were uncles and aunts, adults, they guided me. They said, you come from a family where supporting the revolution is a tradition." She remembered guerrillas accompanying her to see the performances and encouraging her to choose a profession that would benefit the liberation struggle in the future (Nguyen 2023, 12). My's political outlook, then, was shaped not only by her immediate family but also by its wider social circle, which also consisted of guerrillas. Their argument that she should follow family tradition was persuasive, given the importance that Vietnamese society places on loyalty and upholding family honor. However, My also spoke of the immediate connection between her and her father, linking her participation in the liberation struggle to him directly: "I understand now that my revolutionary blood is from him." At thirteen, after some deliberation, she decided to leave her family to serve as a nurse in the battlefields, purposefully not joining the fighting forces because "it is too easy to die there" (Nguyen 2022, 36).

Many families (and subsequently, their children) did not have opportunities to interact openly with guerrillas because the revolutionary operations were underground and secretive. However, my interviewees, such as Duc, still remembered seeing their families and neighborhoods resist the current regime using any means available. Because the southern village-communities could not confront GVN authorities directly for fear of being persecuted, there were many references to peasants employing what Scott (1985) called "weapons of the weak" (i.e., everyday, nonconfrontational forms of resistance that were deliberate in their subtleness and anonymity). Young people's everyday life was shaped by witnessing such political actions that their families undertook. Duc remembers that his family had steel buckets to carry water or fish sauce, which they also used as tools of protest:

> In the evening, after a shout, people would hit and bang on it to make noise. At first, we would hit it quietly, and then everyone else would join. They [GVN] couldn't catch us—we didn't do anything illegal. But it was this unity. If there was a family that didn't make noise—we'd know that they are on the enemy's side. And then when the officials went to check for the buckets, you'd say—oh, my neighbors were making noise, so I followed them, but I don't actually know anything. I just heard the noise so I joined in. . . . They would try to find the person who started it, but no one would tell them, how would they know? (Nguyen 2023, 12).

In many accounts of young people's motivations to enlist in military conflicts, family is often portrayed as a "push" factor, such as fleeing an abusive home or having parents who were missing or unable to provide adequate care (as pointed out by Becker 2009 and Pugel 2009). The stories of my interviewees reveal ways in which positive family relations could directly shape motivations. In line with Nolas, Varvantakis, and Aruldoss's (2017) observation that the intimacy and bonding between family members provide solid ground for political socialization, the relationship between my interviewees and their families played a major role in children and youth wanting to participate in the war. Their decisions were shaped by the cultural expectation to stay loyal to family tradition, interactions with wider social circles (neighbors, friends, and other guerrillas), and the direct transmission of political values from their parents.

Militarized Everyday Life

Not all my interviewees were born into revolutionary families, but the frequent bombings and raids made violence and militarization part of their everyday lives from early childhood. Duc and Nhung, for instance, witnessed destruction, death, and civilians being arrested despite not being associated with the guerrillas. As another interviewee put it: "I never knew what peace was." Ratelle (2013, 167) observes that in such cases, "violence is interiorised as normal, and people adapt to it in order to survive." A Google search of children and youth in the Vietnam War (*thieu nien trong khang chien chong My* or *thanh nien trong khang chien chong My*) shows black-and-white photos of young children talking to revolutionaries, wearing protective straw hats in case of bomb raids, and participating in activities such as digging tunnels. Quynh (2019) confirms the viability of these images with a list of some of the ways that Vietnamese children and youth adapted to living during war: always playing next to bomb shelters in case there was a bombing, bringing first aid kits to school, meeting guerrillas and political cadres frequently, and others.[3]

Through frequent *tuyen truyen* activities, news, and other media being spread over loudspeakers by guerrillas and political cadres, Vietnamese childhood was politicized from a very early age. A close examination of the few Vietnamese written materials left over from the war reveals these dynamics. Those who supported the revolution were referred to as "good children," as in a 1969 letter by Ho Chi Minh (Vietnam Communist Party 2020; my translation). "In general, our children are very good," Ho writes, describing this goodness as follows:

> In the South, the children are very brave, enthusiastically helping the army, helping families with members who are revolutionaries, working as couriers, fighting as guerillas, etc. Many children under the age of ten have already become "Dung si diet My" [an honorary title for fighters]. In the North, the children enthusiastically competed to do "thousands of good deeds" such as helping soldiers' families, returning lost items, courageously risking their lives to save friends, etc. In rural areas, many children organize to help.

As Beier and Tabak (2020, 285) have written, the "naturalization of danger combines with valorizations of particular kinds of responses to produce a normalization of militarization." Jenkins (2014, 28) further notes that "there is an adjustment between an individual's hopes, aspirations and expectations for the future, on the one hand, and the objective situation in which they find themselves." In other words, violent and unstable realities alter perceptions of what is sensible and effective. The young people's habitus—their unspoken, unquestioned attitudes and beliefs with regard to war—was shaped by these realities. For my interviewees, such militarization made the idea of taking up arms realistic and sensible. This was articulated by Si, who stated that enlisting at seventeen simply felt "natural" for him—"it was nothing special."

Children's and youth's familiarity with the political struggle was further reinforced not only by the ongoing war but also by persistent attempts by the guerrillas and political cadres to foster friendly relations with peasants and their mass mobilization campaigns. This brought the revolutionary actors into close contact with young people. Hung, who remembered that guerrillas were always part of his life in a village, often saw them working in the fields alongside other villagers. His eventual work for the NLF involved small errands such as stealing supplies, gathering intelligence, and camouflaging the guerrillas' mines. However, his first errands, at nine years old, were not official missions assigned by the NLF, but rather informal forms of assistance. The first time he stole a gun from the Americans, it was as a favor for a guerrilla uncle, initiated by Hung himself. He overheard his uncle talking about how the American equipment was bigger, heavier, and more beautiful than that which the NLF used. Hung then offered to go up to the American base and steal it for his uncle, who laughed and said, "You're joking." Hung recounts, "It was a favor [for the guerrillas]. The uncle said he liked it [the gun], so I gave it to him. I got it for him as a gift—it's nothing, no problem at all" (Nguyen 2022, 37). For interviewees from revolutionary families, moreover, the struggle was physically brought right into the home when their families sheltered guerrillas. For example, Ngoc referenced her mother cooking food for the Vietnamese army and guerrillas and lying to her that it was for the family's pets. Eventually, however, she worked with her family to host and care for the revolutionary forces.

The presence of revolutionary actors was consistent even (and perhaps especially) during celebrations, with a particularly interesting case pertaining specifically to children.[4] The NLF predecessor, the Viet Minh, implemented a "Revolutionary Autumn Festival," traditionally a children's holiday (usually called the "Autumn Festival"). A published program for one such festival includes not only singing, theater, and handing out presents for children, but also activities such as writing a telegram to the guerrillas or to Ho Chi Minh himself (published in *Báo Cứu Quốc* 1947). Throughout military struggles with the United States, guerrillas and political cadres frequently made an explicit connection between recruits celebrating their childhood and participating in the revolution.

As Pham (2017) writes, almost every year, Ho Chi Minh wrote letters to children and youth, often also encouraging them to study, keep good hygiene, and participate in the revolution in any way they could. In letters from the early 1950s, we already see him alluding to adults fighting for their children's future: "We, uncles, older brothers, older sisters, will do our best to fight in the revolution, destroy French colonizers and American invaders, so that you, children, are free . . . full, and warm"

(Ho Chi Minh 1950, as cited in Vietnam Communist Party 2020). In a 1965 letter, he expresses his hope that one day North and South Vietnam will unite, bringing happiness to both "young and old," shares that he misses children and wishes for each of them to become a "young hero" (Ho Chi Minh 1965, as cited in Ca Mau Electronic Information Portal). In another, undated letter (Phuong 2021), he reminds children that it is thanks to the fighters and the revolution that they were able to be born and grow up in a socialist country.

Although many of my interviewees did not directly interact with guerrillas, stories and narratives about the ongoing conflict also prevailed in their studies through books, images, and other messaging surrounding the potential young recruits. In perhaps one of the few efforts to recover Vietnamese educational materials from before 1975, Tran Van Chanh (2012) compiled texts to be memorized by children from a literature textbook for primary school (*Quoc Van Tieu Hoc*). The textbook mostly contains poems that cover a wide range of themes, including filial piety, encouraging students to study and express gratitude and respect for humanity. However, a significant portion of these poems also involved themes of patriotism, evoking past histories of fighting off foreign invaders. As Tran (2012, 119; my translation) articulates it, "The powerful and galvanizing text of some poems is no different from the urging of battle drums."

Overall, in the DRV, as Dror (2018, 25) notes, "The educational system was geared to produce a new generation of youths and adolescents to become revolutionary fighters who would continue the revolutionary cause of the Party and the nation." Evidence from government directives reveals that there were indeed some deliberate efforts to politicize education. For example, a directive from 1964, issued by the Ministry of Education, stated that "the common requirements for all teachers and professional teaching staff in all sectors and at all levels are: continuously enhance revolutionary enthusiasm, solidarity and unanimity, promote the spirit of self-reliance" (Ministry of Education 1964). More explicitly still, the goal of education was to "actively build national education . . . train the young generation holistically, who know to hate foreign invaders deeply, know to love the Fatherland passionately, have knowledge, training, and health, to continue revolutionary activities" (Circular 44/TT, dated February 13, 1963, of the Central Bureau, as cited in Pham 2020). The leadership approached political education quite seriously. In the Report of the Ministry of Unification (1971; my translation), we can see recommendations such as "the schools need to increase the overall children's awareness of the political situation." The positive image of "people who support the revolution" was socialized into young people from the very beginning; as one report states, most of the children's parents have served in the war against the United States, "so they are, *by nature*, good people" (Ministry of Education 1966; my translation, emphasis added).

In some educational spaces (in both North and South Vietnam) school was also taught by those closely associated with the revolutionary movement. As Pham (2020) writes, teachers were called "revolutionary teachers" (*nha giao cach mang*), strongly implying their association with guerrilla or political activity, while education itself was called a "battleground" (*mat tran*). The teachers were frequently also trained in first aid and evacuation techniques and had to teach while "being ready to hold a gun and kill foreign invaders during sweeps" (Pham 2020; my translation). Many of them, notably, were also very young—Pham's article mentions a teenager who became a teacher at seventeen years old. One of my interviewees located in South Vietnam remembered that his first revolutionary activities started when one of his teachers—himself a guerrilla, although students did not know the extent to which he was involved in activities—asked pupils to disseminate flyers about the revolution and deliver secret messages. Already, then, we can see that performing errands for guerrillas, not to mention the more overtly militarized nature of their learning activities, were integrated into many children's and youth's everyday lives.

Since guerrillas and political cadres were regularly present in their lives since early childhood (and generally had friendly relations with civilians, including the young generation), the possibility of taking up arms was therefore readily imaginable for many young people. In Vietnam and beyond, the importance of strong bonds between armed groups and the population they live in has been well established. Shah (2013, 494) observed that it was the intimacy, "friendship and commitment" that sustained the movement of Maoist guerrillas in India. Similarly, the stories by my interviewees highlight that respect, helpfulness, willingness to hear peasants' personal stories, and a strict code of conduct fostered positive relationships between revolutionary forces and peasants. This was in stark contrast with the relatively impersonal propaganda methods, distant government officials, and frequent indiscriminate violence employed by the GVN against villagers, which only served to undermine the relations between the GVN and the civilian population (also noted by Maranto and Tuchman 1992; Hunt 2008). As American commentators at the height of war noted, it thus came as no surprise that children and youth preferred to join the Vietnamese guerrilla forces (*New York Times* 1964). With respect to the interviewees in this study, violence, militarization, and marginalization eventually led to the desire to address inequalities—and joining the military struggle as one way to do so had already been normalized by the all-people mobilization campaign and revolutionaries' proximity to peasants.

Construction of a "Good" Childhood

My interviewees' motivations to enlist in the conflict as children and youth were further underpinned by Vietnamese societal norms surrounding what constituted a "good" childhood. As I mention in the introduction, my use of the word "childhood" denotes a socially constructed concept that is hardly universal. In mid-twentieth-century wartime Vietnam, "childhood" as a state of life did not always correlate with a specific age range. Moreover, as previously mentioned, my interviewees often did not know what year they were born, having to ask their relatives to look at official records (and other times, the official records were incorrect, and the interviewees gave me both—the date on their official record and that which they knew to be correct). Some were uncertain of exactly when they joined the military struggle and used other means to cite their age—for example, one woman recalled: "I got married when I was seventeen, so that must've been before then."

This flexibility around the chronology of childhood, in turn, had implications for children's and youth's expectations concerning their duties and capabilities. For example, My was very matter-of-fact about working as a nurse at thirteen: "I participated from a very early age, I was thirteen.... At that age, I could participate in the war, I was already mature." Despite asserting that she was a grown-up at thirteen, she later noted: "At that age, you are supposed to sleep and eat well." She did not deny the existence of biological differences between children and adults; however, for her, this also did not contradict the fact that she could participate in the war effort. Her statement is further in line with Huijsmans's (2008) observation that a "good" Southeast Asian childhood is one where you would not only rest and play but also work and contribute to family and community. In line with such expectations and norms, my interviewees frequently mentioned having worked elsewhere prior to joining the political struggle. This earlier work prepared them for carrying out tasks for the revolutionary forces. These jobs varied: some of my interviewees remembered working as a helper in someone's house, being a worker in a factory, or helping provincial committees. Others were not formally employed but nevertheless regularly helped their families with farming and tending animals. Indeed, my interviewees often framed joining the military struggle as a continuation of their previous jobs.

Of particular significance is the story of Vinh, who grew up without a father and assumed the responsibility of caring for his mother and sister. While pursuing his studies until the seventh grade, he simultaneously supported his family. He then joined the Youth Association at sixteen (which, as I mentioned in the previous chapter, was set up to encourage youths to engage in revolutionary activities), helping to organize finances for the provincial committee. When I asked what he did in the two years between ages fourteen and sixteen, he replied that he did "nothing, just staying home." Only after some clarification about whether he helped his family in the fields, he responded: "Of course, I harvested and tended the buffaloes." Such a response highlights that for Vinh, home labor did not count as work, rather becoming something mundane and routine. When he joined the military struggle, many of the activities that he engaged in were suited to his earlier responsibilities at home and on the provincial committee—to cook and prepare meals alongside running small errands like maintaining the camp and buying food, cigarettes, or coffee.

Similarly, other interviewees' initial responsibilities within the armed struggle mirrored the tasks that they performed at home. Hong, who had begun interacting with the guerrillas at age nine due to her family's involvement in sheltering them, recalled instances where the guerillas requested her assistance purchasing products or knitting clothes and scarves—tasks that could be easily carried out amid her other domestic duties. Another interviewee from South Vietnam, Duc, shared that his decision to join guerrillas was driven by a strong sense of communal responsibility—which, as I discussed in chapter 2, already had been communicated to children at a young age. At the age of fourteen, Duc became a spy, influenced primarily by his desire to change the lives of those around him. Witnessing the raids in Cu Chi, he was profoundly affected by the pervasive exploitation of the people: "It was to do with our frustration with the exploitation. The anger, the hate. Those were the feelings. It wasn't about patriotism. . . . The peasants were exploited by the landowners. It makes your heart angry" (Nguyen 2023, 17). A statement from another interviewee alluded that norms and values were timeless and universal, as he presumed that I would do the same in similar circumstances: "Imagine, you want to protect your mother and father; you want to protect your brothers and sisters." He then continued that "of course" I would also go to the battlefield in this case (Nguyen 2023, 1).

As the mass mobilization campaigns progressed, the support for the revolutionary forces was almost "bordering on hysteria" (Marr 2013, 383). Voluntarism became a prevailing norm, especially evident in the liberated regions where a strong sense of solidarity prevailed. Davidson (1968, 77) affirms this, noting that his interview respondents often cited a simple reason for working with the NLF: "everybody" was doing it. Those who did not join the military service contributed to the war effort by engaging in labor and production activities. During this period, the distinction between civilians and guerrillas became blurred, characteristic of the concept of "total" war (Goscha 2012). A consistent theme in the revolutionary messaging was that victory was inevitable, and youngsters all over the country were joining the political struggle.

The mass mobilization led to the prevailing expectation that everyone, people of all ages, would actively support the war effort; in turn, this led to a heightened level of social scrutiny. Opper (2019, 218) recounts an incident where villagers derisively mocked draftees: "Why did you have to be drafted? Why didn't you volunteer? You are cowardly kids!" In such a collectivist society, social ties and public opinion served as potent tools for behavioral control. This sentiment was echoed by some of my interviewees, who revealed that avoiding service would have been nearly impossible without facing judgment from their peers and fellow villagers. The fear of being left behind, not fitting in, and being criticized became strong motivations to join the revolutionary movement. As one of my interviewees put it: "There was of course another thing—not like envy, but something similar to . . . if all of your friends are going, why aren't you going?" The power of social judgment has been similarly observed by Donnell (1967, xii), who acknowledged that while many recruits joined the NLF out of grievance and economic deprivation, a large number were motivated by a "desire to win glory, or perhaps just the respect of their community."

Although almost half of my interviewees were women, it was the men who explicitly referenced a concern with negative social judgment if they did not join the war. The gendered nature of this sensitivity to social condemnation was explained by Minh: "Of course I had to go, otherwise women would laugh at me." The impact of criticism was so strong that it drove another interviewee, Quyen, to find any possible way to leave his village and assist with the war effort, despite having a legitimate reason for not joining the armed forces (they did not allow him to join because he was underage): "But the social pressure is really strong. You will not be able to stay home. Women would say: everyone went to fight, how can you, a youngster [*thanh nien*—while normally referring to youths, this term especially refers to young men], stay home, still working in the fields and carrying vegetables? . . . Sometimes they would say things that would really make me angry." These gendered differences appear to endorse Rydstrom's (2006) insight that Vietnamese boys in particular are brought up to respect and protect notions of honor and obligations, helping to explain the stronger degree of social judgment they would face if they did not carry out their prescribed duties.

This is not to say that girls faced no expectations or judgment. Women were also recruited actively and expected to help with all aspects of the political struggle, from military operations to production and morale maintenance (Taylor 1999). The revolutionary movement often cited examples of several prominent women who led rebellions against the Chinese, as well as a Vietnamese saying: *giac den nha, dan ba cung danh* (if the enemy comes, even the women will fight). As part of the efforts to mobilize women, the Communist Party in North Vietnam developed the "Three Responsibilities" campaign (as cited in Le 2005):

1. To participate in production and other activities in place of men who have left to fight
2. To manage family affairs and encourage men to fight
3. To support the Front and the fighting

This appeal demonstrates that women were expected to hold both supporting and leading roles in the war effort. In particular, as Donnell (1967, xvi) observed, they were expected to help with mobilization because they were "respected in Vietnamese society . . . and [their] judgment and valor can be expected to have a powerful psychological effect and moral influence on the young men." These gender norms affected my interviewees, too. This is particularly reflected in one woman's statement that "of course" she had to join the struggle: "As a woman, I had to go and organize everyone." It is significant that she referred to herself as a "woman," despite joining at around sixteen or seventeen. The Vietnamese definition of childhood, after all, remained flexible. Her perception of her role as a woman, to organize and lead, also echoes Donnell's comments about the powerful influence of women in Vietnamese society. The sentiments articulated by my interviewees, then, not only highlight the importance of fitting in and avoiding being criticized, but wider societal concerns over young people's duties and capacities.

Children's and Youth's Appropriation and Negotiation of Social Norms

When it came to deciding to participate in the war effort, young people were both predisposed and constrained by various social factors that positioned them on a continuum between voluntarism and imposition. Through the many layers of socialization shaping their habitus—through their peers, families, schools, and guerrillas and cadres that they encountered in their everyday life—they came to understand certain courses of action (such as participating in the revolution) as a normal part of their lives, and therefore a conceivable option for them. In some responses, the "common sense" of their decisions was conveyed (such as saying that "of course" one would join the military struggle), in line with Bourdieu's (1990) observation that internalized implicit social rules are a powerful guide of actors' social practices. However, my interviewees also indicated that they did not passively accept indoctrination or the prevalent norms of their social environment. Indeed, many of their responses show that they, on the one hand, internalized the messages about war participation and duty toward community and family, but they also learned to intuitively understand how they could navigate these same social constraints to achieve their goals. In other words, they gained what Bourdieu (1990, 66) calls the "feel for the game"; however, although they were predisposed to reproduce certain practices, they did not do so rigidly. Many of my interviewees still managed to navigate and negotiate possibilities for their young lives within restricted circumstances, thinking critically and demonstrating a willingness to question their own preconceived notions and stereotypes.

Like many interviewees from revolutionary families, Hong indicated her family's influence on her decision to join the struggle. From a young age, she helped her family shelter and provide food for guerrillas, who lived with her and her family. However, despite being surrounded by the South Vietnamese government propaganda that portrayed communists in an unfavorable light, she was willing to challenge her own previous opinions after directly interacting with them: "Back then, the propaganda was that Communists are like monkeys, but I thought that those Communists are very heroic, very strong, very beautiful. So I thought, those puppet-government soldiers—they are lying! The communists are like this—why are they calling them names? I asked my father. . . . He said, here, look at me, I am a Communist, just like Uncle Ho. You see, are we skinny, are we weak?" (Nguyen 2022, 36).

Even after her frequent positive interactions with NLF cadres, however, Hong insisted that her decision to join the political struggle was not reinforced externally. Instead, it came as a consequence of her own independent thinking and deciding, for herself, what would be appropriate: "Those activities [sheltering the guerrillas] made thoughts appear in my head. I was a child of a family like that, with parents like that—how should I behave?" (Nguyen 2023, 14).

It is also important to note that my interviewees described their childhood experience as one where their opinions and wishes were seen as valid and worthy of respect by adults. For example, parents in revolutionary families did not always expect their children to follow in their footsteps. When Hong asked her father to let her join the guerrillas, he explicitly forbade it at first, as he thought that she was too weak to carry out physically demanding tasks in the war. However, he reconsidered his decision later, with the only caveat being that if she absolutely wanted to go, she must complete her mission without deserting. Otherwise, he would disown her: "This is a revolutionary family; if you desert, you will affect our honor. He said, whatever it takes, do your best" (Nguyen 2023, 14). Despite personal disagreement, then, Hong's father still gave her the space to make a considered choice, independent of his opinion.

Children and youth interested in joining the revolutionary struggle also often had to engage in elaborate planning to make this happen. As mentioned before, it was not uncommon for young recruits' requests to join the struggle to be denied at first, by both their parents and the cadres. Many of my interviewees made extra efforts to persuade the group commanders to let them join. The most straightforward way was to argue with the recruitment officers. One interviewee was turned away due to being underweight but argued that he was only skinny and would gain weight after eating and training (the cadre laughed and agreed with his logic, letting him join). Similarly, Quan, who volunteered to join the armed forces at the age of sixteen as a sapper, with the main job of clearing land mines, demonstrated a strong determination to persuade the initially hesitant cadre. He remembered:

> When I went, I was too young and too skinny. At the health check, the doctor rejected me from the beginning because of my weight. So I cried, I pricked a finger and wrote a letter of determination [with blood]. I didn't have enough blood, so I had to ask an older friend for his blood to finish the letter. Then, after begging for a long while, the doctor said, okay, now let's do this: you and I will run seven kilometers. If you can do it, I will accept you. So I agreed. After about one hundred meters, the doctor said: "Okay let's turn back, that's enough." After we returned, he wrote on the medical record: "Underweight, but with potential to develop" (Nguyen 2022, 30).

Similar patterns are seen with young people whose parents did not want them to join the struggle. For example, Sang's father tried to discourage him from joining the Youth Shock Brigades by describing how hard it is to build roads. His father insisted: "With your strength, and your personality [it is notable that he did not mention age as a possible impeding factor], you will not be able to do it. And once you go and can't do it, you will come back. And if you come back, I will not take you back" (Nguyen 2023, 15). Sang, however, told his father to trust that he would not return without finishing his mission, and his father agreed to let him go. Quyen was in a similar situation. When his mother found out that he was going to join the Youth Shock Brigades, she cried. He then had to be the more "mature" one in the conversation and told his mother that her worries were baseless. He then told her that the family knew many people who had joined the political struggle at an even younger age. In addition to highlighting the ability of children and youth to negotiate and defend their positions, these exchanges further demonstrate that regardless of personal beliefs, parents ultimately trusted their children to make their own choices.

Some of my interviewees did not negotiate with either their parents or the cadres, instead coming up with elaborate plans to hide their intentions and run away from home. It is also notable that while expectations regarding "what is done," or a sense of duty, guided my interviewees' decisions, they demonstrated an ability to adapt to and negotiate these norms. For example, Xuan used the expectation that young people engage in labor and production to join the Youth Shock Brigades. Knowing that her parents were likely to object to her joining the war effort, she lied to them, saying that she was going to find a job in another town. She was even careful to explain that the job did not pay very well, thus providing an excuse as to why she would not be able to send money back home. She remembered: "My parents just told me—okay, do as you wish. Just find a job that fits your health and do it. That's fine. We don't need your money, just go if you want to."

Another similar striking example can be seen in the case of Lan, who grew up in Hai Phong, a city in northeastern Vietnam. Her father had been killed in the war, and her brothers both joined the struggle. If she also enlisted, she would leave her mother by herself. In a Confucian society, this would be a serious breach of filial piety. However, after attending a meeting held by the Youth Shock Brigades, she felt that "the opportunity has come to me." Her thoughts echo the aforementioned sentiment that by contributing to the political struggle, recruits felt that they would liberate their parents along with the country and therefore would still be carrying out their familial duties (Halberstam 2007, 92). She reasoned with herself, "I can contribute to the revolution if I stay home, but I can contribute more if I go." She chose to write a letter describing her desire to volunteer, and instead of arguing with her mother about leaving, left in secret. While doing so, however, she demonstrated a significant amount of planning and knowing that she had to lie about leaving so as not to upset her mother, as well as determination to control her own emotions:

> While I wrote, I still didn't let my mother know that I [was] going. I remember, the night before leaving, I lay in bed and cried. My mother asked: "Why are you crying?" I said: "The province chose me to go to study cultural education for women and children, for ten days, at the town school." She asked: "It's only ten days, why cry? When you marry, are you going to cry, too?" So that [not letting her mother know] was easy.
>
> The next day, that was 22nd of December, the youth branch met me. I volunteered on one condition: no one must let my mother know where I went. I was there for about four or five days, when my mother found out. She went up to the base and called for me. But I was afraid that if I met my mother, my determination would disappear. So I hid in the squad. We wore uniforms, wore rubber sandals and caps, so she couldn't see who her daughter was. She searched for me for those four or five days, she couldn't find me, cried and left (Nguyen 2023, 18).

For both girls, the act of hiding their intention to join the revolution is similar to the case I described in chapter 2, where a Viet Minh soldier, who did not tell his parents that he was leaving, was convinced by guerrillas that he was still a filial son because in liberating the country, he was also liberating his parents. Although both of my interviewees were seemingly going against core virtues of filial piety, a closer look at their responses shows that they demonstrated considerable care, affection, and filiality toward their parents—sparing their feelings, deliberating how their decisions would affect their family, and ultimately choosing to participate in a revolution that, they believed, would also benefit their loved ones.

As children and youth, my interviewees' actions echo Madsen's (2012) observations about the meaning of "freedom" and "agency" in Confucian societies. In a society with a distinct hierarchy and strictly assigned roles, "agency" does not always mean the ability to choose or not choose to fulfill one's obligations as desired. Rather, agency manifests itself in the dedication, creativity, nuance—and sometimes, shrewdness—with which one negotiates what their roles and duties could entail. My interviewees' choices may have been limited by their circumstances, and indeed some of the social norms directly contradicted each other, such as choosing to be filial by staying home with parents or leaving to participate in the military struggle. However, my interviewees were able to make their decisions and negotiate the contradicting ideas of what it means to be a "good," dutiful child according to Vietnamese cultural norms. In doing so, they demonstrated the ability to understand, navigate, and make plans within the wartime sociopolitical context.

Throughout the interviews, I discovered a clear and consistent theme: namely, that the social environment was a major factor affecting young people's decision to join the political struggle. Whether children and youth participated because they wanted to help their neighbors and communities escape exploitation or because they were affected by the attitudes of their family and peers, these decisions were not made in a social vacuum. This, then, echoes Schlichte's (2014) point that community—whether real or imagined—plays a significant role in combatants' decisions to join. My interviews reveal that many Vietnamese children and youth were displaying concern for political issues, such as social justice and exploitation, at an early age. For some, understanding revolutionary politics was a journey that progressed as they spent more time with the political and military cadres; others were politicized before they were exposed to this influence. In both cases, the role of politics in their lives was significant.

Moreover, children's and youth's voluntarism need to be evaluated in light of the cultural conditioning that prescribed duties and responsibilities to "good" children: protecting their community, valuing the opinions of those around them, and exhibiting loyalty to family. The influence of both community and revolutionary politics made enlistment feel like a realistic and even desirable decision. In other words, the question that they frequently had to answer was not why they would participate, but why they *wouldn't*. These attitudes and patterns of behavior were also shaped at a very early age, thus challenging the idea that young children cannot be political or proactive in their actions. In turn, this socialization became common sense for them and consequently provided a guiding framework for their decision to join the military struggle.

Despite being predisposed and constrained by their circumstances, the actions taken by my interviewees stand in stark contrast with typical victimized portrayals of children and youth associated with the armed forces. They took pride in being able to join the political struggle and put serious thought into their decision to participate. They often made elaborate plans that may or may not have taken their parents' opinions into account, demonstrating their ability to navigate and, when necessary to achieve a goal, to appropriate their social context. There is, of course, the possibility that my interviewees' recollections were influenced by their desire to be perceived as having been strong and independent, even in their representations of themselves at a young age. Still, their accounts provide a meaningful window into the revolutionary collective expectations for children and youth in wartime Vietnam. Young people of all ages were expected to support the revolution in some capacity and were never assumed to be completely uninformed or without agency.

Chapter 4

"If Everyone Can Do It, I Can Do It Too"
Serving in the War

Children and youth played very specific roles in military struggles and were shaped by the work in their respective groups in a variety of ways. As my interviewees explain, the different jobs and positions that they held often depended on their unit and where they were geographically. While working, many young recruits had to deal with physical hardship, ongoing violence, and lack of food and water. They also had to navigate complex hierarchies, where they were sometimes treated as equal to adults but remained embedded in wider power relations. Although they were often in positions of subjugation due to their young age, they were not as a consequence helpless or passive. In fact, most of my interviewees were treated as workers in lower ranks within a hierarchy, expected to learn with minimal guidance and take responsibility for their actions. As we will see, children and youth recruits learned to take control of many of the restrictive circumstances that they faced while working with adults by ignoring or reinforcing the rules that they learned. This assumed a rich variety of forms, from playing, singing, and joking around to allowing themselves to feel and show empathy and a willingness to cultivate meaningful relationships with their comrades.

Setting Context: Training and Work

Education, Training, and Socialization

After joining the military struggle, new recruits, regardless of age, were trained to evolve from being inexperienced peasants to capable fighters, nurses, or spies (among many other types of roles). I will broadly cover three aspects of this process: military training, political education, and wider socialization.

The military training that young recruits received was quite inconsistent and depended on many factors, including the vulnerability of the educational base to outside attacks and the availability of trainers and equipment (Rottman 2007). Training was often very brief. Popkin (1963, 154), for example, states that 30 percent of the guerrillas "had no real training at all," and 70 percent were given "less than two months" of it. This was confirmed by many of my interviewees, who remembered that they trained only when senior comrades had time, or recalled not having any formal training at all, with most learning on the job or through discussions with their peers.

Many local guerrillas were tasked with staying in their own villages to fight or harass American military personnel. They were generally taught how to handle weapons and throw grenades, as well as tactics in combat such as crawling or camouflaging hiding spots (multiple interviewees jokingly recalled having to crawl through farm animals' feces during their training). Sappers learned to differentiate bombs, defuse land mines, hook wire, coil rope, and sound the alarm on enemy activities. Medical assistants received some training in providing medical help, although reports have characterized this training as rudimentary (Goscha 2010). Those who served in the main combat forces had the most systematic training and more individual instruction: they studied how to use more difficult weapons and rehearsed military tactics, among other activities. Specialized jobs (e.g., mine clearing) required longer training periods of up to three months for sappers, while medical staff trained for about a year (Anderson, Arnsten, and Averch 1967; Donnell, Pauker, and Zasloff 1965). In more extreme cases, new recruits were trained on the job and with minimal supervision, such as members of the Youth Shock Brigades who were tasked with building roads and assisting guerrillas and soldiers off the battlefield (Guillemot 2009).

My interviewees also reported an indispensable part of their everyday life as a part of the resistance forces: criticism sessions (*phe binh*). These sessions, where high-ranking cadres would praise the performance of a specific recruit or criticize someone who had not performed well enough (Davidson and Zasloff 1966), were the "favorite Communist device" for training (Tanham 2006, 33). Used to evaluate the whole unit, they were a common occurrence regardless of what specialty new recruits trained in. The revolutionary leadership believed that criticism, rather than physical punishment, was the best way to maintain discipline and raise awareness (Leites 1969; Donnell, Pauker, and Zasloff 1965). As Rottman (2007, 17) observed, this could be particularly effective for Vietnamese people, as loss of face, or "being forced publicly to admit faults, mistakes, and omissions," was "something that proved extremely difficult for them to accept." Recruits, then, would be subject to honor or shame—both very powerful behavior-controlling tools in a collectivist society (Rottman 2007).

It was common for new recruits to have very little knowledge of political ideologies prior to joining the struggle. For many, their understanding of patriotism or communism was largely shaped during the time that they spent with their unit. Much of this is due to how the political cadres and guerrillas of the National Liberation Front (NLF), like many other groups inspired by Maoism, placed very high importance on political education of their new recruits—"a classic form of socialization" in insurgency groups (Gates 2017, 682). The group felt that weaponry was less important than political education, and thus they dedicated more time to that than to specialized military training (Tanham 2006). As such, study sessions had a constant presence in the life of a revolutionary; whenever they were not fighting, they were studying (Leites 1969).

The political education sessions were organized in lecture format and conducted in small groups. Diverse but centered around similar themes, the trainings made sure to convey to recruits the mission and goals of the revolutionary struggle. Many of my interviewees remembered being told to expel foreign colonizers, hate the enemy, and carry out the mission of uniting South with North Vietnam. They were taught that the struggle would be long, and they should not expect to achieve victory in a few years (similar observations were made by Ralph 1967); on the contrary, they should be determined to fight for as long as it took. In addition, they were instructed to be "brave and heroic" and behave according to the unit's rules: to speak politely and softly to villagers, to not engage in horseplay, to not steal or behave rudely toward civilians, and to not drink

(Elliott and Elliott 1969, 40; Bergerud 2010). One of my interviewees remembered, for instance, that the recruits would be severely criticized if they used swear words. At other times, recruits studied Vietnamese history and politics. One interviewee remembered learning about the "mirrors of bravery" (i.e., martyrs who were hailed as heroes in previous Vietnamese rebellions).

Beyond political and military training, the revolutionary forces consistently employed practices to socialize new recruits into becoming part of the group. This is perhaps most prominent in the way that the groups attempted to subordinate existing loyalty to family to loyalty to comrades. Those joining the groups were described as being "emancipated" (*thoat ly*) from their families. Thoughts of family were not supposed to weigh down recruits during missions; their primary affections should lie with their comrades (Leites 1969). It was during this period, when a recruit was away from home and coping with unfamiliar circumstances and physical stress, that the armed forces attempted to some degree to replace family and other relationships as the new object of the recruit's loyalty (Donnell 1967). The recruits ate, slept, and worked in the same spaces, with little privacy. This in turn strengthened group socialization. Recruits were strongly discouraged from fighting and quarrelling among themselves—even NLF defectors noted that squads were remarkably cohesive (Leites 1969); similar dynamics were recalled by my interviewees who belonged to the Youth Shock Brigades. Such deliberate attempts to socialize new members not only helped the recruits cope with separation from their families but also resulted in increased loyalty to and identification with the resistance movement. Many of my interviewees reported being extremely homesick during their first days of service, but they also directly referenced new friendships and comrades as a source of comfort, which helped them forget their homesickness very quickly.

In addition, political cadres and squad leaders worked hard to maintain the morale of their fighters and eradicate any factors that would make their loyalty toward the group waver. They were instructed to erase pessimism and instill confidence in their fighters so participation in the war would be associated with positive emotions (Elliott and Elliott 1969, 40). As a result, commanders avoided negative topics such as enemy's advantages or mentioning families (Leites 1969). Sometimes they acted as moral support for personal problems: one of my interviewees, who later rose to the rank of general, remembered seeing a soldier's sad face. "Why are you sad?" he asked. The soldier's answer was: "The girls think I'm ugly." My interviewee then recounted having to "encourage" and comfort his junior colleague.

The inevitable hardships, such as life in the jungle, were described as beautiful, noble, and necessary (Jamieson 1995). Commanders were instructed to watch closely the unit's morale and behavior: one document shows a special section where guerrilla leaders evaluated recruits' morale after each session, such as who were the most and least enthusiastic (Elliott and Elliott 1969). If there were signs of morale weakening, they would conduct new education and socialization sessions. Even in their spare time, my interviewees continued to express loyalty to the cause and encouraged further socialization through, for example, patriotic poems and songs. The songs were an extremely prominent part of revolutionary forces' lives, often sung during their spare time or work sessions (Guillemot 2009). Many of my interviewees noted that these performances played an important role in maintaining their own morale and providing a necessary break from work. They found joy and experienced feelings of pride when listening to or singing these songs.

The extent to which socialization was successful remains unclear. On the one hand, the continuous discipline and criticism sessions clearly had an effect, as my interviewees consistently showed concern for "face-saving" as a factor that kept them from deserting or motivated them to be dedicated to their activities as part of the resistance forces. For example, when I asked Quyen whether he thought about giving up and deserting, he said: "If you run away . . . it's very dishonorable. Furthermore, it's very dangerous. . . . So in deserting, you will not only lose your life; you will lose your reputation, too." His answer is notable in that it nearly equates one's life with one's reputation. But at the same time, my interviewees admitted that they were more likely to listen to their leaders and internalize lessons from political education classes because they had made a conscious decision and put much effort into joining the revolutionary forces. Sang, a member of the Youth Shock Brigades who convinced his father to let him join the struggle, stated: "You have to understand, no one forced me to be there. So suddenly . . . the process [of socialization] became very deeply ingrained in my mind." Beyond my interviewees, there are records of defectors who left the guerrilla group for multiple reasons, including homesickness and the harsh living conditions, suggesting that socialization was not always effective (Donnell 1967).

The socialization process was not uniform for all people who joined the military struggle. As will be described later in this chapter, some recruits could carry out their assignments without leaving their families;

for them, the idea of being emancipated from their families did not apply. Others did not become an official part of the armed forces, only helping them in supporting jobs (nurses, messengers, *tuyen truyen* specialists, and other support staff). For example, this was true for Hung, whose "training" to steal grenades from American soldiers consisted of talking with other children and sharing their experiences. Nevertheless, even these cases involved some form of education and socialization. My interviewees who did not leave home still referenced going to political education sessions on days when they did not have missions to carry out. In these sessions, too, they studied, listened to cadres' explanations of class relations and Vietnamese history, and sang songs about patriotism. During their missions, they were similarly encouraged to treat each other with affection and see their squad as a single, cohesive unit. Over time, like their counterparts in the jungle, these recruits would also come to identify themselves as part of a close-knit group fighting for national liberation.

Stepping into Action

After (or even during) training, new recruits began their respective jobs. They performed many activities, belonged to different squads, and operated in different locations with varied access to resources, which resulted in unique experiences for all my interviewees. The units, locations, and assigned jobs determined whether the new recruits operated in their home village or were sent to remote locations; whether they lived in the jungle or in the valleys close to villagers. Their assignments determined the jobs and labor that they performed, as well as their living conditions. The jobs of my interviewees can be broadly categorized into several groups: working for guerrillas, in the main forces, or as rear support.

Local guerrilla units (*du kich dia phuong*) were on the lowest rung of the military organization but nevertheless served as the "backbone" of operations (Tanham 2006, 22). These units frequently operated in their own provinces and were largely able to continue their everyday activities, being a "farmer by day, guerrilla by night" (Rottman 2007, 10). As mentioned previously, these units relied on whatever equipment they could secure, while their training was short, irregular, and depended on the availability of senior cadres. Their main tasks, as outlined by Vo (2015), involved "defending the villages, participating in production, and combining with local forces and regular army in the preparation of the battlefront as well as in the attack." More specifically, these guerrillas attacked

American bases and supply storages, transported food and weapons, and mined or otherwise destroyed roads to sabotage enemy operations, among other important jobs. To a lesser extent, some of my interviewees joined the regular armed forces (*bo doi chu luc*), which were generally better trained and equipped. Their main role was to conduct large-scale offensive attacks, but still using guerrilla tactics (Nguyen 2014; Tanham 2006). For example, they carried little equipment and needed less logistical support, and as a result, they were very mobile, marching across the country with "considerable ease and speed" (Tanham 2006, 80). In turn, this meant that fighters belonging to these forces operated outside their provinces and often lived in the jungle. Even fewer of my interviewees also belonged to the North Vietnamese People's Army of Vietnam (PAVN), which entered the south to fight the GVN regime alongside the guerrillas (Asselin 2013).

The work of the fighters was supported significantly by those who worked on the sidelines (*hau phuong*): porters, nurses, cooks, messengers, and many others. Most of these supporting roles were performed by local villagers—often women and children—as the resistance forces placed very high importance on the total mobilization of all people. Sometimes, due to the nature of their jobs, the rear-support workers could not operate directly from their villages, although most still stayed in the proximity of the province. This was the case with nurses, who had to work from medical bases; on the other hand, young people who acted as messengers for the guerrillas could do this without leaving their village permanently.

An important part of rear support specific to the Vietnam War, of which some of my interviewees were members, were the Youth Shock Brigades. Established during the later years of the First Indochina War, they became an essential part, and eventually the "forgotten heroes," of the Vietnam War (Guillemot 2009, 18). As we have seen, some of my interviewees could not join the armed forces due to being underweight or underage—for them, joining these brigades was an alternative way to participate in the war. In the north, about 2.5 million youngsters signed up for the Youth Shock Brigades (Le 2015). They took most of the jobs in the rear support, which was reflected in their slogan, "arrive to the battlefield first and leave last" (Le 2015). "[Arriving] to the battlefield first" meant that the Youth Shock Brigades built roads to transport the military troops, dug tunnels to shield them, and carried weapons and equipment to the battlefield. By "[leaving] last," they cleared the battlefields, carried wounded fighters to safety, and performed simple medical duties. The Youth Shock Brigades lived and operated according to the military regime and discipline, adhering to rules of proper conduct and always speaking politely to the villagers. Their work was essential to the outcome of the struggle. It was the Youth Shock Brigades that built the thousands of kilometers in underground tunnels along the Ho Chi Minh Trail with minimal training and using only simple equipment, including shovels, hoes, and nail hammers (Guillemot 2009). These tunnels were not only used for hiding and sheltering the revolutionary armed forces but also as offense sites: for example, where they could hide under tunnel covers and fire at the enemy forces undetected (Rottman 2007). Unlike local rear support forces, the Youth Shock Brigades were very mobile, reflecting their slogan to "be anywhere they are needed" (*o dau chien truong can la Thanh nien xung phong co mat*) and "go wherever there are enemies" (*o dau co giac la Thanh nien xung phong xuat quan*), both recorded in Bao Bien Phong (2021). They served in some of the most dangerous locations along the Ho Chi Minh Trail (Weaver 2010).

Regardless of the jobs they undertook, my interviewees indicated that their service was characterized by multiple hardships. It was also physically demanding. This was particularly true for the armed forces traveling from North to South Vietnam and for the Youth Shock Brigades, who were required to live in the jungle, away from their home provinces. They acutely felt the lack of food, water, and clothing. Allowances and salaries generally varied between units and depended on resources. For guerrillas, it is often suggested that they received no salary and relied on villagers for food; if they were paid, the amount was "meager" (Davidson 1968, 11; Hunt 2008). Reports by Vietnamese veterans suggest that sometimes fighters had only 100 grams of rice to eat every day—quite often, this was the only food available (Phuong 2019). Similar numbers were remembered by one of my interviewees, Vinh. He admitted that he was in a more privileged position, however, maintaining a camp for Laotian cadres, who were given better food because they were "foreign friends." Even then, he remembered that dying of starvation was perhaps a bigger threat to him than bomb raids—during some of the worst months, each person was rationed only 400 grams of rice per *month*. The Youth Shock Brigades were in a similar position with regard to food and salaries. Guillemot (2009, 31) elaborates: "The available data on food rations are shocking. Regulations stated that each recruit was to receive twenty-four kilograms (53 lbs.) of rice per month, but bombings and other disruptions frequently caused rations to dwindle to almost nothing. Consumption sometimes dipped to as little as four kilograms (9 lbs.) per person."

Indeed, my interviewees, when answering the question "What was the most difficult part of the war?" frequently described hunger, lack of sanitation, and prevalence of illnesses. Hong, who joined the military struggle after her father's change of heart, remembered being so hungry at times that it was difficult to see. Some of their difficulties were extremely specific: Si was part of the armed forces and thus participated in many battles, facing injury and death frequently. However, it was the lack of salt provisions that he found the most troubling: "It makes me shiver just thinking about it, even today." Such were the consequences of operating in the hot, humid jungle: those recruits were in particular need of salt due to how much they sweated. Yet the food provisions were too irregular to provide it consistently. Another interviewee, Cuong, similarly referenced lack of salt as being one of his most memorable wartime experiences, recalling that soldiers almost never put it in food to avoid waste. Instead, they ate unsalted rice and vegetable broth while keeping salt grains wrapped individually. Whenever soldiers wanted to have some salt, they would take it out and lick a grain, then put it back in the wrapping paper.

Local guerrillas or rear-support helpers who lived in their home provinces, and thus did not depend on food rations, were still not protected from the physical effects of the war. Villagers also suffered from poverty and hunger; after defeating France in 1954, Vietnam was "one of the poorest and least developed countries in Asia," with many villagers confirming a life full of hardship (Bryant 1998, 241). Bombing raids were still a common occurrence that inevitably shaped the villagers' lives. As Duc remembered, during his childhood he spent as much time in his family's bomb shelter as he did in the house. Whenever bombings began, they would study, sleep, and eat in bomb shelters, using oil lamps as a source of light. Sometimes they would study there even when there were no bombings, afraid that fighting could break out in the night. The next day, everyone's nose mucus would be completely black from inhaling smoke from the lamps.

Physical labor was also a regular part of life, especially for the PAVN and the Youth Shock Brigades, who traveled thousands of kilometers on foot to the south. Si remembered walking through jungle on blistered and swollen feet, sometimes without any shoes—the shoes that were distributed to the units were rarely the right size. They often did so while carrying heavy food packages, equipment, or weapons ("I carried 30 kilograms of food at the time," remembered one former Youth Shock Brigade member). Many of my interviewees, especially women who were part of the Youth Shock Brigades and thus were responsible for toting equipment and food for the armed groups, could not explain how they were able to carry such heavy loads. Both the Youth Shock Brigades and local guerrillas also frequently described the physically demanding task of digging tunnels. Apart from digging, this job also required handling the soil, carrying it to the nearest lake for disposal, and camouflaging it with leaves, different soil, and tree branches so enemy forces would not detect the tunnels.

In addition to the physical labor, there was constant exposure to violence and loss. Multiple interviewees told me stories of witnessing, running from, or losing their comrades in raids. For example, Lan, whose story began with lying to her mother about joining the Youth Shock Brigades, remembered a particularly painful incident:

> [We had just completed our jobs for the day.] The guy on duty passed by our tunnel—we were all sitting there, singing.... He was holding a book. Back then, we loved books and stories, so I jumped from the trench to take his book. He shoved me, and I fell. A second later, I heard a loud boom. I thought he was joking around and playing pranks. I scolded him, "What are you doing?" He pulled me to sit up. I remember sitting in his lap, scolding him harder. Suddenly, he said: "They all died, Lan."
>
> I turned around, and just a meter from me, there were thirteen people, including seven from my squad—I would [have been] the eighth, but I jumped—they were all dead. Thirteen girl volunteers, all dead, lying on the trench. There was blood everywhere, somebody with a broken skull, someone without a leg, somebody's stomach was showing.... There was a girl, younger than me, in my squad. Her head was hanging over a Casuarina's tree. And two more girls—one girl's skull broke, and another girl—her leg was broken and you could see the white from bones.
>
> I screamed. Everyone ran towards us. I didn't think of anything, I just took off my uniform and bandaged those people. Another girl saw me doing it, and she did the same. Only when people took my comrades away to the dam for the burial, we looked at each other and realized we were practically in our underwear. We didn't know what to do, so we hugged each other and cried.

Her story is not unique. Multiple interviewees remembered joking around one moment and hiding from bombs or being hit with bombs the next moment. Other stories included near-death situations. Many times, my interviewees would tell me stories of bullets passing through their uniforms but not hitting their bodies, or instances when they were meant to go on a dangerous mission but swapping with someone at the last minute—and surviving as a result. The prevalence of death and violence was encapsulated by many interviewees as: "It's death avoiding you, not you avoiding death," implying that it was simply impossible to reliably escape bombs, persecution, and bullets. There was some luck involved in their survival, as if the bombs and bullets themselves did not "want" to hit my interviewees.

Working as part of the revolutionary forces was emotionally and physically demanding. The leadership knew this and thus put in much effort to socialize, educate, and train their recruits to endure hardship. By portraying suffering as necessary and beautiful, or simply by requesting that their fighters withstand it, they cultivated loyalty to the revolutionary cause. While such socialization was not always successful, as records of defectors indicate, large numbers of new recruits were transformed into loyal group members, who—regardless of the jobs that they undertook—were dedicated to their missions and assignments. The next sections look closer into the social relations that my interviewees had to navigate.

Flattened but Not Erased: Hierarchies and Power Relations

While working alongside the revolutionary forces, my interviewees experienced a complicated interweaving of efforts to treat children, youth, and adults as equals and presumptions of young people's subordination. As mentioned in chapter 2, Vietnamese peasant childhood involved working alongside studying and playing; it was also not a space where children and youth would be free of duties and responsibilities. Due to the local understanding of childhood and young people's capabilities, my interviewees were expected to work alongside adults with minimal supervision and scaffolding. This was indicated, for example, in how the Youth Shock Brigade members, despite sometimes being comprised of teenagers, received almost no training and were expected to learn on the job. One of the slogans of the organization was *"khac lam, khac biet,"* which roughly translates as: "You'll know once you start working" (Guillemot 2009, 27). Quyen, who struggled with being shamed in his home village even though he had a clear reason for not joining the resistance forces (they rejected him due to his age), described arriving at the job site during his first days as a Youth Shock Brigade member. His group had never seen some of the tools that they were being asked to use and received almost no instruction on how to build roads, apart from someone reading them a brief manual. He recounted:

> We did everything ourselves. We learned it from each other, no one taught us. No one taught me how to cut stones, or how to use a hammer. But we still managed to learn it, day by day. You look at other people and how they do it. Then you learn: one person has to hold the rock, and two people need to use hammers. Click, then rotate again. No one knows it professionally, it's just self-taught, comrades telling each other. Fifteen- and sixteen-year-olds, just doing it by themselves.

In part, such autonomy in young recruits' jobs was likely to be an unintended consequence of the little training that the revolutionary armed forces and the Youth Shock Brigades could afford to provide. However, in taking for granted that children and youth would learn to do the jobs themselves, the adults still demonstrated the unspoken presumption that young people are not subjects in constant need of care. They were expected and trusted to be independent in coming up with their own solutions without much teaching or guidance.

Interpersonally, the revolutionary forces attempted to treat their recruits equally, regardless of rank, gender, or age. This was noted even by defectors. One defector reported high-ranking cadres always speaking to recruits in a friendly and equal manner; they all remained close and "never fought among themselves" (Leites 1969, 188). Indeed, there has been much discussion in the scholarship of the equality between the higher and lower ranks: it was "surprisingly rare" (Leites 1969, 24) for lower-ranking guerrillas or soldiers to be criticized by higher-ranking cadres without being able to do the same right back to their seniors. My interviewees confirmed that power relations between age groups were also reduced in this way. Quyen recalled: "There were no beatings. If someone did something wrong, he'd get criticized. Young, old—it'd be the same. The young could call out the old, saying something like—'it doesn't matter that you are my commander, what you did is not good.'" The notion of the Vietnamese revolutionary armed groups placing high emphasis on equality (including class and gender equality), flattening of hierarchies, collective decision-making, and self-criticism is consistent with records of other leftist guerrilla movements. This can potentially be attributed to the communist ideologies that guided such groups (e.g., Weinstein 2007; Wood and Thomas 2017).

However, even if there was a theoretical commitment to equality, the presence of hierarchy was still very strong in practice, which is also recorded to be a frequent feature of Maoist groups. Shah's (2013) analysis is particularly illuminating in this sense. She points out that Maoist groups in India placed much emphasis on overcoming caste and class divisions, but hierarchical organizations still remained. Similar dynamics occurred in the experience of my interviewees. There was a clear tension that my interviewees had to navigate: on the one hand, some hierarchies were flattened, but on the other, young recruits were still subordinated on two levels—first, within a hierarchy of rank that distinguished their jobs from more experienced cadres or commanders; and second, within the Confucian understanding of age and power relations.

With regard to specific age-based power relations, the use of language in the resistance groups distinctly illustrates how young recruits' places in the group were equalized on the surface while, at the level of who had real power, their subordination was maintained. As Bourdieu (1990) noted, language can reinforce established social structures and systems of dominance; as an individual learns how to speak in different contexts, the rules of this discourse become incorporated into the habitus. Vietnamese is a relational language: there is a different word for "I" for different situations, and the speaker is constantly defining their position vis-à-vis the conversationalist. While there are many factors that affect pronoun usage, age is the most important: "How old are you?" is one of the first questions that Vietnamese people ask their acquaintances, so they can adjust their pronouns accordingly. The child would then be expected to use appropriate markers of politeness and formality in sentences, which an older conversationalist would not be expected to do. In this sense, speech constantly reinforces and redefines social relationships between speakers—which in turn translates into different power relations. This is in line with the Confucian framework, with language being an important tool to ensure that each person acted according to their role (Luong 1988).

Revolutionary groups attempted to change the pronouns that recruits were used to relying on in their civilian lives, thus also changing power dynamics within their squadrons. As children and youth, many of my interviewees worked with people between thirty and forty years old—at least old enough to be younger siblings of their parents. In most contexts, the correct pronouns for communication between people of these ages would be *chau* (equivalent to nephew/niece) for the children and *co/chu* (aunt/uncle) for their addressees. Speakers of central or southern Vietnamese dialects often use *con* instead of *chau*, which literally translates to "son/daughter," making the relationship more familial but denoting similar age differences between the speakers. Yet, according to many of my interviewees, within their units, the pronouns were deliberately changed to *anh* (for men) and *chị* (for women) to refer to older comrades (older brother/sister), while they would refer to themselves as *em* (younger brother/sister). Markers of politeness, commonly used by younger people toward their elders, were often dropped. In other cases, as described by Sang, no pronouns other than *dong chi* (comrade) and *toi* (neutral and formal "I") were used while working; however, outside of work, the pronouns switched to the older and younger brother/sister forms.

It is important to note that while the use of different pronouns minimized the age difference, it was not completely deemphasized. Pronouns referring to "older brother/sister" and "younger sibling" still came with set power relations and social hierarchies—they could not be treated as complete equals. In line with Luong's (1988) observations, each pronoun came with a set of expectations and roles, and pronouns denoting younger and older siblings were not an exception. In Nguyen's (2016) observations of Vietnamese families, for example, it was still presumed that younger siblings were required to listen to their elders and accept that sometimes their older siblings would have more freedom when choosing how to treat them. As children and young people, then, my interviewees were constantly reminded of their own position within their respective group through the language that they used—and thus reminded of their own subordination. Further, younger recruits would not be able to suggest changes to more equal pronouns themselves; this would be seen as being rude and entitled. Young people were therefore expected to exercise certain autonomy and capability in their jobs but had little power to subvert existing power relations.

In addition, most of my interviewees were in subordinate positions with regard to the jobs that they carried out. For example, those who worked as messengers often did not know exactly what documents they were delivering, or to whom. Even Quyen, complicating his earlier reflections about having relative equality in criticism sessions, stated that while they were free to point out shortcomings in adults, young recruits still ultimately had to defer to their elders' orders. This is consistent with records of how the revolutionary forces organized their military hierarchy: as Rottman (2007, 45) observed, in the units, every person had a "distinct place and role." The leader was a fatherlike figure who worked harder than other members, carried responsibility for the whole unit, and promoted mutual well-being (Leites 1969). Lower echelons of the groups were responsible for carrying out tasks assigned to them but often did not know the big picture of the operations (Rottman 2007). They were also subject to strict discipline by unit commanders; failure to complete tasks would not result in physical beatings but would bring a "loss of face" which, for my interviewees, was a sufficiently powerful punishment. Sang, for example, noted that the possibility of being criticized was one of his primary motivations to always do his best on the battlefield.

Another interviewee, Ha, perceived children and young people as generally having little say in military operations. She remembered being assigned a mission to carry a backpack with important documents, money, and a radio to another unit in the valleys. A guerrilla saw that she was too small for the backpack and offered to carry it for her. They walked on a train railway that Ha had used many times before, which she assumed was safe. However, that night, they were attacked by the Government of Vietnam (GVN) forces. The male guerrilla died, while Ha survived by pretending to be dead. She then remembered not being able to retrieve the backpack and thinking that perhaps losing the documents while dying would be better than losing them and living; that way, she would not be criticized. Inevitably, she had to face the criticism of higher-ranking cadres, who accused her of "[not wanting] to protect important documents, but letting other people take care of it." She described her reaction: "I said—we were from the same village, he saw that I was walking with a big backpack and he wanted to carry it for me. I didn't think of anything. That's the truth." In the end, however, she said, "If I [were] criticized, I [would] just accept it." Despite being trusted with many important jobs, then, many young recruits were still constrained by power relations stemming both from their age and subordinate position at work.

Gendered Structural Constraints

Within the revolutionary groups, young girls' position as subordinates was further complicated by their gender. Adhering to communist principles, the resistance forces strived to treat everyone equally (Taylor 1999). Turner (2002, 94) observed that women "were almost never denigrated as burdensome distractions from the work at hand, especially by the men who worked closely with them," and noted that the problem of sexual harassment was not recorded to be common. I could find very few records of women being pressured to sleep with their male comrades (Quinn-Judge 2001) or enter relationships with them. In a case investigated by Guillemot (2009), both the girl and her boss, who were discovered to be in a relationship, were subject to shame, with the girl facing group social pressure and the boss being mocked by the rest of the group for abusing his power. This is in line with earlier findings that guerrillas could be criticized or purged for raping, molesting, or even flirting with women (Davidson 1968; Leites 1969). Donnell, Pauker, and Zasloff (1965, xiii) suggest that the communists' conduct protocol required a "strict, puritanical sexual code." Others suggest that this had less to do with puritanism and more with the pragmatic idea that recruits could not focus on their duty and complete their missions if they were distracted (Taylor 1999). Turner (2002) offers another explanation, observing that harsh living conditions made survival the primary—indeed, often the only—concern. The hardships of life on the frontlines and in the jungle, health problems, and lack of privacy led to little room for concerns about romance or sex. Another problem was morale: a woman in Turner's study (2002) suggested that the guerrillas and political cadres were afraid that if women were routinely harassed by men on the battlefield, morale would be endangered—a very important factor for groups that otherwise had few resources.

While condemning rape and illicit sexual activity, the revolutionary forces were discouraging but generally tolerant of romantic relationships, realizing that completely prohibiting such relationships would lead to alienation of potential recruits (Turner 2002). However, they urged their fighters to wait until after the revolution to marry and have children (Taylor 1999). In cases when women did get pregnant, commanders sent them home, where women could provide better care for the children, sometimes with marriage certificates to protect them from judgment by conservative neighbors (Turner 2002). Only one of my interviewees, Tam, mentioned having a boyfriend during the time of service—a comrade in her squad when she was about nineteen or twenty years old. Their relationship was short, as he later died in an attack; however, her account did not indicate any condemnation from the unit commander.

Despite efforts to promote equality, the influence of Confucianism meant that women were still in disadvantaged positions relative to men. This was particularly reflected when women struggled for positions of power. Nguyen Thi Dinh, the first and only female general from the Vietnam War, herself noted that both American and Vietnamese men "do not like to talk about women generals. Even Vietnamese men, and we have a history of famous women generals" (Pelzer 2015, 107). Portrayals of Dinh's character in Vietnamese sources also praise qualities traditionally associated with men, such as "strong" (*manh me*) and "unyielding" (*kien cuong*) (Bac 2020). Overall, there was much resistance to women's leadership. Turner (2002, 105), for example, cites guidelines issued by the Communist Party requesting that male party members "overcome their belief that "women cannot lead but must be led."

In addition, as Turner (2002, 104) states, "erotic sentiments" were still more likely expressed toward women by those *outside* the revolutionary forces, rather than by their comrades. In particular, girls were very vulnerable to sexual violence from the American soldiers, whose rape of Vietnamese women has been much more widely recorded (Weaver 2010, 5). There is still, however, very little information on the issue of rape and sexual violence within or outside the resistance forces, especially in the Vietnamese sources. Such questions, as Weaver (2010) points out, carry a stigma for women. This, in turn, would have resulted in secretiveness and an unwillingness to share their experiences with researchers and journalists. Nevertheless, the few accounts that do exist demonstrate that girls' bodies were not completely protected from harassment by men (Weaver 2010).

When I raised questions about gender-based violence and discrimination in my interviews, my female interviewees spoke of being generally comfortable around male comrades, mentioning that they "didn't know anything at that age." Tien, for example, explicitly said that love and relationships "were for older ones." Lan remembered that even at twenty-one, she "didn't know anything." When her first boyfriend (who was not a guerrilla) invited her to his house after the war, "We just slept in the same bed every evening. I met him the other day and he teased me—how could I be so innocent back then? But I really didn't know anything." The extent of how comfortable my female interviewees were around men is shown in Hong's account. She once had to treat a male guerrilla about her age (sixteen or seventeen) who was hit by a bomb. His genitals were burned, and she asked him to remove his trousers so she could clean and disinfect the area. He did not let her, saying that he did not dare to take off his uniform in front of her, a girl. In her words: "I said, comrade, you have to listen to me, it's my job. So he did. The sand, the soil—it got all in there, his skin was completely sore. I took a pair of scissors and cut, it hurt very much. And there weren't any antibiotics or anything." She then took him to the hospital, laughing and remembering: "Afterwards, we got teased—you have to marry him now! You've seen all of it!"

While sexual violence did not surface as a major problem during my interviews, the presence of war still resulted in wider structural violence against women. Lack of resources and poor living conditions resulting from the fighting were most acutely felt by girls. During the Vietnam War, described as "predominantly masculine . . . for men, against men, led by men," women's needs were often marginalized or completely ignored (Guillemot 2009, 47). My female interviewees frequently mentioned the effect of lack of water for washing on girls' menstruation. Water was already so scarce that some of my interviewees reported having to drink their own urine to stay hydrated; when they did have water, it was prioritized for food and drink.

Different girls dealt with their periods differently, as indicated by two former Youth Shock Brigades members' interpretation of their circumstances. Girls in Xuan's unit had to travel to streams and rivers to wash themselves (thus potentially exposing themselves to additional dangers). She recalled being able to get off work half an hour earlier if she was having her period, and generally spoke of it as if it was difficult, but not particularly traumatizing. By contrast, Lan, another Youth Shock Brigades member, perceived it as extremely hard, describing the problems in great detail:

> We didn't have sanitary pads like now—we had to take mosquito nets. After one cycle of menstruation was over, we washed it and used it for the next one—for the whole year. It was thick and tough, and we didn't have any soap. We would wait for rain and leave the "pad" under it, so that the acid goes into the "pad" and "washes" it. Or we peed on it, and let it soak.

She further described sometimes going into the forest to pick fruit and specific types of nuts to use as soap. Lan explicitly said that female hardships were more significant than those faced by men. Girls were distributed only two uniforms per year. During sunny days, it was easy to wash and dry the uniforms; however, during the rainy season, they had to wear wet clothes. Girls' hair was always full of lice. Lan recalled having difficulty adjusting to the rough material of the uniform; the girls' nipples were sore and red, while their genitals, constantly rubbing against the rough material of the trousers, were "completely black" and in constant pain.

Although each Vietnamese girl clearly had her own gender-based issues to contend with, differences in how my women interviewees interpreted their experiences can also be traced to geographical contexts. Xuan was working mainly in the north, where the conditions were poor but still allowed access to water and basic sanitary products. By contrast, Lan worked in the south, where the fighting was much more intense. Indeed, when I asked Xuan whether she had problems with access to water, she mentioned that her circumstances were still better than those in central or southern Vietnam, places that lacked water. This highlights the extent to which the experience of children and young fighters participating in the military struggles cannot be conceptualized as uniform, as even female-specific hardships varied based on the girls' own interpretations and circumstances.

One theme that surfaced in my interviews was the importance of specifically female spaces to bond and cope with the war. It first has to be emphasized that all interviewees mentioned camaraderie as an important coping mechanism. The general reports by my interviewees echo observations by Rottman (2007) that during their life with the revolutionary forces, personal concerns were seen as less important than collective needs. Indeed, Xuan recalled nostalgically that at the time, there was "nothing personal, no one thought about themselves." She remembered, for example, that once she needed to go home, and the whole unit gave her their monthly allowance to help her travel. From the accounts of my interviewees, it becomes apparent that the sense of camaraderie was extremely high among members of the revolutionary groups, regardless of recruits' rank.

However, it was women who shared with me two specific instances when friendship with other girls helped them overcome the physical and emotional hardships of war. The first example came from Lan, who joined the Youth Shock Brigades right before Tet—Lunar New Year, which is traditionally a family holiday in Vietnam. She remembered missing home "horribly" at first, hiding in the bush to cry. Another woman heard her crying and "consoled and encouraged" her. As Lan recounted: "She said, I will take you as my sister. And I calmed down; I didn't cry anymore."

The second story was shared by Tien, another former Youth Shock Brigades member, who fell sick with fever one day while carrying out a mission. At around three in the morning, her unit left for work while she lay in a tunnel. She remembered hearing no human voices, only wind and birdsong, and thinking that she was going to die soon. One of her male comrades later went to check whether she was dead or alive and asked a female comrade to feed her some milk. Since the Youth Shock Brigades did not have any milk, the comrade asked local guerrillas for some. The young female comrade proceeded to care for Tien, telling her that she was alive and making sure that she rested, as well as helping her wash her clothes. The rest of the unit did not go into the tunnel, afraid that Tien's sickness might be contagious. Her comrade, then, exposed herself to further danger by caring for Tien.

Women in Vietnamese culture are expected to take on a role of caregivers, providing comfort and their own resources to others (Rydstrom 2002). Compassion and self-sacrifice (such as being the only person to care for a potentially contagious comrade) were generally expected of them; it is thus not surprising that girls displayed such qualities and volunteered to perform these roles. However, no male interviewees reported similar specific instances of a female friend or caretaker helping them get through a difficult physical or emotional situation, even though instances of women's emotional labor, which "makes wars work," have been recorded by other researchers (Howell 2015, 141). There seems to have been space for female-centric bonding, then, which left a deep impression on the girls. Women, especially young girls, were embedded in the hierarchies and subordination outlined in this discussion—they could not make major decisions with regard to the use of water, for example. Nevertheless, these instances demonstrate how, in circumstances in which women's physical and emotional needs were generally neglected, girls made space to support each other and reject passive suffering.

Between Equality and Hierarchy

While the revolutionary forces often aimed to minimize traditional hierarchies by fostering a sense of collective effort and equality, these ideals coexisted with Confucian values that upheld age-based authority and reinforced power imbalances. This created a complex environment for young recruits, who were treated as capable and equal contributors and yet had to navigate through unspoken hierarchies that often contradicted these ideals (although, as we will see, they still found ways to negotiate even these hierarchies). This is a combination where ideology, social practices, and localized understandings of childhood reinforced each other in some places (e.g., equal treatment with regard to children's and youth's capacities came both from communist understanding of quality and local expectation of peasant childhood), but contradicted in others (e.g., despite equal roles, young people would continuously be reminded of their subordinate position via language). It also shows how the presence of resistance forces (and the consequent intersection of communism, Confucianism, and local peasant practices) produced a new set of norms that both reinforced and disrupted established hierarchies.

Understanding these tensions offers insight into how social dynamics in revolutionary forces were far from monolithic: rather, each young recruit was positioned in a layered, complex system where age, job specifics, and authority intersected in ways that were both enabling and restrictive.

Such understanding of childhood stands in stark contrast to more universalized or Western notions of childhood as a period of protection and vulnerability. In the context of Vietnamese military struggle, childhood was not a distinct phase, sheltered from adult responsibilities, but rather a fluid category where young people were expected to perform similar roles as adults, while still contending with age-based power dynamics. Such an understanding of childhood evades the binary "either child, or adult" conceptualization. Instead, it points to a more complex reality, where *some* aspects of young people's lives are equalized (sometimes by adults themselves), but overall power relations persist. Yet, even in the context of complicated hierarchies and subordinate positions (and physically dangerous and demanding environments), my interviewees learned to negotiate, challenge, and sometimes strategically take advantage of the rules imposed on them, finding pockets to assert their presence and agency despite the constraints. These examples are detailed next.

Children's and Youth's Navigation of Social Context

Children and youth who enlisted in the military struggle found themselves in a new and challenging environment. Novel jobs required new skills and physical endurance; new information had to be learned about patriotism, communism, and conduct; and they had to find their places within the hierarchy of their respective groups' social relations. I use Pierre Bourdieu's thinking about habitus to help trace how children and youth internalized and navigated the expectations of the environments in which they lived and fought as members of the resistance forces.

Bourdieu (1977, 86) conceptualized habitus, or what he describes as "internalized structures, schemes of perception, conception, and action," with one's history being absorbed to the point of being second nature, durable but also flexible and open to change. On the one hand, habitus might also be viewed as a "structuring structure" (Lau 2004, 377), in the sense that it produces actors who internalize new practices to the extent that they end up reproducing and reinforcing the given structure. This was a prominent theme in my interviews: education and training by guerrillas and political cadres added a layer of socialization to my interviewees' lives, adding to how they were previously socialized within their families and communities. As children and youth became more familiar with the wartime context and expectations for them as contributors to the revolutionary cause, they themselves began actively perpetuating and reinforcing the notions of patriotism and unity—which in turn would guide them as they sought to complete their assigned duties. By memorizing the codes of conduct and communist teachings well, in addition to actively perpetuating them, young recruits maintained their status as respected members of the group while avoiding critique during criticism sessions, thus also gaining more symbolic and social capital. They gained honor and respect, in other words, by enacting teachings and cultivating social relationships.

This is not to say that the new structures were passively internalized by my interviewees. There was still much space for showing their commitment in creative ways—within highly constrained circumstances, young recruits still managed to find spaces to express their own voices and agency, similar to Bourdieu's (2000) example of composers who create new music despite being constrained by the same musical keys. Children and youth also sometimes challenged and negotiated the surrounding norms and messaging. Indeed, previous research has shown that children and youth rarely accept change without first reflecting on how it might fit into their existing worldview (Winther-Lindqvist 2009). While clearly memorizing and internalizing communist *tuyen truyen* messaging and lessons, my interviewees similarly infused their new understanding of the world with their own existing thoughts on what is right, desirable, and possible. Going further, my interviewees indicated that with time, they mastered the new rules, knowing subconsciously when they could break them without having to face criticism. This indicates that children and youth became familiar enough with their new life—or gained enough "feel for the game," as Bourdieu (1990, 66) has put it—to be able to anticipate how others might react to their breaking rules. This mirrors the tendency that I described in chapter 3 where, despite being predisposed by social norms to join the military struggle, many young recruits still demonstrated an ability to critically reflect on these same norms and sometimes bypass or use them to achieve their own goals. Multiple layers of socialization and internal deliberations interacted with each other rather than the new norms being passively accepted.

Reinforcing Social Practices

As I outlined in the introduction and chapter 2, young people's agency does not always manifest as rebellion or resistance, but rather as a willingness to *engage* in the social practices promoted in the surrounding context. This is strikingly demonstrated in instances where children and youth continued working, remaining optimistic and dedicated despite the physical and emotional hardships of war. When I asked Son about his perseverance as his unit marched from North Vietnam to South Vietnam, especially when facing exhaustion and weather conditions that made taking the next step through the jungle seem like an impossible task, he responded: "It was very simple. I thought—if everyone can do it, I can do it, too. That's it."

Other social practices within the resistance forces and ideological messaging were similarly reinforced by young recruits. For example, many willingly contributed to the *tuyen truyen* messages given to them by cadres, creatively coming up with their own ways to assert the importance of patriotism in their own lives. Songs and dances, as discussed earlier in this chapter, were used as tools to raise fighters' morale and cultivate patriotism—and sometimes children and youth did not simply internalize these songs but also participated in creating them. Phong, for example, recited a song that he wrote as a thirteen-year-old cadet. In the song, he expresses his resolve to train diligently, acknowledging the youthful spirit around him, full of rhythm and life. He describes scenes of holding hands and singing together, feeling joyful and in harmony with the sun. The youngsters in his song were vibrant and full of life, singing with the hope that their efforts will lead to a brighter future ("so flowers will bloom"). The poem also emphasizes Phong's commitment to self-discipline, stating that his training was to prepare for his future as an adult and, eventually, a proud member of the Ho Chi Minh Communist Youth Union.

While she did not write her own songs, Hong similarly used singing as a way to help her comrades: "You know, back then, bombs burned people—they couldn't open their eyes. So one soldier from the Tay ethnic minority, we had to feed him by spoon, bit by bit. He requested specifically for me to serve him. Because other people, sometimes they would spoon-feed him too much, he wouldn't be able to eat it, he would cry. So I fed him every day like this." She then decided to sing for him because he couldn't open his eyes or his mouth, but he could hear her sing. Other people "who were conscious" could hear her sing and told her that "they were very happy, they didn't feel the pain anymore."

Hong's case also provides an illustration of the complexities of young people's internal thought processes. On the one hand, she mentioned that she wanted to do everything she could "for citizens, for our country," echoing some of the slogans that guerrillas and political cadres used in their *tuyen truyen* messaging. However, she spent much longer elaborating to me how she became determined to work harder after her own encounters with people she treated as a nurse:

> There were people who injured their eyes, their legs . . . their whole bodies were burnt. It was very tragic. I saw people like this, and I was already sad, but then, there was a smell. It smelled so bad! If it was normal life, I wouldn't be able to tolerate it. . . . They lay on two beds, and their faces were completely burnt. The doctor washed them, but then maggots crawled all over the place. That's how rotten the injuries were.

She remembered pitying the injured fighters so much that she cried over their pain and injuries. Her compassion motivated her to work harder. As she articulated: "But I felt empathy for these soldiers—they lost their life for peace. I thought—those people lost their lives for the country, for us—I would have to do everything to help them, too." The idea of soldiers losing their lives "for peace," or "for the country," is indicative in itself of the guerrillas' and political cadres' messaging. However, the subsequent justifications for her work came through applying the teachings to what she witnessed herself. Hong's activities, then, were underpinned by a complicated combination of her own emotions of empathy and pity, her experience and external socialization.

I was particularly struck by Hong's story, not least because she demonstrated such a close awareness of the people around her. Her story, combined with the aforementioned accounts of friendships and bonding, again highlights that the experiences of children and youth cannot be separated from their social environments. Indeed, for my interviewees, the ability to cultivate relationships with their peers and villagers or predict reactions from different adults became one of the defining features of their experience. Their environment provided a sense of camaraderie, humor, and play, as well as becoming a space for mutual learning and teaching, emotional bonding, and empathy. Paying attention to instances when young people demonstrated competence, empathy, and dedication to their friends and comrades, in turn, challenges the stereotype of the passive, dehumanized, or robotic child associated with armed forces. These examples are particularly worthy of emphasis because they underline that while working as part of the revolutionary forces, the people whom I interviewed never lost their humanity but indeed actively sought to cultivate it.

Children and youth associated with the revolutionary forces also displayed a willingness to work hard and excel at their tasks. We saw in chapter 3 that My, after being exposed to guerrilla performances, decided to join the struggle as a nurse. While living with guerrillas, she worked hard to become the best nurse at her medical base; eventually, as she recounted, the doctor always requested that she assist with his surgeries, while scolding some of the older nurses for not doing their job properly. Vinh, who was tasked with maintaining a camp for political cadres, including Vietnamese and Laotians, described always striving to do his job honestly. For example, when given a budget, he always bought exactly the amount that was needed for the camp. He did not buy excess products such as cigarettes or coffee and sell them on the black market, as many others did during the war. For him, this was a matter of principle: he decided to carry out his duties in the most honest way possible.

Even in situations where their lives were threatened, some of my interviewees managed to come up with creative solutions that they believed were superior to the "adult" ones. This is strikingly portrayed in the story of Loan, a sapper who mainly operated in southern and central Vietnam. After witnessing her father, a communist, being beaten up by GVN officials, she became determined to participate in the struggle. Helping her mother cook food and shelter guerrillas, she later began working for the guerrillas herself. In 1965, at fourteen years old, she was almost captured by the GVN officials. As they were chasing her, she had no way of escaping into a secret tunnel, nor could she contact other guerrillas for help. In these circumstances, she came up with a plan: to wear her shirt inside out and knock on a villager's door. She remembered:

> I knocked on this woman's door and asked her to let me in. She said—it's four in the morning, why are you running into my house? I then explained that I was carrying out my mission and the GVN were chasing me. I asked her to pretend to be my aunt. She immediately said—come in, come in. After a while, the South Vietnamese officials came in. I said—I am a normal villager, my foot is crippled and I am going up to Saigon to get treatment.

She then described pretending to crawl as if her foot were crippled. Her creative solution to the problem notwithstanding, her thoughts portray how she felt smarter than the adults who were chasing her. She described thinking about one of them: "That official was so stupid—if I am crippled, my foot should look small. But my foot was fine, and he still believed me." In this instance, then, she demonstrated not only the ability to think quickly and resolve a situation in a creative way under highly stressful circumstances, but also produced a tactical assessment of how this situation should have been responded to by another person (in this case, the adult official).

Gaining a "Feel for the Game": Learning When Rules Could Be Bypassed

While always respecting the communist code of conduct and approach to discipline, children and youth also eventually learned which rules might be negotiable. This is reflected in an anecdote from Tien. When she and her friends in the Youth Shock Brigades kept chatting and joking around during work, her frustrated unit commander ordered them to stop talking, shouting: "You fucking chatterboxes!" Given the strict hierarchy in the group, obedience to the commander's orders would be expected. At this point, however, the group was already familiar enough with the commander to know that even when using harsh language, he would be unlikely to punish them for chatting; his comment, in fact, only made them laugh harder. Tien mentioned that this is still a very "dear memory" for the veterans in her unit. During study sessions, they would quietly tie pieces of paper to someone's shirt and laugh at the way it moved, again showing their willingness to ignore rules in a supposedly strict situation. In another instance, Phong remembered that the young cadets in his school were so frustrated by the lack of food that they tied up the "older brother" cook and threw him in the river as a prank (without actually endangering his life). The choice to direct their frustrations at the cook is noteworthy—they knew that he was less likely to punish them than teachers. However, they then realized that if the cook were tied up, there would be no food at all. As a result, they promised not to touch him again—imposing their own rules on this experience—and vented their frustrations onto teachers instead.

Sometimes young recruits would steal villagers' fruit and leaves—behavior that was clearly not in line with the rules. Xuan remembered pretending to need to do something in villagers' houses, but in reality going there to steal cassava leaves to grow in her own unit (she also mentioned that they probably knew about it). Cuong, a member of the forces who spent time marching through the jungle, remembered a particularly elaborate scheme that involved pranking senior commanders to get access to food. Each unit was often given square pies wrapped in banana leaves, he recalled. They were not allowed to eat them until given permission; unit commanders often conducted random checks, touching the wrappers to make sure that the pies were still there. The young recruits, then, often ate the pies and replaced them with square-shaped pieces of wood; the commanders touched them, felt the consistency of the wood being similar to the pie, and would not question them any further.

Earlier in this chapter, I described how the commanders and political cadres worked to maintain the morale of their units. However, accounts from my interviewees also suggest that, as children and youth participating in the conflict, they cultivated a sense of optimism for themselves in a distinctly "childlike" way, as Jeffrey (2011, 250) put it: with fun, jokes, and playful mischief. Confirming this, Tien said that "younger Youth Shock Brigade members always had something to laugh about, unlike older ones." The importance of laughing and joking was repeatedly stated to be an important coping mechanism for my interviewees—for example, Quan articulated that "if it wasn't for the optimism and fun, I wouldn't be able to tolerate it." What is notable, however, is how their jokes deliberately poked fun at their circumstances and the rules that they had to abide by. For example, Xuan remembered that the Youth Shock Brigades members "found everything funny. Every time we heard bombs, we would laugh while running to the tunnels; by the time we stopped laughing, the bombing would be over." One "funny" thing was how the bombings disrupted rules about relationships: "During work, boys and girls were not allowed to be in relationships, but when running to the tunnels, they would hold hands or jump into each other's laps. We did it spontaneously, without thinking, and then discovered it once we're in the tunnel. Everyone found it very funny, so we would laugh at that."

Other young people, knowing that they could not escape the harsh living conditions or complain directly to their superiors, would come up with parody songs making fun of their circumstances. For example, Phong recalls that another cadet changed the song "Healthy for the Fatherland" to "Getting Rashes for the Fatherland," reflecting the poor hygienic conditions in the jungle. Sometimes they would sing these parodied lyrics quietly during times when patriotic songs were playing to uplift the cadets' morale.

Strategic Navigation of Childhood Stereotypes

So far, I have described children's and youth's lives and roles within the resistance forces (local guerrillas, the main forces, PAVN, and the Youth Shock Brigades). Beyond their own groups, however, many of my interviewees interacted with American soldiers, who also constituted a part of their social environment. Competent and creative when carrying out their missions, these young people displayed often lifesaving social awareness of what the American soldiers were like and how they were likely to react to their actions. Documents and photos from the war show that American GIs generally approached children as subjects to be protected rather than as threats. This is indicated, for example, by a photo taken in 1968 published by *Time* that shows an American GI caring for a child, walking with an injured toddler in his arms. The commentary describes how in doing so, "Hard Marines suddenly became the most gentle, loving persons" (Gabriner and Rothman n.d.). In another instance, Stur (2011, 154) shares the text from a pamphlet published by the US Department of the Navy in 1967 as part of the Marine Corps' Civic Action Program: "Battle-scarred hands of a Marine infantryman . . . giving a little girl—destined by the fate of guerrilla warfare to spend her youth in an orphanage—her first real doll."

Resourceful young recruits fighting on the side of the revolutionary forces, therefore, used their own young age to carry out their missions more effectively. In some cases, their youth saved their lives without them needing to intentionally use their age to protect themselves. Tam, who transported weapons for the NLF, described being caught by the GVN forces during one of her missions. Two of her comrades died in the attack; only she and the unit commander were left. She remembered making her way to a bakery, where the commander told her to hide in the oven while he distracted the GVN soldiers—in reality, he probably accepted that he was going to die. Eventually, however, she was captured. The GVN soldiers were almost prepared to shoot her until one of them said: "Look, she's so small. She probably tagged along for fun without knowing anything. . . . What Viet Cong [the GVN name for the NLF]? What's the use of killing her?" They did not know that out of all my interviewees, Tam articulated the most explicitly political motivations for joining the guerrilla cause; she found the Saigon regime too exploitative. She was tried in court by the GVN and sent to a number of prisons—however, she was also the only person in her unit whose life was spared.

Other young recruits deliberately exploited the belief that their age (in American eyes) presupposed ignorance, innocence, and vulnerability. As such, children and youth were effective at performing tasks while remaining unsuspicious, particularly keeping watch, delivering documents, and running small errands for the guerrillas. One of my interviewees, Linh, began working as a messenger from ten years old, later participating in larger-scale guerrilla operations. She sewed a small pocket inside her underwear where she hid important documents. Sometimes American officials would suspect that she was making a delivery and search her; however, they never made her take off her underwear because she was a child, so she was never caught. She remembered, however, that adults would be requested to take off their underwear during these searches. Knowing that American soldiers tended to check children less thoroughly, she was eager to help the guerrillas.

In the pamphlet shared by Stur (2011), a soldier giving a doll to a small girl is portrayed as an important act of humanity; and indeed, the American and GVN forces must have thought of playing as an inseparable part of childhood. This assumption was also exploited by children and youth to aid them in stealing American supplies. This kind of theft was important to the revolutionary armed forces, who were underequipped and compiled many of their supplies by stealing from the enemy or taking things from dead bodies (Tanham 2006). Hung, for example, recounted not being afraid of American soldiers because he knew that they liked children—as he stated: "Just say 'hello,' 'OK' to them, they liked it very much." The soldiers were very willing to play with him and frequently offered him fruit and chocolates. Sometimes he would specifically ask for American coffee or chocolates to bring to the communist cadres. After playing with the Americans for a while, he would make sure that they trusted him and would suggest rubbing their backs in order to be able to go inside their bases, which had piles of grenades lying in the corners. He remembered having to rub their backs very carefully, "so that they are really happy" and distracted. While doing this, he would simultaneously use a thin string to hook grenades and drag them quietly toward himself. Sometimes children and youth would work in pairs or threes—one person, for example, would play with the soldiers while others stole the supplies.

On another occasion, Hung was asked to make special baskets from banana leaves and cover mines that the NLF planted along the roads. Since the GVN often scanned the roads for mines, these leaves would intercept the metal detectors' signals. Hung remembered that collecting large amounts of banana leaves could lead to suspicion. Every time a GVN official asked him: "What are you doing, child, collecting these leaves?" he would say: "I'm making a gun out of the leaves!" and then pretended to shoot a gun. "You know, since I was a child; children are mischievous." He was careful to pretend to play when in sight of others, but in fact he was collecting leaves, which he was drying and using to cover mines. In these examples, we see that children's and youth's intelligence went beyond their immediate ability to steal grenades or deliver messages. They displayed very high levels of social awareness: understanding the cultural meanings attached to childhood, foreign and familiar, they could predict adults' expectations and use their misguided assumptions to achieve children's own goals.

Ultimately, young recruits were free to exercise a good amount of creativity and autonomy (in keeping with the guerrillas' and the Vietnamese peasant understanding of childhood that I have been describing), resulting in many of them enjoying their time with the revolutionary forces. My interviewees grew up in dangerous and violent environments; however, many saw their work in the military struggle as a way to learn to navigate highly restrictive structures in an innovative way, and to survive even in some of the most challenging circumstances. Learning new things and consistently seeing results constituted a rewarding experience for many. It was common for my interviewees to remember being very proud when they managed to come up with creative solutions to problems that would be challenging even for adults. Many of them, like Quan and Vinh, treated their revolutionary activities as a job, stating that the opportunity to hone their skills through training and real-life experiences eventually shaped them as workers and as people.

The experiences of children and youth serving in the Vietnam War were far from homogenous. They were given specific jobs that they were required to carry out wherever they were sent to, geographically. In addition, their lives were inevitably shaped by contradictions that came as a result of new social environments, situated at the encounter between communism, Confucianism, and local understanding of peasant childhood. Here, children and youth generally found themselves negotiating power relations despite attempts to equalize relations between group members. It is notable, however, that their childhoods did not necessitate presumptions of inherent passivity or additional guidance from adults.

As with their motivation to join the struggle, the children's and youth's time during their service is best understood as involving an interaction between social structures and the young recruits' own inner lives. Children and youth internalized many of the messages that they received from guerrillas and political cadres about patriotism, liberation, and proper conduct. However, they rarely adopted these messages without questioning them—and sometimes they ignored the rules altogether. In other instances, they internalized part of the teachings, combining these lessons with their own observations as they gained more experience.

Their subsequent courses of action—whether they were striving to be the best nurse on the medical base, distracting Americans while stealing grenades, or simply trying to help a fellow soldier in pain—were always underpinned by the attitudes and beliefs that they developed as a combination of both external socialization and their own ideas. As we will see in chapter 5, the wartime service habitus—internalized messages about patriotism, the habit of discipline, and endurance of hardship—became a very important part of my interviewees' identities, which they carried with them into the postwar period. Rather than forgetting or dismissing their youth as members of the resistance forces, they viewed it as a distinct period in their lives—as important and worthy of respect as other periods.

CHAPTER 5

"My Country Is Still Poor, but I Will Persevere"

The Return to Civilian Life

Whether members of the National Liberation Front (NLF), the armed forces, or the Youth Shock Brigades, many children and youth found themselves in the middle of political and economic turmoil after completing their missions; they had to navigate still-unstable environments while rebuilding their civilian lives. For example, My—nineteen years old at the end of her time serving—returned to her village on the outskirts of Saigon to resume school. Si, who worked as a part of the main forces, stayed in the south for a few months to manage villages with the rest of the units before returning to the north. Tien, having just turned eighteen years old when the war ended, remembered having absolutely no idea where her life would go from there, what occupation she would later prepare for, or how she would achieve her goals. Upon returning, many of my interviewees found their villages burned and their fields destroyed. Not all of them went back strictly at the end of the war (i.e., in 1975), and I will provide timelines where needed.

Yet the general trend of my interviews revealed that their transition from war to postwar life was relatively seamless. One part of it was my interviewees' own choice not to be victimized. This choice was facilitated by several factors. The first is the environment within which my interviewees were operating—they were the victors of the war, and thus their starting point was one of privilege, especially in comparison to their counterparts who fought for the defeated Government of Vietnam (GVN). In turn, they were given opportunities for employment, and their communities did not stigmatize their war experiences. This is not to say that they found reintegration easy—as we will see in this chapter, there were discrepancies between what they expected upon their return and their realities. As children and youth, their adaptation was further facilitated by a second factor, the habitus acquired through their time as part of the resistance forces. This proved to be particularly useful in a context where the government was implementing socialist policies that revolutionaries were already familiar with.

The accounts of my interviewees are quite different from the accounts of children serving in contemporary armed forces (e.g., the Lord's Resistance Army in Uganda) who struggled to reintegrate, facing significant challenges with socialization, employment, education, and generally going back to daily civilian life. While these cases are common, they are linked to the specific social contexts within which this reintegration took place—often, the scholarship focuses on children and youth who fought in a group in which there were no opportunities for or interest in implementing their own support structures or gaining privileges within their communities (e.g., Veale and Stavrou 2007; Bloom 2019). By contrast, the cases of my interviewees demonstrate what happens when former young fighters are reintegrated into their community as victors and are allowed access to institutional support, social privilege, and spaces to preserve—rather than discard—their past.

Postwar Context

By the end of the war with the United States, Vietnam was left in crisis. Two-thirds of the villages, agricultural land, roads, and railways were destroyed by bombs, with many more mines remaining unexploded (Dang 2010). Agent Orange left many people and livestock permanently mutilated. The United States refused to provide any reconstruction aid; on the contrary, it imposed a nineteen-year-long trade embargo on Vietnam, prohibiting any US businesses from importing or exporting goods (Castelli 1995). It further pressured its allies and other international institutions to follow suit (Davies 2015). Overall, as Bradley (2021, 175) notes, Vietnam was "on its own" to solve its economic and social problems.

Over the next decade, Vietnam ran on its centrally planned economy. This economic model had already been implemented in North Vietnam after the Viet Minh's victory against the French forces in 1954.

This resulted in a range of policies, such as reallocating land to peasants, establishing collective farming and co-ops, and running a variety of literacy and educational programs (Kerkvliet 2005). Many reasons were outlined to justify the changes: peasants would be able to use land more efficiently, raise more livestock, and produce beyond their needs. As a 1958 national pronouncement remarked, such changes would "strongly encourage our peasant compatriots in the south to exert every effort in the struggle against the United States and Diem in order to push ahead for reunification of our homeland" (as cited in Kerkvliet 2005, 11). In sum, this shift was articulated as both a way to a better economic life for everyone and an act of patriotism. Kerkvliet (2005) notes that peasants were grateful for these reforms, as they believed that the changes would improve their economic situation. Indeed, due to the government's programs, statistics show that North Vietnam (in 1945/1954) had better rates of literacy, education, and women's political participation than South Vietnam in later years—that is, 1975 (Grosse 2015).

When the fighting ended in 1975, the same economic institutions that had been operating in North Vietnam for more than two decades were introduced in South Vietnam. Yet while the socialist economic model had run relatively well in North Vietnam, many South Vietnamese peasants refused to accept the implementation of these institutions (Kolko 1995). Thrift (1987, 424), for example, recorded how peasants in the Red River Delta "refused to harvest crops, abandoned land, even clandestinely killed their livestock to avoid taxes." Some of my southern interviewees recalled the disincentive and lack of interest with which farmers participated in co-ops—for example, immediately tossing their hoes aside as soon as they heard the end-of-the-day gong, often leaving their work unfinished. Despite this, they were still required to work in co-ops. Hung, who ran small errands for guerrillas in the south, recalled that some children could be denied education if their family refused to participate in collective agricultural organizations. In these circumstances, many South Vietnamese civilians chose to flee—even those who did not initially support the GVN. The end of the war saw waves of refugees in the south fleeing to the United States, as well as general social tensions between those who supported communism and those who did not. Some of my interviewees also remembered an increase in the presence of small armed groups that remained loyal to the old regime, harassing villages for food and produce instead of joining the co-ops. The economic hardships were also further complicated by other wars that followed almost immediately—military conflict in Cambodia in 1978 and the Sino-Vietnamese War in 1979.

This context, therefore, led to underperforming economic outputs. The next years were characterized by a collapsing economy and widespread poverty. While the government predicted a 14 percent increase in the economy following 1975, in reality it grew by only 0.4 percent; the industrial sector grew by 0.6 percent and agriculture by 1.9 percent (Nguyen 2012). Moreover, the country's poverty rate stood at 60 percent (Davies 2015). Inexperience in economic management and lack of incentives were among the primary reasons for the economic crisis that Vietnam experienced in the 1970s (Harvie and Tran 1997). As Kolko (1995) noted, many former Vietnamese revolutionaries asked in the end whether their sacrifice was worth winning the war if they were losing the peace.

Privilege of Former Revolutionaries

Despite such economic and social hardships, my interviewees' return to civilian life was characterized by relative calmness. Several factors contributed to their seamless transition. As victors of the war, not only had my interviewees returned home as winners, but the side that they fought for implemented a range of programs and resources aimed at stabilizing the political and social situation. The communist supporters' position of privilege relative to the GVN supporters in the aftermath of the war is worth exploring, as it directly affected the reintegration experiences of my then-young interviewees. Significantly, this treatment is different from the majority of contemporary cases of children's recent participation in armed conflicts. Groups like the Lord's Resistance Army, the Union of Congolese Patriots in Congo, and Fuerzas Armadas Revolucionarias de Colombia (FARC) did not have the opportunity for or interest in establishing formal institutions to support their fighters (Thomson 2020; Borzello 2007; Smith 2012). In addition, such fighters have frequently belonged to the losing side in political conflicts, which meant that the children fighting for them had to face the stigma of being in the defeated group, similar to what the GVN collaborators were exposed to. In cases where children and youth did fight for a group that eventually established its own government, most accounts once again point out children's victimization amid the political chaos and weak government structure. For example, Mekonnen and van Reisen (2012) and Binadi and Binadi (2011) describe the circumstances in Eritrea and South Sudan, respectively: despite winning their conflicts, these governments have weak records of instating reintegration programs for children and youth associated with the armed forces (and ex-fighters more generally).

Indeed, most children and youth fighting in armed conflicts across the world have not received the privilege and status, including institutional support and community acceptance, afforded to my interviewees.

By contrast, in Vietnam, as a result of its socialist policies, the local and national government authorities organized and managed labor, assigning jobs to all citizens fit to work in various state offices and co-ops. This is highlighted in regulations such as "All levels of the government are responsible for arranging suitable jobs for all working people in their localities, enabling them to both have a source of livelihood and contribute to society" (Ministry of Public Security—Ministry of Labor 1974; my translation). The state kept records of who was or was not unemployed, who had the capacity to move to another location, who needed to work in their own village, workers' different health conditions, and other useful data. Local government branches were required to send this information to the Ministry of Labor regularly, so it could "coordinate with the production sectors to arrange and assign jobs" to fill labor quotas (Council of Ministers 1974; my translation). The same regulatory body noted that there were still many unemployed people in the country, despite many jobs being available through regional branches. The unemployed were subject to investigation and could be forced to work by the police if needed (Ministry of Labor 1972).

Within these circumstances, finding a source of income, whether by working in an agricultural co-op or in a local state office, was a realistic possibility for youth. Most Vietnamese peasants (around 97 percent, according to Luong 2003), including youth, joined co-ops. The government also passed several regulations that prioritized the employment of veterans and former revolutionaries. In a directive issued in 1980, the Ministry of Defense and the Ministry of Labor were asked to arrange for youth who served in the revolution to attend high school or vocational school, coordinating this effort with the training and recruitment targets (Prime Minister 1980). The Ministry of Defense was to provide exact statistics on how many people were leaving the armed forces so other government departments could "arrange allocation according to recruitment and enrolment demands of branches and localities" (Prime Minister 1980; my translation). The regulation pointed out that demand still existed for cadres in industries such as accounting, taxes, finances, and nursing, and it directed the Ministry of Labor to instruct provinces to prioritize recruitment among those who had recently left the military. Various secondary sources confirm that posts of authority in communes or provinces were quickly filled by former revolutionaries. For example,

Malarney (2002b, 77) noted, "The experience of having served in the military, for many, has become an important qualification for assuming leadership roles in the commune." Special schools were opened for former revolutionaries, who would be educated and go back to serve in roles of authority in their home provinces (Dang 2018; also seen in Prime Minister 1980). Luong (2003) records an instance of a villager who was drafted (rather than applying) to head a co-op, suggesting that the government played a major role in controlling job assignments.

Most of my interviewees acknowledged that there indeed existed a separate priority system for former veterans (regardless of their age). The priority systems varied. People who finished their service could present at various factories or offices a certificate confirming their completion of a military mission. Like many former revolutionaries, Minh, who was initially in the main forces, was asked to help rebuild his northern province after the war ended. He used the word "manage" to describe his activities: identifying what buildings needed to be restored, what materials were left, and how they could be used, among other data. He explained that large military teams would do similar management jobs for bigger cities, while local teams would manage smaller towns and provinces. For those wishing to pursue higher education, their military background awarded them extra points that would give them an advantage to achieve the required grades on college entrance exams.

A more complicated system of allocation existed for those who wanted to continue working in the military while studying. For example, Quan, whose journey we followed in chapter 3, joined the revolution at sixteen and worked as a sapper, afterward choosing to stay in the military, continuing his schooling while moving up the ranks. However, as he explained, several factors needed to be considered during such allocations: the number of people with similar career choices, the number of positions available, and whether the commanders felt that the candidate was well suited for such a trajectory. In his case, for example, he was chosen to study at a university; however, his initial choice to become an engineer was not granted due to the small number of such positions allocated. Instead, his commanders asked him to study politics and train as a political cadre.

The same arrangements existed for Youth Shock Brigade members. In general, these young people were almost immediately sent to work in the service of postwar society, as demonstrated in a Ministry of Finance (1976) regulation directing that communes arrange work (most often production in local co-ops) or education for Youth Shock Brigade members.

A further regulation issued in 1978 mentioned that they should be prioritized when being allocated jobs: "depending on the requirements of production, work and circumstances of each member, the branches at the central level and the People's Committees of provinces and cities employing Youth Shock Brigade members will prioritize the placement of them to work in economic branches or to enroll in schools and training classes according to the State regulations" (Prime Minister 1978a; my translation).

My interviewees confirmed that finding a job immediately after war service and reintegrating into society were not difficult tasks for Youth Shock Brigade members. Quang, for example, explains:

> After I came back, I went straight to work. Whatever job I applied to, I was accepted immediately. If you wanted to work somewhere else [in another province, for example], they would be able to arrange it. Some people went to work for the national authorities, and whoever couldn't, worked for the province. That's how they managed the life after war. . . . Back then, Youth Shock Brigade members had a recommendation letter that they could present when asking for a job.

One of my interviewees, Hung, noted that the privileges that the veterans enjoyed caused tensions in society. He acknowledged that while these priorities were "a repayment of gratitude," they were not always beneficial to the economy or the people. Being a child from South Vietnam, he witnessed those with potential and capabilities being denied entry into good universities or turned away for jobs because they came from families that supported the GVN. He himself was chosen to join police forces because he "had a good background" (i.e., came from a family that supported the revolution throughout the war). He also witnessed those without such a "good background" doing manual labor rather than being placed in better jobs. Many people, he remembered, left the country because they could not see a future for themselves or their families in Vietnam.

Former GVN supporters were not the only people to suffer economic hardship—former revolutionaries also experienced the negative consequences of the Vietnamese postwar economy. Despite these complexities, however, my interviewees were deeply aware that they were in a position of relative privilege, and many acknowledged that they received good jobs and financial remuneration due to their status as former revolutionaries.

Perception of Young Revolutionaries

According to my interviewees, the general community perception of people who joined and supported the military struggle against the United States and their Vietnamese allies varied from positive to neutral. On the official level, young recruits were celebrated on the same level as older ones. The sentiments that existed prior to young people's recruitment—like the idea that the revolutionaries were carrying out a noble and historic mission—persisted. After the wars ended, the government further portrayed the work of former revolutionaries as deserving praise by giving them awards and medals and/or financially supplementing families of injured, perished, or missing fighters. This is indicated in regulations issued immediately after the Vietnam War. For example, in a 1975 circular, the government urged: "Now that the war against the United States for national salvation has ended successfully, localities need to ... complete commendation [of former veterans]" (Government 1975; my translation). The circular further stated that the localities needed to pay special attention to families with soldiers who were injured or who had died.

It is notable that direct participation in combat was not necessary for someone to receive awards and medals—for example, one of my interviewees was awarded a medal of bravery for sheltering guerrillas and cooking food for them. The importance of family is continuously underlined even in these awards. A regulation issued in 1978 is particularly illustrative of the authorities' honoring family as a unit (Prime Minister 1978b; my translation): "A condition for parents to be considered [for the award] and commended is if they agreed and encouraged their children to emancipate themselves from family and participate in the revolution; not commit crimes against the Fatherland, harming the interests of the people and the revolution; not sentenced to imprisonment or probation by the revolutionary government." Many of my interviewees, while recounting their experiences, showed me their medals and awards, explaining how different military roles would result in different types of awards. Many of these medals were also accompanied by certificates of acknowledgment of their bravery and achievements hanging on the walls in their houses—signs of accolades worthy of pride.

None of my interviewees reported experiencing the same glorification at the village level as on the official level; but returning young recruits, often remaining active in village life, were generally accepted by villagers and lived in close proximity to peasants. The image of a child pulled from a life of relative tranquility and sent to faraway locations to fight for armed forces does not apply to many of my interviewees. For many of them, delivering messages, cooking food, digging tunnels, harassing local American soldiers, or running small errands could be done directly from one's village. As mentioned in chapter 3, many young recruits continued to be "farmers by day, guerrillas by night," maintaining village activities such as farming, studying, and socializing with neighbors and friends. For example, one of my interviewees became part of the local guerrilla group and participated in most of her activities at night. She would work in the fields during the day, have dinner at home, take a shower, then go to guerrilla meetings or carry out her assigned missions. At around one o'clock in the morning, she would come home to sleep. Her everyday life, then, was largely undisrupted. Knowing that work in the fields in Vietnam starts very early, I asked if she got enough sleep. "Who cares about sleeping?" she responded. Other interviewees such as Duc and Hung, who mostly ran errands and stole guns, grenades, and food from the Americans, did so alongside their usual chores. For them, again, there was no reintegration—they were already a part of, and never left, their own communities. The return to farm work was also simple: many interviewees were already used to it (having done some of it when they were even younger), so coming back was no problem.

Some of my interviewees did have to leave their villages as part of their journey from the north to the south; even then, however, they were not completely removed from wider society. As discussed in previous chapters of this book, Vietnamese revolutionary forces made a deliberate effort to understand villagers' cultures and grievances. This is particularly well illustrated in Ho Chi Minh's own words: to strive to do anything that is good for the people and avoid doing anything that is harmful for the people (as cited in *Thanh Nien* 2006); for examples of soldiers internalizing this philosophy, see Nguyen (2020). While the resistance forces did have a strong identity and spent much time cultivating it among their fighters, this identity was largely defined against the American forces, not Vietnamese civilians. Some sources on combatants from the Vietnam War similarly allude to veterans being welcomed warmly upon their return and having no problems building relationships, including with their own families (e.g., Nguyen 2020).

This close relationship between villagers and resistance forces was an important characteristic differentiating guerrillas and their supporters from the "foreign invaders." My interviewees frequently referenced casually chatting with villagers, learning about their lives, and helping them with small chores such as sweeping or carrying heavy loads. This was encouraged, as readers will recall, by the leadership. Si, an interviewee who participated as part of the main armed forces, also remembered being trained in interacting with civilians "to encourage people to do their jobs, to participate in opening a route, lead us (soldiers) to a certain place, or if we need food, to feed us. That is a way of communicating so that they understand that I am a good person and a soldier." He explained that quite often, he applied the same techniques in his postwar life to foster relationships with villagers. In other words, many people who served in the war did not lose their social skills but maintained them; in some cases, their military experiences strengthened their ability to cultivate meaningful relationships with civilians. As such, upon their subsequent return, young former recruits perhaps understood the villagers' ways of life more rather than less acutely.

We have also seen that this relationship was often reciprocal: it was common for villagers to shelter and help the resistance forces and their supporters, and the guerrillas specifically reinforced this bond through their principle of the "three togethers": sleeping, eating, and working with the villagers. Indeed, it is through this sheltering that some of my interviewees, such as Linh, first encountered the NLF. As described in chapter 4, Linh delivered documents and helped the NLF navigate her home village as a child. Later, at the age of sixteen or seventeen, she began working as a full-time guerrilla—but still in her home village. However, the GVN authorities were persecuting her, and it was not safe for her to live in her house. She was thus especially reliant on villagers who hid her from the GVN authorities and provided her with food and shelter. She recalled one specific GVN official, who was tasked with catching her, offering rewards to those who might turn her in, once even locking a group of villagers in a room and demanding they reveal her location to him. "But the villagers are very smart, no one told him anything," she remembered. Even when not allowed to continue their normal lives as farmers, members of the armed groups and rear-support workers—and by extension, the young people who were associated with them—still maintained close relationships with villagers. In turn, this meant that young recruits remained integrated within wider social structures, which helped facilitate their smooth reintegration into postwar society.

On the family level, most of my interviewees who left home recalled being welcomed back warmly by their parents and extended families. For example, My, who left her family to serve in Saigon without telling them, remembers their relief and happiness upon seeing her again. "When they learned that I left for Saigon, they assumed that I went to work for the GVN," she said. "They were disappointed. But when I came back, they were very happy because they realized they were wrong about me and I was a good person," again indicating that as a former revolutionary, she enjoyed more social acceptance than those who supported the South Vietnamese regime. Loan recalled her mother and other villagers preparing a big meal when she returned, singing and celebrating all night.

Hardships of Postwar Life

My interviewees had access to economic, social, and symbolic capital that enabled their transition to postwar life—capital not always available to supporters of the GVN. Young former revolutionaries, therefore, were allowed to continue their normal lives without being forced to experience the contempt of those around them, which in turn had a positive impact on their mental health in the aftermath of the war. Yet, after the celebrations, my interviewees still had to face the realities of living in a country that had to rebuild itself from war. Many veterans found that postwar life did not grant them immediate happiness. Perhaps the best articulation is made by Quan: "After liberating South Vietnam, everyone was happy, everyone was excited. But then, many people became disappointed, because many thought that after the liberation, they would immediately get rich, be happy, get to eat a lot. But later they found that it is not easy; so many people were shocked and had to endure hardships in many aspects of life."

In other words, their position within the field—"a network, or a configuration, of objective relations between positions," as defined by Bourdieu and Wacquant (1992, 97)—has changed, as they went from being young recruits in resistance forces, with an established regime and lifestyle, to becoming civilians who had to once again navigate the new realities and build new lives. This new field—continuing the game analogy—came with new rules, with which they had not yet become familiar. There were several reasons for the difference between expectation and reality. First, the collapse of the Vietnamese economy meant that even with veterans' privileges, life would be difficult. The salaries, financial remunerations, and food rations were often not enough, and there were often not enough products to buy: for example, after the struggle with the United States, Vietnam had to import rice despite being full of rice fields (Davies 2015).

In addition, the socialist regime, which was going through economic crisis, did not always compensate former revolutionaries with the promised rewards. Youth Shock Brigade members, in particular, suffered the most; they were seen as a rather informal and temporary group set up specifically to help the armed struggle from the rear, rather than a branch of a liberation force. As described previously, Youth Shock Brigade members lived according to the discipline and rules that also characterized the guerrilla experience. The tasks that they carried out were essential to guerrilla operations on the battlefield and were as physically and emotionally demanding. Many members of the organization expected to receive social prestige as a result of their involvement in the political struggle. However, this recognition did not seem to go beyond prioritization in employment. On the contrary, while guerrillas' and armed forces' contributions were recognized on the official level via medals, awards, and some form of financial remuneration, Youth Shock Brigade members were largely overlooked by the government and society (Guillemot 2009).

Tien also admitted that many of these youth "lived like cavemen," knowing only how to carry out their jobs and never thinking much in advance about what society might look like after the war or how to survive in it. She articulated that this was particularly the case for younger Youth Shock Brigade members; older members were better at calculating the possible difficulties and challenges associated with their futures. As such, in postwar society, many young volunteers "weren't very smart." "Smart" in this context is not a reflection of their capabilities—rather, it referred to being sufficiently cunning and shrewd to live and build a career in the harsh postwar conditions and poverty. As a result, Tien remembered some of her comrades hiding from other villagers the fact that they participated as Youth Shock Brigade members because they were embarrassed to be so poor despite serving in the revolution. In her words, it almost did not matter that they won the war—when they came home, their economic situation was not much different from those who lost. Their role was largely forgotten until at least the 1990s, when former Youth Shock Brigade members began demanding acknowledgment of their history and sacrifices (Guillemot 2009). Even the privileges that Tien experienced were not always what she expected: for example, her new workplace did not count her Youth Shock Brigade membership years as "work experience." Instead, they classified her time in the brigade as "studying," which affected her salary and position in the organization.

Quyen's case, in particular, also highlights that levels of privilege varied among the veterans. As we saw in chapter 3, he tried to join the armed forces but was denied due to being underweight and underage. Still intent on joining the war to escape the constant judgment of his fellow villagers, Quyen then signed up to participate in the Youth Shock Brigades. Throughout his work, he reported learning from his peers, helping villagers, and always doing his best at his assigned jobs. In his accounts, we can see the importance of discipline and his emphasis on "saving face." Determined never to desert, he coped with difficulties by thinking of "when the victorious day comes," reflecting his internalization of revolutionary messaging.

When talking about his immediate postwar life, however, he articulated that things were not as he expected. He was disappointed to see society moving away from the lifestyle that he was exposed to for so long before and after joining the struggle. He initially found the postwar environment "materialistic" and difficult to navigate. For Quyen, this directly affected his ability to find a job after coming back. The provincial authorities said: "Comrade, you are a wounded veteran . . . please bear with us while we look for a suitable job for you." Quyen "waited and waited until he was tired." Later, he spoke to his other veteran friends, who told him he was "stupid"—he needed to give money to the cadres to receive a job. This was when he realized how different his circumstances had become. In the following fragment from our conversation, Quyen assesses his own realizations:

Quyen (*quietly*): You know [after coming back], negative things started happening in the society. In reality, corruption appeared immediately after establishing peace [with regard to him needing to have money to get a job].
Interviewer: I am surprised to hear this. I would expect people who served in the war to be respected.
Quyen (*louder*): That's right! I thought so too! That I would be welcomed . . . as a hero, welcomed back to work. But those are our innocent thoughts. But people on the outside of the battlefield, their thoughts were very materialistic.

He did admit that his case was not very prevalent, and he explicitly pointed out that it was a more common occurrence among lower-ranking cadres (not government or leadership), who were the ones with whom he interacted. However, it also serves as an illustration of a boy for whom the postwar realities did not meet expectations.

Another factor that led to a divergence between expectations and reality for returning young revolutionaries was the difference between everyday life as a part of armed forces and as a civilian. Although this issue was particularly relevant to the interviewees who left their homes, differences between the military and civilian lifestyles affected everyone's consequent postwar reintegration. As young recruits, my interviewees lived according to specific rules, with strict discipline—for example, military groups would have set times for waking up, eating, and going to sleep. Their lives were full of a sense of camaraderie, governed by an emphasis on honor and self-sacrifice. Indeed, many became familiar with a life where everything was shared—for example, Xuan remembered having to go back home and her whole unit giving her what little money they had, while other interviewees gave examples of comrades sharing utensils or reading letters from family to each other.

Such widespread sharing, however, seemed to disappear beyond tight-knit revolutionary force units. As analyzed by Kolko (1995) and observed by Marr as well (2000, 793), the disappearance of revolutionary idealism contributed greatly to returning soldiers' disillusionment. The general consensus among my interviewees was that having a common enemy during the war forced everyone to focus on one common effort; yet, in peacetime, everyone returned to caring for themselves first and foremost. This contradiction provided a difficult test for those who were loyal to the revolution's professed values and experienced the military's tight-knit camaraderie. This shift to individualism, accompanied by rising competition, conflict, and ruptures in social life, stood in stark contrast to the unity projected during fighting (Malarney 2002b).

My interviewees echoed very similar sentiments on this issue. In general, they found it hard to adjust to a shift from unity and strong camaraderie to what they perceived as a competitive, materialistic, and more fragmented society; this point is also reinforced by some Vietnamese commentators, such as Lai (2019). Cuong, for example, expressed his sadness about the war coming to an end:

> After war, I have to say this . . . even though no one had to die, you only waited to go home, there was still something very sad. Sad, because there was no more comrade spirit. . . . I mean, the war was over, we were alive, there was no death—especially in the South. Everyone wanted the war to be over, to end the grief, but there were many times when I thought—the war is over, and suddenly, the human love is over, too. Sometimes I feel sad about that.

Moreover, even though my interviewees reported maintaining amicable relations with civilians—none mentioned feeling particularly lonely and isolated—some admitted not being able to relate to their friends as much when they returned to their home villages. Si recalled catching up with old friends after he came back from the war:

> It is true that there are a few things where I was more outdated than others. For example, there was a number of friends who came back from overseas, they talked about how China was, how the Soviet Union was, but I didn't know about this. At the time, there was no radio to listen to, either. Sometimes I did feel a bit lost. I didn't understand anything about the outside world, while they talked about flying, eating bread and soup, and I didn't know what those are.

The lived experiences of my interviewees demonstrate a contradiction where formal markers of success in education and employment coexisted with deeper struggles. Despite relatively seamless transition to civilian life, these aspects of social integration were not sufficient to shield them from the other challenges of their daily lives: economic hardships of postwar Vietnam, as well as drastic changes in routines and lifestyles. Such lived experiences indicate the complexity of the reintegration process: it encompasses many aspects that go beyond education and employment. Stability of the overall economy (e.g., control for scarcity and inflation) would have helped my interviewees immensely, as would immediate formal recognition of supporting roles. However, my interviewees were still capable of adapting and negotiating the harsh postwar reality, as I explore next.

Negotiating the Mismatch: Refusal to Be Victimized

When asked about how they coped with postwar difficulties, many of my interviewees stressed the importance of making an active decision to be optimistic and rely on themselves while rebuilding their civilian lives. In doing so, they highlighted that their ability to weather the conflicts arising from the mismatch between their expectations and the postwar reality was a result of their own reflections and an active refusal to be victimized. For example, some former young revolutionaries I interviewed chose to be content with the privileges that they had already received. Si's thoughts were particularly illuminating in this regard. When I mentioned the disappointment that many former veterans felt, he agreed that this was a common sentiment, but he had reflected on it many times. He came to this conclusion:

> You [former revolutionaries] already have people caring and asking about you, about those who joined the resistance. This led to . . . some people demanding, without striving to be better, for everyone to care about them. But that's only making their lives more difficult. I've thought about it already—veterans already have a pension, financial assistance, social benefits, little gifts for holidays . . . that's a sign of respect. If you ask for more, it would be sad. After all, the country has gone through decades of war, and your contribution is only a small part in the overall success. If you demand more, it will be very difficult for you.

In a similar vein, many interviewees recounted quickly coming to terms with the fact that they should not expect much from the state benefits or society in general. This was, for example, the case with Loan. After she completed her job as a sapper, she came back to her village after the war. She quickly discovered that she was not qualified for any available jobs at the time—most open positions were looking for someone with scientific and technological knowledge, which Loan did not have. In addition, she was a wounded veteran, and her health barred her from being able to take factory jobs. Despite her quick thinking and strategizing skills, which were valuable qualities while she was a guerrilla, she still faced many struggles at the beginning of her life as a civilian. She described feeling lost, confused, and unsupported despite her family welcoming her back and receiving a small financial remuneration for her service. But she understood very quickly that she would have to "take care of myself by myself. . . . There were too many people suffering . . . it would be too long until the government would be able to take care of me." I asked whether she was shocked or disappointed at that realization. She replied that this was something that she was already prepared for. She had observed the socioeconomic situation and witnessed severe food shortages. She knew of "stories that you'd think would only exist in books," such as scooters running on coal because there was no gasoline, or local shops selling car tires instead of rice. She understood that she had to be self-reliant in building her life for herself, displaying an optimism that she described as common to her family and village. "But I was not sad," she remembered. "I was just so happy that national liberation had been achieved, that sleeping on the floor was good enough."

We can see how my interviewees' reflections led to their active choice to make the best of their circumstances and to find ways to build a civilian life however they could. This is illustrated, for example, in My's story. At nineteen, she returned to her village after the war and continued studying while also working as a nurse. Being a nurse was a very demanding job, yet due to Vietnam's struggling postwar economy, her salary was still not enough, and she recalled having financial struggles constantly. For example, she often went to sleep not knowing where tomorrow's food would come from. Despite this, she remembered always trying to be optimistic: "I slept at night thinking that I don't have any money today, there is nothing for my family to eat. But I would only think like that for two seconds. Then I would tell myself: OK, sleep first. Thinking about it all night won't solve anything, food isn't going to appear, and I will be more tired tomorrow." Her specific way of overcoming difficulties was taking side jobs that employed her other skills; for example, sometimes she worked at a provincial office, typing documents. The main source of her resilience, she asserted, lay in her choice to maintain the belief that she could deal with any challenges that might come.

A similar sense of optimism was echoed by Duc, who reflected on the fact that many veterans did not receive a good job or adequate financial assistance, while others led comfortable lives:

> I can't compare myself to others, I can't wonder why this person is rich and I am not. I just cheer myself up—everyone has their own destiny. So instead, I try to help those who are less fortunate. Because if we compare ourselves with other people, we feel sorry for ourselves—we can't live like that.... I will just live my way, lead a simple, normal life, and don't think too much.

We can see, then, that despite not always receiving what they may have been entitled to, my interviewees were able to reconcile contradictions between their expectations and reality by refusing to see themselves as victims. In their perception, this was a consequence of their own actions and internal reflections. However, a deeper analysis of their responses also reveals the role of their habitus in helping them weather the harder, more disappointing aspects of their postwar situations.

Reconciling Contradictions Through Habitus

The misfit between familiar practices and a new social environment prompts different reactions: resistance (Adams 2006), discomfort and insecurity (Reay, Crozier, and Clayton 2009), becoming a source of adaptation (van Eijck 1999), or generating new responses as required by the new rules (Sutherland and Darnhofer 2012). However, as Aarseth, Layton, and Nielsen (2016, 158) have observed, ultimately the conflicts between habitus and the field do not always "doom" a subject "to a life of suffering." Rather, these discomfiting tensions can be reconciled with each other. Aarseth, Layton, and Nielsen (2016) suggest that an individual can emerge with a revised habitus within a new field of experience by deploying heightened reflexivity, assessing differences and similarities between the old and new environments, finding positive things about the new circumstances, and working through conflicting emotional states.

Thus, while my interviewees' internal reflections and choices certainly played a role in their ability to adjust to their new realities, the picture was more complicated; their habitus, formed in the context of being peasant children, and later revolutionaries, sustained their hopes for the future and helped them adapt to their postwar lives as civilians, workers, and students. When describing how they were able to readjust to civilian life, their explanations often focused on how they learned to observe the surrounding environment, navigate it, and find the best ways to integrate themselves into their new realities—often specifically using the skills and knowledge that they acquired as part of the revolutionary forces. In other words, their ability to adapt but also draw on familiar dispositions helped them negotiate the misfit between their subjective situations and the changed objective structures that they encountered after the war.

Loyalty to the Ideological Goals

Despite the many hardships that former revolutionaries encountered after the wars ended, they chose not to disconnect from their military past, even though at least part of the reason why they experienced such strong disillusionment during reintegration was their socialization in their respective units. Indeed, my interviewees suggest that they wanted to preserve revolutionary ideals—and by extension, their identities as former guerrillas, soldiers, youth volunteers, or revolution supporters more broadly. For example, one of my interviewees stated that he simply does not give himself permission to forget his time serving in the war, as a sign of respect to his memories and his past. Again, this memorialization may be because the communist supporters won the war, thus leaving space for former revolutionaries to express loyalty and use it to aid their postwar reintegration. By contrast, the GVN supporters would be asked to discard their previous loyalties. My interviewees did not face this additional layer of ideological conflict, facilitating an easier transition and adaptation to the difficult postwar years.

Moreover, my interviewees' training proved to be both ideologically and practically useful to them—particularly for those from the south, where the socialist government began to introduce co-ops and policies for land allocation. Unlike civilians for whom these programs were new, my interviewees were already familiar with the programs and the justifications that the government used to implement them (more efficient production, utilization of available resources, and ultimately bettering the lives of peasants). As such, most of them reported not being surprised by the policies—on the contrary, these changes were expected. Indeed, a frequent answer to my question of how they coped with economic hardships was "I lived according to ideology" or "I was already prepared." They understood the reasons for implementing agricultural co-ops, knew how they operated, and devised coping strategies to adapt quickly to the new economy—for example, cooperating with the government or agreeing to protect the regime regardless of their personal hardships. Hung remembers seeing many people leaving South Vietnam to become refugees in the United States; even as a child of a revolutionary family, he found many policies issued by the socialist government inefficient. However, he asserted that he was determined to support socialism anyway: "People like me are responsible for defending this country, this regime, because we believed that the society will be better." Similar sentiments were echoed by Duc who, after being discharged from the war, found himself "dying just over trying to figure out what to eat." Nevertheless, he insisted:

> My country being like that, I accepted it. But I lived according to ideology. I believed in the leadership of the Party. I thought—this period is difficult right now, my country is still poor, but I am a citizen, I will try to strive to overcome difficulties. I will persevere. Then the economy developed. I believed in the future: if I build the country with the government, then I will overcome it all. Since I followed the Party, I accepted it. But there were also people in Saigon who crossed the border; they found it too difficult. Because the state took the regime in North Vietnam and applied it in South Vietnam, many people did not like it. But whoever understood the revolution knew that we had to cooperate with the state to build the economy.

CHAPTER 5

Transferring Wartime Skills and Experience to Everyday Life

While the socialist government often prioritized former revolutionaries and Youth Shock Brigade members in job and education allocation, my interviewees still found that they had to rely on themselves to succeed in their respective studies or jobs. Many former young recruits that I interviewed, particularly those who went on to study, recalled that they were able to become some of the best students in their classes, and they attributed their success to the discipline, resilience against hardship, and determination shaped by the lifestyle in the military. They were not the only ones—as Duc remembered, many who served in the army could build lives for themselves because "they were used to hardships, and now they work hard to make money when they came home."

In chapter 3, I outlined how being involved with the military struggle from a young age, for many of my interviewees, was continuous with childhood work practices that were common in mid-twentieth-century Vietnam. Moreover, active participation in the revolution was often part of being a "good" child. These sentiments persisted after the war: participating in the revolution was thought of as an activity that helped children and youth gain useful skills. After returning from the wars and starting work, many of my interviewees—then in their twenties—discovered that they were able to use the creativity and relationships developed during their wartime service to aid them in their civilian work lives. This is a sentiment echoed by Turner (2002, 95), who interviewed a Vietnamese veteran and military professor about the conditions and training that Youth Shock Brigade members received during their time on the battlefield. The professor suggested that the military life "offered many young people the chance to learn new skills" and thus contributed to their quality of life after the war.

Vinh's story is perhaps the best illustration of such continuities. As mentioned previously, he was tasked with maintaining the military camps, acting first as a cook and eventually as a kitchen manager, and running various errands between his usual duties. For him, these tasks were continuous with work that he had already been doing as a child. When he finished his mission toward the end of the war, he returned to his home village. His mother asked him to help her in the fields; however, he told her that this line of thinking was "outdated." After working with foreigners, becoming a kitchen manager, and leaving home, he wanted to explore more jobs outside his village. In the next years, Vinh "went wherever they sent" him, reflecting the CPV's tendency to allocate jobs and prioritize former veterans. He wound up working in different places: a radio station, a film factory, a bank, and other positions. He stressed that while the government made many people redundant, they always gave him work even when others were let go. He attributed this privilege to his previous experience running errands for the military camp. He learned "from real life" how to do everything honestly and carefully, how to speak with equals as well as seniors, and how to manage problems creatively. In his eyes, this made him a good worker, so not surprisingly, he was valued in his workplace.

Similar sentiments carried through in the accounts of former young revolutionaries who went on to study. A few of my interviewees finished their education immediately after coming back from the battlefield. Some only finished high school and went to work; others went to study in universities and academies. Different interviewees adapted to studying in different ways. For example, Quan knew even before he joined the military struggle that his passion was studying. Yet he initially wanted to study engineering but was allocated to train to become a political cadre. He remembered being bored with the subject and feeling demotivated. Eventually, however, he felt that as a former soldier, studying was a duty assigned by the Party that he needed to fulfill. This, in turn, motivated him to study hard: from the second year on, his grades were consistently "Excellent" or "Outstanding." In addition to his own ambitions, he acknowledged that his experience with the military struggle granted him resilience:

> War trains us in terms of difficulties, and hardships. . . . After the war, no hardship was too difficult for me. Later, as a student, sometimes I also felt disappointed, depressed, like I didn't care. But once you've fought in the war, then you won't be afraid of any hardships. . . . Former revolutionaries who have a passion for studying, they are very scary. Because they apply the same determination forged in fighting to studying.

Quan succeeded at his studies in part because he was passionate about acquiring knowledge; however, this was not the case for everyone. He recognized that some of his comrades could not get used to learning: "Once they opened a book, they fell asleep." Another of my interviewees presents a similar case. Si became a fighter in the main forces, overcoming physical hardships of war like lack of salt, long distances walked barefoot, and frequent illnesses. However, when he came back, he realized that he "did not know how to study," feeling sad and surprised by this. His reasoning for eventually understanding how to study well was similar to Quan's: "This is the core of a soldier during the war.... Our mentality was this: just carry out missions according to the assignment. Once something is assigned, it has to be carried out." While their initial feelings about studying were different, their ways of approaching the task echo each other—to appeal to one's past as having served during wartime and to apply core features of this military identity to civilian life.

Camaraderie as a Source of Support

The importance of camaraderie, which was continually reinforced throughout military life, continued in the postwar period. Former young recruits whom I interviewed actively maintained relationships with their comrades, often prioritizing these relationships over those with friends who did not participate in the struggle. Many of my interviewees stated that during celebrations, they would gather with comrades first, and with friends and neighbors second. This is in line with the idea of comrades becoming their "second family"—a notion emphasized consistently by resistance forces. Many recounted holding gatherings and forums where they reflected on their past experiences, setting up their own organizations to provide social and financial support. The importance of these networks is implied in Quan's statement that those who did not participate in the revolution might think that veterans are "not normal" for always recounting stories of the past; yet former comrades did so frequently while drinking and eating together. Camaraderie, they felt, was an especially noble type of friendship.

These friendships had many avenues where they could be exercised, both formal and informal. With regard to formal networks, perhaps the most notable is the Veterans' Association set up by the new government in the late 1980s. This organization was instrumental in providing a support network for former revolutionaries—a space where they could socialize, connect, and participate in charitable and promotional activities. Indeed, I found some of my interviewees through Veterans' and Youth Shock Brigade member associations; when visiting them, I was greeted in a common room with several members drinking tea, passing around sweets, and catching up. No one paid much attention to me, only asking me to sit and drink tea with them while waiting for my interviewee to arrive. The casual and relaxed atmosphere suggested that these gatherings were a frequent occurrence.

The Veterans' Association outlined several goals—notably, the promotion of support networks "to care [for] and help veterans improve their material and spiritual lives" (as laid out by Nguyen 2021). Such associations were instrumental in providing the veterans with a space where their communist and fighter identities were continually reinforced (a particularly prominent example of this is how on their website, the Veterans' Association (n.d.) refers to its members as "Uncle Ho's soldiers"). Throughout its three decades of existence, the Association organized multiple campaigns that aimed to promote the socialist regime and cultivate positive relations among its members.

Thanh (2021), for example, reported Ninh Hai's association branch campaigning for a fundraiser (called "Camaraderie's love") to donate money to repair veterans' housing; other branches helped veterans find employment. There are also records of the Veterans' Association collaborating with the Women's Association and Youth Association to tackle issues of crime, drug use, and poverty (e.g., Thu 2021). Like the Veterans' Association, Youth Shock Brigade members also have their own "Ex-Youth Shock Brigade Members" Association, with many similar roles and activities. They organize charity campaigns (specifically to help low-income members); help with manual work, including house-building; and give gifts to members on special occasions like national holidays commemorating the wars (as reported by Khanh 2020).

Many of my interviewees noted that these associations played an instrumental role in helping them feel celebrated, respected, and cared for. For example, Duc mentioned that members of the Veterans' Association frequently brought him gifts, visited him, and "cheered me up from time to time"; he believed that this was very "precious and shows special care" for veterans. He was not the only one who expressed such sentiments—my interviewees made frequent references to fellow association members visiting, gift-giving, inquiring about their health, and chatting "to cheer them up." This meant that these veterans had a constant and reliable source of material and social support, which was reinforced on a state level. Their social ties and identities as part of resistance forces, then, were recognized, providing them, once again, with a support network that helped them weather the disappointment that they felt in their more fragmented postwar reality.

The importance of more informal support networks, moreover, cannot be discredited. My interviewees consistently referred to their friendships with their comrades as crucial to helping them find their footing in postwar society. Duc even referred to having his own (informal) network of former revolutionaries who served specifically in his village. They frequently carried out their own fundraising campaigns to help comrades in financial difficulty, who were ill or unemployed, for instance. He remembered often participating in such activities, helping with what he could.

The relationships also seemed to be instrumental in navigating potential trauma after the war. The issue of trauma from witnessing violence and death and losing comrades is not widely discussed in Vietnam; generally, my interviewees reported some instances of posttraumatic stress but approached it as an individual, one-off issue rather than collective trauma. The difference is particularly stark when one compares this absence to the prevalent discussions of trauma endured by American veterans coming back from the Vietnam War (Wong and Cook 1992, for example, explicitly call posttraumatic stress disorder a legacy from the war). By contrast, I could not find any references to mental health in the context of former Vietnamese revolutionaries. This could be due to a variety of reasons—for example, the postwar state was more preoccupied with allocating resources to economic development and employment, rather than to offering psychological help. There is also a stigma in Vietnam attached not only to the mentally ill but also their families (Niemi et al. 2010). In turn, this stigma could result in many former revolutionaries not wanting to seek help or to share related details with outsiders.

Nevertheless, I found frequent allusions to paying respects to those who died in the war as a way to navigate this loss. Earlier, I recounted Lan's story of a bomb raid that killed her whole unit. She then told me that after the war, she went back to the same location and arranged proper burial rituals and set up appropriate graves—which, at the time immediately after the raid, she could not do. For her, it was a way to not only pay respects to comrades but also give them a dignified burial. Duc also remembered going to old battlefields every year to light incense and pay respects over his comrades' graves. He stated that sometimes even the soldiers' families and spouses could not come on the exact days of celebrations or anniversaries, while he and other comrades would come every year, regardless of the weather or their own circumstances. "At the same time, while lighting the incense, I am reminded of the past and reminded to live well," he stated. Reports on former revolutionaries similarly highlight that the memories of camaraderie, friendship, and indebtedness that they felt to those who died in the war served as a motivation to live in a way that was worthy of these sacrifices (Bao 2017). In a way, it sometimes also enabled them to reintegrate amid a chaotic and unstable environment: many of my other interviewees remembered that they did not want to complain about postwar life, no matter how difficult it was, because they were always aware of how lucky they were simply to survive.

These former young revolutionaries displayed a remarkable capacity for empathy while honoring the importance of social ties, even toward those who were no longer present in their lives. This contrasts with portrayals of children and youth being irreparably damaged by witnessing death and losing their friends. In the case of my interviewees, the love and empathy that they felt for their comrades were a source of strength during their subsequent reintegration. The articulation of "living well" as a duty toward comrades who died, again, highlights this sense of camaraderie, forged and practiced through their time in resistance forces. It also points to the ability of children and youth to turn negative emotions into an important source of resilience. Similar sentiments have been articulated explicitly by Watson (2015): casting a negative emotion like grief as an automatic and inseparable feature of victimhood, she asserts, ignores how young people can—and do—channel such feelings into activism, political participation, and rebuilding their lives.

Depending on the conflict and the postwar environment of a specific country, the outcomes of reintegrating children and youth who participate in armed forces may vary. In some cases, children have exhibited antisocial behavior (Boothby 2006; Veale and Stavrou 2007) or shown major signs of depression and posttraumatic stress (Boothby 2006). Other returning children have suffered community stigmatization (Özerdem and Podder 2011; Denov and Marchand 2014) or difficulty returning to civilian life after being excluded for years (Denov 2011). In addition, as Watson (2015, 55) has observed, in many instances job creation for youth would "simply not be a priority for either donors or the presiding government," translating into a lack of opportunities for former youth combatants (Annan, Brier, and Aryemo 2009; Blattman and Annan 2008).

The need to redefine one's entire identity is another factor often mentioned as a challenge in postwar lives of children and youth associated with the armed forces (Honwana 2009; Denov 2011). Problems can further stem from former young combatants being under eighteen years old, thus hindering their ability to access financial and reintegration benefits (Zyck 2011; McMullin 2011). Another predominant theme is loss of power and agency, particularly for those who held positions of authority prior to demobilization (Zyck 2011). This in turn can lead to reports of youth having to "forget" their past to start a new life (Annan, Brier, and Aryemo 2009).

Simultaneously, much research has highlighted the abilities of former young combatants to adapt and display resilience, even amid unstable economic and political postwar environments (Özerdem and Podder 2011). Ex-youth soldiers have often developed strong leadership abilities (Jordans et al. 2012; Kryger and Lindgren 2011), with many eventually reintegrating with their communities and finding employment (Veale and Stavrou 2007; Blattman and Annan 2008; Jordans et al. 2012). Further, Özerdem and Podder (2011) observe that successful reintegration can depend on the outcome of a conflict. Victors, as they state, "integrate easily and often dominate the political scene" (Özerdem and Podder 2011, 314). By contrast, those who fought for unpopular rebel factions lose more social capital and can be excluded from the social landscape (Blattman and Annan 2008).

The case of my interviewees, then, presents an account of what happens when former youth combatants find themselves on the side that won. Their victory allowed them to escape stigma and enjoy certain privileges, especially compared to young people who supported the GVN. Moreover, left to their own devices, the Vietnamese state and communities were the primary agents facilitating reintegration, without interference by the international community. The Vietnamese sense of childhood further shaped this response. Since their lives were never free of labor, duties, and responsibilities, the former young recruits whom I interviewed did not feel disempowered as a result of joining the military effort. And the government's policies with regard to education, employment, and financial remuneration privileged former revolutionaries—young or not—while refusing to characterize them as lost or dangerous. Instead, the state perceived its returning young combatants as loyal and capable people who could be beneficial for rebuilding the economy. Finally, the revolutionaries were deeply integrated into peasants' lives, meaning that these young recruits were never truly cast as outsiders within their communities.

Despite these privileges, the fact that postwar life came as a disappointment to many of my interviewees cannot be discounted. Many expected to improve their economic situation immediately upon returning, while others anticipated more substantial prestige and respect than they received. They reported feeling that postwar life was difficult in unimaginable, unpredictable ways—but they also actively refused to feel like victims. Some of my interviewees explicitly referenced having consciously, deliberately chosen to approach life with hope and optimism and come to terms with their position in society. As with recruitment and their time serving in the war, then, children and youth displayed complex internal lives, which, in turn, was an important factor in shaping their futures.

The conflict between their postwar expectations and reality was also reconciled in large part because of their habitus. Being young recruits, who were socialized into joining the revolution from a young age and later spent considerable time learning about communism, they were able to retain faith in the CPV following the war, articulating hardship as a necessary step toward rebuilding the country's economy and future. In addition, the attitudes toward labor that they formed at a young age helped them view their experience with the revolutionary forces as a time where they learned to be resilient, capable workers—common features of a "good" revolutionary. These aspects of my interviewees' habitus helped them live through the difficulties of postwar life: already accustomed to the hardships of war, they believed that they could weather similar hardships during peacetime. Furthermore, they cultivated camaraderie and unity with their fellow fighters, creating social circles where they could express and reflect upon their identities as revolutionaries.

The experiences of my interviewees highlight the importance of education, employment, and community acceptance, as well as macro-level factors (wider economic conditions), and micro-level dynamics, including everyday interactions and social networks. Another insight from their narratives is the value of recognizing and fostering familiar or transferable skills and attributes from their prior roles—skills that can offer a sense of continuity and purpose during their transition to civilian life. Of course, this approach must be critically attuned to context: the applicability and emotional resonance of these experiences vary greatly among young people.

Conclusion

This book has analyzed children's and youth's participation in the Vietnam War, tracing how local constructions of childhood shaped the militarized lives of the young people who made the decision to join the military struggle. Why did children and youth join the revolutionary forces during the Vietnam War? Once they joined the conflict, how did they understand their own experiences? How did these young recruits reintegrate into civilian life once the military conflict came to an end? On a theoretical level, I was also explicitly interested in how the politics of a military conflict like the Vietnam War shapes the social context within which young fighters operate: How does ideology influence the sociocultural practices of young people and youth who participate in armed conflicts?

To address these questions, I conducted life-history interviews with former young Vietnamese recruits, analyzing their experiences prior to, during, and after the military struggle with the United States. Influenced by Bourdieusian relational sociology—particularly his ideas about how one's habitus, or "system of acquired dispositions," is formed and reinforced (1990, 13)—I came to view my interviewees' decision-making in light of multiple relationships, circumstances, and social contexts. Children and youth working for the National Liberation Front (NLF), the main forces, People's Army of Vietnam (PAVN), and the Youth Shock

Brigades had the capacity to make complicated decisions even within the constraints of an ongoing war. Although their experiences were shaped by widespread social practices that they often took for granted—including, in addition to communist messaging, the influence of Confucianism and local understanding of childhood—my interviewees nevertheless found ways to navigate these multiple constraints, use them to achieve their goals, and demonstrate creativity and social awareness while doing so.

Most of my interviewees stressed the voluntary and nonpolitical nature of their recruitment as children and youth. Upon analyzing their responses, I found that many believed their participation to be nonpolitical because they did not articulate it to themselves in terms of formal Marxist ideology. Their motivations were still political, in the sense that they were deeply concerned with issues of justice, equality, and foreign intervention. Further, while many of my interviewees consistently highlighted that they were volunteers, multiple social practices, which existed before they joined the military struggle, predisposed them to see joining as a viable option. Several of these practices stood out in particular. First was the role of family loyalty and filial piety, two of the most significant values stressed in Vietnamese Confucian peasant villages; joining the resistance forces was a practice that already existed in many of their families. Second, the prevalence of children and youth working in Vietnam at the time meant that young people were used to assuming demanding responsibilities, often viewing enlistment in the military group or in the Youth Shock Brigades as just one of many jobs available to them. Third, everyday life had been militarized for Vietnamese young people from a very young age, as many of them would have already witnessed the Viet Minh's struggle against the French. This meant that the idea of participating in the war was not alien to my interviewees' worldview, but instead was seen as a realistic, normalized path to take.

Once children and youth became part of the revolutionary forces, they were given intense political and military training. Indeed, political education appeared to be a particularly important feature of their lives as revolutionaries; this is where many of my interviewees first learned about and could explicitly articulate the ideological tenets of communism, patriotism, and anticolonialism. In addition, unit commanders worked hard to socialize young people into developing a distinct "revolutionary" identity, teaching them the code of conduct, and explaining the meaning behind their activities. Young people were given relative freedom and autonomy by commanders to conduct their missions as they saw fit; in general, there was an expectation that children and youth would do their work with as little guidance as possible. Despite the expected independence, however, young people were highly restricted by their positions as subordinates. In this sense, their independence remained confined to what their commanders saw as appropriate, with minimal input from the young recruits themselves. However, even within that limited space, young people demonstrated their ability to navigate their new social context with a sense of agency: they learned to fuse newly learned political concepts with their own sense of justice and to ignore the rules of the hierarchy when they knew that they could get away with it. They learned to use other people's expectations of childhood to fulfill their missions successfully, and they carved out space for friendships and mutual support to navigate the hardships of living in the middle of a war. In doing so, they demonstrated their capability for adaptability and problem-solving.

Postwar, many young recruits expected their lives to improve. Yet, in reality, the Vietnamese economy descended into economic crisis immediately after the war due to sanctions and challenges of postwar reconstruction. However, many of my interviewees were in a position where their previous military conflict experience enabled them to navigate their postwar hardships without feeling discouraged or defeated. Their resilience was shaped by the context within which they volunteered and reintegrated into their communities. First, all my interviewees were on the winning side of the war, which meant that they were in a position of relative privilege. Second, they were already familiar with, and indeed expected, many of the policies that the communist government implemented. Due to their internalization of revolutionary messaging, they also retained faith that the government would be able to overcome any economic and political hardship. Finally, they cultivated strong social networks—both formal and informal—with other former young recruits, which sustained them in the postwar environment.

Without claiming to be universally representative, my findings suggest that children and young people, rather than being apolitical, were deeply embedded in the Vietnam War. Much as with adults, their experiences were shaped by social and historical contexts. Multiple factors specific to their habitus—such as the idea of a "good" Vietnamese child or youth and later military socialization—facilitated their mobilization to join the armed struggle, their performance as members of military forces or rear-support workers, and their later postwar reintegration as former revolutionaries. Furthermore, the stories of my interviewees showed that children and youth are multifaceted, knowledgeable individuals with rich and diverse internal lives. These findings are in line with multiple calls to not only attend to young people's political subjecthood in research but also to approach youth as a distinctive source of knowledge who are more than capable of shaping the world around them (Watson 2006; Beier 2020).

Participation in Military Struggle as a Socially Embedded Phenomenon

Throughout my interviews, several themes surfaced as particularly important to the experiences of young Vietnamese recruits. Families not only predisposed children and youth to join the military struggle and helped them maintain their fighting spirit once they became part of the struggle but also reinforced the importance of "face-saving" and honor as values to be upheld during their service. Moreover, despite the expectation of their independence, children and youth generally remained in a position of subjugation, confined to a strict social hierarchy within their families and, subsequently, within their respective revolutionary groups as well. These factors can be traced to the Confucian social order, indicating that prevalent cultural frameworks affect how children and youth joined the military struggle.

The Importance of Filial Piety

In many contemporary cases of children and youth participating in military struggles, family—whether nuclear or extended—rarely appears as the *primary* motivating factor predisposing children and youth to join military conflicts. Rather, family appears either as a tranquil environment from which young people are kidnapped (e.g., Denov and Maclure 2007) or a broken institution from which children are forced to flee (e.g., Yinusa et al. 2018). My exploration of young people participating in Vietnamese military conflicts reveals a different context, where family can serve as a political motivator for children and youth. My findings show that for many young recruits, the decision to enlist did not derive from the absence of a loving relationship between them and their parents, but rather from its presence. The decision to leave one's family, to join an armed group, and often to purposefully replace one's family of origin with a higher sense of a "national" (communist) family was an expression of filial piety and subsequent fulfillment of their expected familial and communal roles.

While on the surface, the idea of young people leaving their families and joining the military conflict appears to conflict with core Confucian tenets (which frame leaving one's family as a breach of filial piety), this decision would still be in line with the Confucian social order. Many children and youth came to view joining the struggle as protecting their parents and contributing to their family's ability to thrive. This meant doing what they did not want to do—generally, leaving their homes to go and fight a war—because they believed that this was the best way to keep their families and villages safe. In addition, for many children and youth, joining the revolutionary forces was a way to express their loyalty to family traditions—if their parents had already participated in a war, they were expected to uphold their reputation and honor. Throughout the hardships that they endured during the wars, young people's thoughts often turned to their parents, which served as a motivation to lift their spirits. As such, the idea of children and youth taking up arms conforms to the wider Confucian societal order, which places filial piety and loyalty to one's community above self-interest.

The presence of the guerillas and political cadres within villages deepened young people's predisposition to join the military struggle even further. As I pointed out in chapter 2, the revolutionary forces implemented a careful strategy of mass mobilization and message-spreading that combined the notion of filial piety with revolutionary aims: by participating in the liberation movement, the guerrillas and cadres argued, young people will help liberate Vietnam and subsequently, their parents. The effects of such *tuyen truyen* were twofold. First, it helped to attract many enthusiastic members who had faith in the revolutionary mission—and who, in turn, shared their enthusiasm with their children. Drawing on the Vietnamese expectation of filial piety, the resistance forces therefore expected that children and youth would follow in their parents' footsteps. This helped solidify a direct connection between being a "good" child (or young person) and joining the military struggle.

Many of these themes were never explicitly mentioned by my interviewees but were consistently present throughout their stories. While no one explicitly said, "I love my family," they expressed their love in descriptions of crying when they left home and missing their families while serving in the war. While no one explicitly articulated participation in the war as an expression of filial piety, statements such as, "I wanted to protect my parents, so of course I went into the battlefield directly," placed in the context of the Confucian value system, highlight how cultural and societal values shaped young people's decisions. In turn, these findings emphasize how seemingly apolitical spaces such as family can be powerful political motivators—not because they are broken or dysfunctional, but precisely because of their affection, intimacy, and mutual loyalties.

Influence of Social Environments

Among my interviewees, the influence of their wider social environments manifested in two ways. First, face-saving and honor, core values in most mid-twentieth-century Vietnamese communities, were major factors motivating military recruits. Interestingly, face-saving does not appear to be a particularly important factor motivating children and youth to join more contemporary conflicts; it has not been highlighted in Shepler's (2014) or Rosenoff's (2010) studies, for example. However, going beyond young people's war participation, Parker (2001) argues that reputation is an essential value among those who have joined violent gangs. In the cases she discusses, though, this value is inherently tied to marginalized youth's struggle against the "hopelessness of their existence" (Parker 2001, 153). One's place in such gangs would often be determined by the person's leadership skills, dressing well, and popularity in relationships (Parker 2001, 155)—all qualities that must be displayed if one is to "save face." For my interviewees, by contrast, face-saving was less a way to cope with marginalization and more a widespread societal value traceable to the Confucian social order.

Among Vietnamese young people, saving face was an important part of maintaining strong relationships with family and community; one's personal reputation, in other words, was seen as a reflection of one's community. Children and youth were therefore constantly aware that their own reputations would also have implications for their families, thus making them especially focused on acquiring and maintaining this symbolic capital. Outside the context of anticolonial struggles, face-saving and respect would most likely be accumulated by, for example, doing well at school or holding a certain prestigious job. However, in wartime, it translated into participating in the political struggle and doing it well. Similar arguments have been articulated by Bultmann (2015), who observes that taking part in a certain number of battles or carrying out certain missions becomes a symbolic resource, valued specifically in the context of insurgency. While his work focuses specifically on adult Khmer Rouge insurgents, my interviewees' experiences indicated that his arguments are also applicable to young people's struggle to gain social capital.

This concern for face-saving explains many aspects of the lives of children and youth who participated in Vietnamese revolutionary struggle. For example, carrying out one's duty carelessly, showing fear, or deserting one's mission would not result in physical punishment, but in being criticized in front of one's peers. Even in the absence of physical punishment, the discipline in the revolutionary forces was rigid and effective. This was because public criticism sessions, a common communist disciplinary device, constituted a sufficiently powerful behavioral-management tool. This preoccupation with face-saving also can explain some instances of young recruits' enlistment in the first place. Since children and youth often lived in areas where joining the military struggle was a normal social practice, refusing to do so brought shame not only to themselves but also to their families. Therefore, whether my interviewees decided to join the military struggle, were considering leaving the hardships of guerrilla life, or were contemplating the best ways to carry out their missions, a concern about their personal reputations always guided their actions.

Many of my interviewees also expressed great affection for their friends and neighbors, citing concern about their wider circles of belonging as an additional motivation to join the revolutionary cause. They continued to display this care even as they had to leave their home villages, helping civilian villagers whom they also relied on for shelter and food, or helping friends and comrades overcome hardships. During wartime, Vietnamese children and youth displayed a deep social awareness and an ability to empathize with others, diverging from the stereotype of a lone, isolated child becoming associated with the armed forces (an image criticized by scholars such as Lee-Koo 2011). These findings are also in line with those of scholars who pointed out the ability of children and youth in armed groups to navigate, interpret, and engage with people around them (e.g., Utas 2011; Cortes and Buchanan 2007). Like the veterans in the study conducted by Schlichte (2014, 380), young recruits were "social beings in the sense that their attitudes, modes of action and reasoning [were] heavily shaped by their social context."

Hierarchy and Subjugation

Vietnamese young people of peasant background in the mid-twentieth century were expected to engage in difficult and complex tasks, including work and participation in politics, with minimal guidance from adults. Indeed, children and youth appeared as relatively independent, even autonomous individuals in my interviewees' accounts. Since Vietnamese revolutionary forces strived for communism-inspired equality, they also strived to treat young members as equal to their older comrades. However, a deeper reading of my interviewees' responses reveals that they never were completely equal to their elder counterparts due to the abiding influence of Vietnamese-Confucian values that established a hierarchy among differently positioned members of communities. Although "equals" with their comrades in some aspects of work, children and youth remained constantly aware of their social position relative to other (older and higher-ranking) comrades.

Indeed, young Vietnamese recruits were expected to obey the rules and submit to discipline established by more senior commanders without any further argument, as prescribed by Confucian tenets. Even if they rose through the ranks, it would be impossible to escape such differential power relations due to the importance that Vietnamese society—and particularly the language—places on age. As detailed in chapter 4, so long as they continued to use the relational pronouns that revealed their younger age in conversations, they would be expected to perform the role of a younger person. These language requirements came with certain expectations with regard to politeness, behavior, and speech. Although revolutionary forces deliberately tried to neutralize the age difference by changing these relational pronouns, children's and youth's obedience was still expected, simply because they were younger. The difference in terms of who occupied substantive positions of real power within the group's hierarchy could not be completely erased.

Yet there is more nuance to their positionality than a simple contrast imparts. To start with, although located lower in the hierarchy, young recruits had space to exercise their own creativity without much intervention from adults. Indeed, even when carrying out difficult and dangerous tasks, my interviewees often implied that they did not expect any help from adults. Further, they often received only minimal guidance with regard to mastering difficult skills such as cutting stone, using road-building tools, or stealing American equipment.

The specifics of Vietnamese childhoods, combined with communist efforts to promote equality while still adhering to Confucian tradition, resulted in young people finding themselves in a complicated position: not completely marginalized, as is often the case with children and youth fighting in contemporary conflicts, but not completely autonomous, either. My findings provide an explanation for the puzzling question of why some young recruits were given much freedom to make decisions in risky situations, while at the same time often not given basic information—for instance, to whom they would be reporting or what kind of document they would be delivering. Contradictions within the revolutionary forces' efforts to promote both communist equality and familiarity with Confucian hierarchical order, then, affected the experiences of young recruits significantly.

Interaction of Political Ideology with Social Practices

The impact of ideology was another prominent factor that significantly shaped the motivations and experience of the people whom I interviewed. None of my interviewees explicitly named a particular ideology as the cause they were fighting *for* or stated that they enlisted with an aim to establish a communist government; as we have seen, most Vietnamese young people had little idea of what communism even was. Rather, communist ideology influenced the social practices that young people were exposed to in their everyday lives. Even if a young person does not know political slogans by heart, ideology can still infuse their attitudes and behaviors. In other words, as Malarney (2002a, 9) observed, practices in social and cultural contexts have become "powerful and important principles" guiding Vietnamese people's lives, not just "ideological window-dressing."

For example, many of my interviewees remembered that it was difficult to escape communist ideas when interacting with guerrillas and political cadres, even before they officially joined the military cause. This can be traced back to the tactics of mass mobilization, drawn by the revolutionary forces from Maoist techniques that included disseminating revolutionary messages, informally talking with peasants, and holding informal meetings—all of which resulted in many people knowing someone who had worked for the revolutionary cause. The language of and concerns for social justice, patriotism, and anticolonialism became integrated into young people's everyday lives, even if they did not always register this consciously. The war was brought close to children and youth, and it therefore was expected that they would also participate in the political struggle in some form.

The effects of being exposed to communist ideology continued to manifest as my interviewees became integrated into military life. Beyond educating their young recruits on the core tenets of communism, nationalism, and anticolonialism, the revolutionary forces were systematic and deliberate in how they cultivated a common communist identity among units; they understood that their recruits' morale must be maintained for their young members to continue to see communism in a positive light. As such, they encouraged recruits to cultivate positive relationships with one another and allowed the young recruits to sing, play, and joke around. Orders to work could sometimes be weighed against young people's own subtler, playful counters. No dynamics between the members, regardless of their age, were ever fully black and white. They also gave space for some autonomy, creative thinking, and independence during the times when the young recruits were carrying out their jobs. Notably, my interviewees specifically remembered an absence of physical punishment, threats, and coercion throughout their time of working with their older or higher-ranking comrades, which further contributed to maintaining morale. All these features, in turn, affected my interviewees significantly: many reported finding the experience of participating in the military struggle and being part of the revolutionary forces genuinely useful and educational, while others found it meaningful.

This is not to say that an explicit understanding of communist principles did not also shape my interviewees' experiences. On the contrary, knowing and understanding the core ideas of communism helped many people who formerly served in the war to reintegrate into postwar society. This, again, is not highlighted in the current research on children and youth associated with the armed forces, most likely because the majority of children and youth involved in contemporary conflicts are joining groups that do not have the opportunity to carry out systematic campaigns to achieve their political missions. By contrast, the Vietnamese communist government, being victors, were able to implement a range of diverse policies, which former revolutionaries were expecting. This helped them sustain their optimism and resilience while navigating many postwar hardships, even when the policies implemented by the communist government were sometimes ineffective. In the words of Duc, one of my interviewees, living in the difficult postwar context was easier for him because he "lived according to the ideology."

Communist ideologies accompanied many of my interviewees throughout their early childhoods until the end of the political struggle. Their memories of the "nationwide revolutionary spirit," the idea that a "good" person will participate in the political struggle, and their faith in the communist government can ultimately be traced to multiple intentional messaging campaigns conducted by guerrillas and political cadres. These campaigns, in turn, drew their inspiration from Maoist philosophy and political tactics. As with filial piety, my interviewees did not specifically cite the impact of communism on their decision to enlist in or support the revolutionary cause. However, the ideological principles existed in their lives long before they decided to join the military struggle. Such findings further highlight the political nature of childhood or the extent to which young people are willing to be involved in political activities.

My findings stress that political ideology is best understood not only as a framework within which institutional and military strategies are carried out, but as a normative structure that aids socialization and maintains morale, among other functions (this is in line with Sanín and Wood 2014). The responses of my interviewees demonstrate that ideology is a *social practice* that merges with existing sociocultural practices and becomes internalized as part of an individual's habitus. As a result, ideology has become so normalized that its practices are taken for granted as unquestionably true. This is shown in instances of Vietnamese young people volunteering to enlist or support the revolutionary cause in part as a result of mass mobilization, *tuyen truyen*, and sentiments of injustice, while explicitly articulating their motivations as nonpolitical. Later, as they joined the struggle, my interviewees received more formal communist education, and this ideology continued to shape their actions and what they perceived as desirable and possible in the aftermath of the war.

There is still much space for investigating the role and effect of ideology on children and youth who are associated with armed groups; as Sanín and Wood (2014) have observed, this is an underresearched topic in conflict studies in general. This is because young combatants are often associated with the "new war" paradigm, which does not regard ideology as a primary driver of social action (see Malešević 2008 for an analysis of ideology within the "new war" paradigm). Yet if we go beyond the limited number of cases in the researched canon on children and youth associated with the armed forces, we can gain more insight into these understudied areas. Doing so requires shifting our attention to "old wars" which, although not so strongly associated with children and youth participating in conflicts, nevertheless also relied on young people as volunteers, fighters, and support staff. Kucherenko (2011), for example, shows that Soviet young people were exposed to intense Stalinist propaganda in their families, schools, and through mass media—institutions that obsessively disseminated the value of civic duty and loyalty to the Motherland. Yet she notes that "despite the many books written on the subject of the Soviet-German war, the story of these young people eluded systematic investigation, either in the Soviet Union or outside of it," precisely because Soviet historians tend to downplay the "social factor," including cultural practices and ideologies (Kucherenko 2011, 4). Similarly, Özerdem, Podder, and Quitoriano (2010, 305) have explicitly stated that there needs to be more research into how taking up arms is a "natural progression in social existence" and how both ideology and sociocultural practices affect potential young recruits.

The lessons that we can learn about the impact of ideology on children and youth participation in wars pertain not just to so-called old wars but also to contemporary conflicts. For example, jihadist groups display a similar dedication to ideology, which in turn has been shown to become part of their everyday practices, including toilet habits, cooking, and sports. Yet Hegghammer (2017) further noted that the rituals observed in jihadist groups do not steer far from ordinary Muslim experiences. He then explains this counterintuitive finding: jihadist groups make themselves easier to join because potential recruits do not have to abandon their own religious background to do so. Other hints of how jihadist ideology affect ideas about childhood are articulated by Pokalova (2019, 197), who cited Abdullah Azzam's view that young people "are not exempt from defensive jihad which is an individual duty upon the Muslims close by, 'where the young people will march forth without the permission of the parents, the wife without the permission of her husband.'" Again, here we see an interweaving of culture and ideology, which together affect everyday practices and young people's own conceptions of themselves.

As Ugarriza and Craig (2013) further argue, empirical evidence on many contemporary conflicts (frequently coming from fields such as social psychology) points to an important role played by ideology in shaping participants' specific understandings of the world, manifesting itself in doctrines, myths, and symbols that many rebel groups use to guide their actions. Approached in this way, ideology cannot only be reduced to an instrumental means for mobilization. Rather, as Sanín and Wood (2014, 214) assert, we need to refocus our attention on the political, as "all armed groups engaged in political violence . . . do so on the basis of an ideology." A deeper understanding of these practices, in turn, could shed light on why young people volunteer to become soldiers or why they choose to remain in armed groups, and how their military identity can be "unmade" to suit their civilian life. Such insights are clearly applicable to cases beyond old wars and help to uncover structural conditions that guide individuals' behaviors in a variety of military contexts.

Reconceptualization of Agency as Relational and Contextual

My research highlights the usefulness of a relational approach when conceptualizing how children's and youth's agency takes shape. More specifically, Bourdieu's concepts—habitus and field, in particular—have

CONCLUSION

helped me explore and better understand how agency is produced in interaction with one's sociocultural context. In this book, I employed a theoretical framework drawing on the work of scholars of childhood and young people associated with the armed forces who have employed a Bourdieusian approach. Shepler (2014) and Rosenoff (2010), for example, explore the strategies, motivations, and lived experiences of young people involved in contemporary military conflicts. This work was especially useful to me when examining the role that children and youth played in the military operations in the Vietnam War. It allowed me to understand how young people can exercise agency while navigating the structural constraints presented by an ongoing military conflict. In particular, Shepler's findings about many child-soldiering practices being continuous with Sierra Leonean childhood were instrumental in shaping my own thinking about the necessity of considering the social context surrounding children and youth before they even make the decision to enlist in or support an armed group. Similarly, Rosenoff's (2010) explanation of strategies that youth utilize to survive in a violent conflict highlights the usefulness of concepts like habitus in helping researchers understand youth's decisions and motivations—even if, to outsiders, their actions might not always make sense. I built on many of these theoretical insights to similarly put the actions of young revolutionaries in their social and political context. Beyond the Vietnamese context, moreover, my work emphasizes the importance of acknowledging children's and youth's agency as a starting assumption—that young people possess a complex inner life, including their own ideas, beliefs, and ability to make reasoned decisions—rather than the end point of an argument (as outlined by Thomas 2016).

In paying close attention to young people's social context, my research has also uncovered the influence of militarization on young people. It has shown that Vietnamese young recruits made choices, particularly with regard to participation in revolutionary and military activities, based on their previous experience and exposure to militarization. Children and youth who have been exposed to violence, war, and political discussions with their families and friends eventually internalize the "feel for the game" (Bourdieu and Wacquant 1992, 223) and gain skills and understanding of strategies that are most likely to help them function in highly militarized environments (Velitchkova 2021). Further, my findings have demonstrated the children's and youth's capability for change and flexibility. Rather than passively internalizing new rules as they start to become a part of a new social environment, young people learn when to bend them, when to infuse them with their own understanding of what is right. In other words, as in a similar observation by Winther-Lindqvist (2009, 71), young people always internalized new rules that they also "spiced up with their own ideas about good behavior, friendship, and justice."

These insights can be applied to wider debates about the militarization of childhood and to cases of young people who are not direct participants in war: even when they do not become combatants, children and youth still continue to be political subjects, who are shaped and who can shape "everyday militarisms" (a phrase that includes supporting the war and conforming to the set of wartime values, as defined by Zheng 2021, 105). This book, then, contributes to the strand of literature on the militarization of children and youth that posits that "militarization does not just happen to young people; as complex political subjects, young people navigate, engage with militarisms and through them, interpreting, (re)producing, remaking, and resisting" (Beier and Tabak 2020, 287).

Bourdieu's work, moreover, has helped me move toward an examination of how young people's actions, thoughts, and motivations have been shaped through the interaction of both agency and structure. Through this lens, children and youth are perceived as multifaceted social actors: capable of intelligence and creativity, they also find themselves in a position of relative subjugation and marginalization when compared to adults. While the Vietnam War environment predisposed young recruits to have certain kinds of experiences, they did not merely internalize and reinforce existing sociocultural practices in a passive way. Rather, they creatively navigated their circumstances and made sense of the ongoing war, bypassing the victim versus perpetrator binary. Like adults, they were complex social beings that were living in almost impossible circumstances.

In the context of Vietnam—a predominantly Confucian society in which individuality, as a value, is downplayed in favor of fealty to family and community—one also must come to understand how, for children and youth participants in the military conflict, agency often expressed itself as something other than active resistance to authority. Indeed, a Bourdieusian relational approach has allowed me to understand the restrictions imposed by the context in which these young people participated in the military struggle. This is in line with calls by scholars such as Gleason (2016), who have advocated for conceptualizing young people's agency beyond their defiance of adults or overt attempts to assert their self-interest. There can still be room for agency when young people obey authorities, carry out their assigned missions to the best of their ability, and reinforce rather than challenge dominant social practices. Similar observations have been made with regard to the Khmer Rouge, where some young soldiers learned to play musical instruments to gain the favor of the commanders and therefore ensure their own survival (Kar 2020). This understanding is particularly relevant when analyzing the experiences of young people who fight in extremely restrictive circumstances, such as for armed groups that forcibly conscript their recruits and threaten to kill them if they desert.

Going Forward

The case presented in this book is a historical one, specific to a particular geographic and cultural context over a certain period of time (roughly 1950s–1970s Vietnam). Some of its features may not be applicable to the kind of recruitment of children and youth that we see today: my interviewees were not recruited via forced methods and did not even witness such instances, nor did they recall experiencing coercion or threat of bodily harm by their own commanders. Their observations are confirmed by the secondary literature. Yet instances of coercion, kidnapping, threats, and violence toward children and youth caught up in military conflicts unfortunately exist, such as in instances of children and youth being recruited into armed groups in Myanmar (Chen 2014). My interviewees were also on the winning side, which in turn afforded them many privileges regardless of their age—employment and study opportunities, a small remuneration, and social capital in the form of respect, honor, and friendly relations with civilians. Observations by Bloom (2019) also highlight that in cases of many armed groups, children's jobs are seen as distinct from those of adults'—that is, they were not recruited to do "adult" work. This did not seem to be the case with my interview participants. On the contrary, many highlighted the equality with which they were treated, be it in the jobs they were assigned or the food they received. Perhaps such a tendency can be traced to the tactics inherent in mass mobilization that the "people's war" strategy presumes, again highlighting the differences between this historical case and the many contemporary instances of children and youth taking up arms or enlisting in armed groups.

Throughout this book, however, some core themes emerged that still resonate and therefore could be used to inform our understanding of cases beyond Vietnam. The first is the importance of treating children and youth as political actors in their own right. As my research shows, even though the revolutionary forces never placed children and youth at the heart of their mass mobilization campaign, Vietnamese childhood was profoundly embedded in politics. Seemingly private spaces such as family and peer groups became sites where children and youth first learned about the armed struggle. This also demonstrates that young people joining a military struggle is a *process* over time—one that is fostered through multiple social, institutional, and historical mechanisms. These mechanisms are often taken for granted by children and youth themselves, but a holistic view of the situation can contribute to a critical and more empathetic analysis of their experiences.

My findings speak to very similar calls to attend to the complicated processes of socialization in the academic literature; for example, Bloom (2019, 5) lists "structural conditions" (or "social ecologies"—"parents, families, peer groups, ... and other community-based institutions") that, while not being directly coercive, contribute to predisposing children and youth to join military efforts. We must treat each case as unique and distinct. My research also highlights that these influences inform young people's navigation of war and postwar environments, in some cases enabling a smoother transition to postwar life.

While keeping in mind that my interviewees were the eventual victors of the military struggle, their responses do highlight the importance of employment, educational opportunities, and ties to community as factors aiding their postwar reintegration. Once again, social context matters: there were cultural presumptions about childhood that caused my interviewees to not be seen as "damaged" due to their participation in the war; many were also rarely removed from their communities, which eased their reintegration. However, these findings also speak to earlier observations by scholars such as Lee (2009) with regard to the frustrations of many children and youth associated with the armed forces who were denied employment opportunities or financial help due to their youth. Drawing on the idea that being involved in an armed group is a process—one which individuals enter, but ultimately *leave*—allows for space to explore how wider social, cultural, and economic factors influence the process of reintegration and what institutional support is appropriate.

That said, the wider reflections of my interviewees regarding the poverty and destruction that contributed to their difficult postwar lives also emphasize that they would have benefited from greater structural support as Vietnam strived to rebuild its economy. To approach such problems, researchers and policymakers alike must strike a balance between soliciting international support, engaging local expertise, and taking into account children's and youth's unique personal needs. In this respect, Bloom's (2019) recommendations and calls for the international and local communities to collaborate, invest in countries affected by conflict, and engage the public sector are particularly relevant and important suggestions. Vietnam was left to rebuild on its own due to international sanctions, which was one of the reasons for its difficulties in delivering the promised economic growth. This experience need not be repeated for children and youth associated with armed forces all over the world today.

Young people have constituted a significant military presence in a variety of roles. This reality will most likely not disappear any time soon. Therefore, to borrow Denov and Maclure's (2007) wording, to understand how to "unmake" occurrences of children and youth associated with the armed forces, there needs to be an understanding of how, precisely, they are "made." Doing so necessitates a serious consideration of their cultural context and personal histories.

Yet little remains known about young people's experiences in war and their own perspectives on such experiences, particularly with regard to conflicts not typically associated with children and youth—historical, anticolonial struggles in Asia being one such example. The Vietnamese military conflicts have been discussed more extensively than many other conflicts occurring in Southeast Asia, laying the grounds for some of the most well-known theories and research on insurgency participation. However, even with this wealth of research and discussion, there is a surprising silence on the roles, experiences, and positions of young people who participated in Vietnamese conflicts, even though the phenomenon is widely known in Vietnam and occasionally acknowledged in Western scholarship.

Former young fighters from understudied conflicts still have much to say. Their accounts can provide valuable insight into how the ongoing militarization of everyday life, sociocultural practices, and the wider political context can shape children's and youth's wartime experiences. They also highlight that young people are deeply political actors. Acknowledging young people's place in military conflicts will help uncover a multiplicity of childhoods—and therefore foster a more sensitive and nuanced understanding of their experiences.

Acknowledgments

The process of bringing this book into existence is one that would not have been possible without the help and kindness of many people along the way. As a Vietnamese person who has spent much of my life abroad, this research journey allowed me to connect more deeply with the history of Vietnam. First and foremost, I am profoundly grateful to my interviewees, who shared their stories with laughter, emotion, and vulnerability. I hope to convey their courage, heart, dedication, and resilience—qualities that have inspired me beyond this project. This work is a tribute to the strength and spirit of those who, regardless of their age, guided and protected their communities and loved ones through challenging times.

I am deeply grateful to my academic mentors, without whom this journey would have taken a very different path. Ali Watson first sparked my interest in children and international politics when I was an undergraduate student at St. Andrews and has guided me through my first steps in data collection and analysis. My PhD supervisors, Jeremy Larkins and David Brenner, provided invaluable guidance and insight with impressive amounts of patience and kindness. Rajyashree Pandey helped shape this project in helping me to think through the historical and cultural contexts of childhood. I also thank Melissa Sevasti-Nolas, my internal examiner, for her thoughtful feedback and engagement beyond our PhD viva.

My parents have been a steadfast source of support, providing both logistical assistance and emotional encouragement throughout this journey. I am equally grateful to their network of friends and colleagues, whose guidance and connections were instrumental in introducing me to war veterans. Their support has been essential to this project.

To my PhD colleagues Mabel, Ekaterina, Carla, Katarina, and Dimitra—thank you for always being a safe space where I could share and shape my underdeveloped ideas. I am also grateful to my dear friends Maria, Josie, Hiep, Dimitra, Freya, Farid, and Duong, who read drafts, provided feedback, and always had unwavering faith in me.

My colleagues at the School of Oriental and African Studies generously helped me to refine the arguments in this book further. Many thanks to Vino Kanapathipillai, Fiona Adamson, Amelia Odida, Ralph Emmers, and Salwa Ismail for reading my work and providing kind and constructive feedback that always seems to inspire yet more papers! I also thank Mark Laffey for our conversations as I navigated the book publishing and peer-review process.

I also want to acknowledge the incredible community of scholars dedicated to childhood and international relations, especially Marshall Beier, Jana Tabak, Kate Macfarlane, Helen Berents, Mark Drumbl, Erica Burman, and Stacey Hynd. They are brilliant scholars whose work continually inspires me. Our meetings and conversations are few and far between due to our distance and professional commitments; and yet their thoughtful feedback and insights have significantly shaped (and keep shaping) my understanding of global childhoods.

During my research, I had the privilege of accessing archival documents preserved at the National Archives of Vietnam. I am deeply grateful for the exceptional support provided by the staff of the National Archives Center II and National Archives Center III. Their professionalism, efficiency, and willingness to assist were invaluable to my work. The National Archives of Vietnam store a rich collection of valuable documents and also provide an inspiring space for research, for which I am immensely thankful.

Finally, a special thank you to my editor at Cornell University Press, Sarah. Her professionalism, steady guidance, and calm demeanor were invaluable throughout this process—especially when met with my frequent, sometimes panicked emails! I cannot think of a better editor for this project.

The financial assistance for this project came from Goldsmiths PhD Scholarship, the Laidlaw Foundation, and the Sir John Plumb Trust. I am particularly grateful to Joachim Whaley, from Sir John Plumb Trust, for his kindness and trust in my work.

Thank you all for being a part of this journey.

Notes

Introduction

1. Although my interviewees worked for a number of armed and nonarmed groups and organizations (detailed in chapter 3), I will use the terms "revolutionary forces," "resistance forces," or "liberation forces" as shorthand when referring to them as a general group. While scholarly debates continue over whether the Vietnam War should be framed as a war of national liberation (Miller 2024), my interviewees consistently described their participation as part of a broader revolutionary struggle. I have therefore chosen terminology that reflects their shared perspectives. Similarly, I will at times refer to the military struggle as "revolutionary struggle" or "resistance movement," which is in line with how my interviewees understood their actions.

2. Given the ages at which my interviewees enlisted, I draw on literature about child soldiers for analytical framing. However, I will not be applying this term to my interviewees to avoid pejorative connotations (as also noted by Podder 2011), and to allow an understanding that they were involved in a range of tasks beyond combat duties. Instead, my preferred terms are "children and youth associated with armed forces" or "young recruits."

3. For example, Taylor (2010) refers to it has having taken place between 1955–1975; however, Miller (2024) also points out that some scholars define its start as early as 1945 or as late as 1960.

4. This project has received ethical clearance by the University of St. Andrews, when I did my first round of interviews, and Goldsmiths, University of London, when I did my second and third rounds.

3. "You Would Do the Same"

1. Some parts of this chapter have previously appeared in the following journal articles: Mai Anh Nguyen, " 'Little People Do Little Things': The Motivation and Recruitment of Viet Cong Child Soldiers," *Critical Studies on Security* 10 (1) (2022): 30–42, https://doi.org/10.1080/21624887.2022.2073740; Mai Anh Nguyen, "Parenting Patriots: Filial Piety, Family Socialization, and Insurgency in the Vietnam War," *Journal of Vietnamese Studies* 18 (4) (2023): 1–29, https://doi.org/10.1525/vs.2023.18.4.1.

2. Statements of guerrillas' selectivity were also confirmed by my interviewees who participated in the Viet Minh's struggle against France. One female guerrilla, who worked with a local Viet Minh force sabotaging the French sweeps,

told me that before she was accepted, the cadres needed to check whether she was "smart and hard-working enough." Another interviewee, who worked in the same group, insisted, "It was harder to join the guerrillas than become a member of the Party nowadays. Back then, they would give you many trial jobs before accepting you." Such jobs generally consisted of asking the children to run errands, deliver messages, help to hide weapons, keep watch for the arrival of the enemy soldiers, and other useful tasks.

3. More images can be found in a book published by Kim Dong Publishing House, *Tre Em Thoi Chien* (Children at War, 2017).

4. I use the term "children" here because the documents that I consulted use the word *thieu nhi*, equivalent of "young child" in Vietnamese.

References

Aarseth, Helene, Lynne Layton, and Harriet Bjerrum Nielsen. 2016. "Conflicts in the Habitus: The Emotional Work of Becoming Modern." *Sociological Review* 64: 148–65. https://doi.org/10.1111/1467-954X.12347.
Adams, Matthew. 2006. "Hybridizing Habitus and Reflexivity: Towards an Understanding of Contemporary Identity?" *Sociology* 40: 511–28. https://doi.org/10.1177/003803850663672.
Anderson, Mary, Michael Arnsten, and Harvey Averch. 1967. *Insurgent Organization and Operations: A Case Study of the Viet Cong in the Delta, 1964-1966*. Santa Monica, CA: RAND.
Annan, Jeannie, Moriah Brier, and Filder Aryemo. 2009. "From 'Rebel' to 'Returnee': Daily Life and Reintegration for Young Soldiers in Northern Uganda." *Journal of Adolescent Research* 24 (6): 639–67. https://doi.org/10.1177/0743558409350499.
Asselin, Pierre. 2013. *Hanoi's Road to the Vietnam War, 1954-1965*. Berkeley: University of California Press.
Asselin, Pierre. 2018. *Vietnam's American War: A History*. Cambridge: Cambridge University Press.
Atkinson, Alexander. 1973. "Chinese Communist Strategic Thought." *RUSI Journal* 118 (1): 60–64. https://doi.org/10.1080/03071847309428712.
Atkinson, Paul, and Amanda Coffey. 2003. "Revisiting the Relationship Between Participant Observation and Interviewing." In *Postmodern Interviewing*, edited by Jaber F. Gubrium, 109–22. Thousand Oaks, CA: SAGE.
Audin, Judith. 2017. "Civic Duty, Moral Responsibility, and Reciprocity: An Ethnographic Study on Resident-Volunteers in the Neighbourhoods of Beijing." *China Perspectives* 3: 47–56. https://doi.org/10.4000/chinaperspectives.7411.
Bac, Binh. 2020. "Nữ Tướng Duy Nhất Của Quân Đội Cách Mạng Việt Nam" [The Only Female General of the Vietnamese Revolutionary Army]. *Thanh Nien*, January 16. https://thanhnien.vn/thoi-su/nu-tuong-duy-nhat-cua-quan-doi-cach-mang-viet-nam-1172605.html.
"Bác Hồ Gửi Thư Cho Các Cháu Thiếu Nhi Nhân Này 1/6" [Uncle Ho Sent a Letter to the Children on June 1]. 2020. *Báo Điện Tử - Đảng Cộng Sản Việt Nam* [Vietnam Communist Party Newspaper], May 29. Accessed September 17, 2023. https://dangcongsan.vn/multimedia/mega-story/mega-story-nhung-buc-thu-bac-ho-gui-cac-chau-thieu-nhi-nhan-ngay-1-6-555924.html.
Baird, Adam D. S. 2011. "Negotiating Pathways to Manhood: Violence Reproduction in Medellin's Periphery. Exploring Habitus and Masculinity to Explain Young Men's Decisions to Join Armed Groups in Poor Urban Neighbourhoods of Colombia." PhD diss., University of Bradford.

REFERENCES

Bao Bien Phong. 2021. "Thanh niên xung phong: Biểu tượng tinh thần yêu nước của tuổi trẻ Việt" [Youth Shock Brigades: Symbol of Patriotism of Vietnamese Youth]. Accessed January 25, 2025. https://www.bienphong.com.vn/thanh-nien-xung-phong-bieu-tuong-tinh-than-yeu-nuoc-cua-tuoi-tre-viet-post441582.html.

Báo Cứu Quốc [National Salvation Newspaper]. 1947. "Chương Trình Tết Trung Thu Kháng Chiến" [Resistance Mid-Autumn Festival Program]. September 29.

Bao, Duy. 2017. "Đồng Đội Ơi, Chúng Tôi Mãi Không Quên" [Dear Comrades, We Will Never Forget]. Accessed September 19, 2023. https://tinhuyquangtri.vn/dong-doi-oi-chung-toi-mai-khong-quen.

Barbieri, Magali, and Daniele Belanger. 2009. *Reconfiguring Families in Contemporary Vietnam*. Stanford, CA: Stanford University Press.

Becker, Jo. 2009. "Child Recruitment in Burma, Sri Lanka and Nepal." In *Child Soldiers in the Age of Fractured States*, edited by Scott Gates and Simon Reich, 108–20. Pittsburgh: University of Pittsburgh Press.

Beier, Marshall J. 2015. "Children, Childhoods, and Security Studies: An Introduction." *Critical Studies on Security* 3 (1): 1–13. https://doi.org/10.1080/21624887.2015.1019715.

Beier, Marshall J. 2020. "Introduction: Making Sense of Childhood in International Relations." In *Discovering Childhood in International Relations*, edited by Marshall J. Beier, 1–20. Cham, Switzerland: Palgrave Macmillan.

Beier, Marshall J., and Jana Tabak. 2020. "Children, Childhoods, and Everyday Militarisms." *Childhood* 27 (3): 281–93. https://doi.org/10.1177/0907568220923902.

Berents, Helen. 2009. "No Child's Play: Recognising the Agency of Former Child Soldiers in Peace Building Processes." *Dialogue e-Journal* 6 (2): 1–35.

Berezin, Mabel, Emily Sandusky, and Thomas Davidson. 2020. "Culture in Politics and Politics in Culture." In *The New Handbook of Political Sociology*, edited by Thomas Janoski, Cedric de Leon, Joya Misra, and Isaac William Martin, 102–31. Cambridge: Cambridge University Press.

Bergerud, Eric. 2010. "The Village War in Vietnam, 1965–1973." In *The Columbia History of the Vietnam War*, edited by David Anderson, 262–96. New York: Columbia University Press.

Bernal, Martin. 1968. "Vietnam: A Primer on the War." *Cambridge Quarterly* 3 (4): 318–40.

Binadi, Dilli Raj, and Pratisha Dewan Binadi. 2011. "Reintegration of Child Soldiers in Nepal: Grassroots Reflections." In *Child Soldiers: From Recruitment to Reintegration*, edited by Alpaslan Özerdem and Sukanya Podder, 284–305. London: Palgrave Macmillan.

Binh Phuoc. 2018. "'Thập Ác' Thời Xưa" ["Ten Evils" of the Past]. *Binh Phuoc*, October 25. https://baobinhphuoc.com.vn/news/376/116853/thap-ac-thoi-xua.

Blattman, Christopher, and Jeannie Annan. 2008. "Child Combatants in Northern Uganda: Reintegration Myths and Realities." In *Security and Post-Conflict Reconstruction: Dealing with Fighters in the Aftermath of War*, edited by Robert Muggah, 103–26. London: Routledge.

Bloom, Mia. 2019. *Small Arms: Children and Terrorism*. Ithaca, NY: Cornell University Press.

Boothby, Neil. 2006. "What Happens When Child Soldiers Grow Up? The Mozambique Case Study." *Intervention: International Journal of Mental Health, Psychosocial Work & Counselling in Areas of Armed Conflict* 4 (3): 244–59. https://doi.org/10.1097/WTF.0b013e32801181ab.
Borton, Lady. 2000. "Working in a Vietnamese Voice." *Academy of Management Perspectives* 14 (4): 20–29.
Borzello, Anna. 2007. "The Challenge of DDR in Northern Uganda: The Lord's Resistance Army: Analysis." *Conflict, Security & Development* 7 (3): 387–415. https://doi.org/10.1080/14678800701556537.
Bourdieu, Pierre. 1977. *Outline of a Theory of Practice*. Cambridge: Cambridge University Press.
Bourdieu, Pierre. 1986. *Distinction: A Social Critique of the Judgement of Taste*. London: Routledge.
Bourdieu, Pierre. 1990. *In Other Words: Essays Towards a Reflexive Sociology*. Cambridge: Polity.
Bourdieu, Pierre. 1992. *The Logic of Practice*. Cambridge: Polity.
Bourdieu, Pierre. 1996. "Understanding." *Theory, Culture and Society* 13 (2): 17–37. https://doi.org/10.1177/026327696013002002.
Bourdieu, Pierre. 1998. *Practical Reason: On Theory of Action*. Stanford, CA: Stanford University Press.
Bourdieu, Pierre. 2000. *Pascalian Meditations*. Cambridge: Polity.
Bourdieu, Pierre, and Loïc Wacquant. 1992. *An Invitation to Reflexive Sociology*. Cambridge: Polity.
Bradley, Mark P. 2010. "Setting the Stage: Vietnamese Revolutionary Nationalism and the First Vietnam War." In *The Columbia History of the Vietnam War*, edited by David L. Anderson, 93–119. New York: Columbia University Press.
Bradley, Mark P. 2021. *Vietnam at War*. Oxford: Oxford University Press.
Brigham, Robert K. 2010. "Vietnam Society at War." In *Columbia History of the Vietnam War*, edited by David L. Anderson, 317–33. New York: Columbia University Press.
Brigham, Robert K. 2024. "The National Liberation Front." In *The Cambridge History of the Vietnam War*, edited by Andrew Preston and Lien-Hang T. Nguyen, 174–88. Cambridge: Cambridge University Press.
Bryant, John. 1998. "Communism, Poverty, and Demographic Change in North Vietnam." *Population and Development Review* 24 (2): 235–69.
Bui, Ngoc Son. 2013. "The Confucian Foundations of Ho Chi Minh's Vision of the Government." *Journal of Oriental Studies* 46: 35–59. https://ssrn.com/abstract=2677680.
Bultmann, Daniel. 2015. *Inside Cambodian Insurgency: A Sociological Perspective on Civil Wars and Conflict*. Farnham, UK: Ashgate.
Burman, Erica. 1994. "Innocents Abroad: Western Fantasies of Childhood and the Iconography of Emergencies." *Disasters* 18 (3): 238–53. https://doi.org/10.1111/j.1467-7717.1994.tb00310.x.
Burr, Rachel. 2014. "The Complexity of Morality: Being a 'Good Child' in Vietnam?" *Journal of Moral Education* 43 (2): 156–68. https://doi.org/10.1080/03057240.2014.893421.

REFERENCES

Ca Mau Electronic Information Portal [Cổng Thông Tin Điện Tử Tỉnh Cà Mau]. 2016. "Thư Trung Thu Của Bác Hồ Viết Cho Thiếu Nhi" [Uncle Ho's Mid-Autumn Festival Letters Written for Children]. Assessed September 17, 2022. camau.gov.vn.

Campbell, Duncan B. 2012. *Spartan Warrior 735-331 BC*. Oxford: Osprey.

Caplan, Pat. 1997. *African Voices, African Lives: Personal Narratives from a Swahili Village*. London: Routledge.

Carrier, Joseph M., and Charles A. H. Thomson. 1966. *Viet Cong Motivation and Morale: The Special Case of Chieu Hoi*. Santa Monica, CA: RAND.

Carver, George A. 1966. "The Faceless Viet Cong." *Foreign Affairs* 44 (3): 347–72. https://doi.org/10.2307/20039173.

Castelli, Beth. 1995. "The Lifting of the Trade Embargo Between the United States and Vietnam: The Loss of a Potential Bargaining Tool or a Means of Fostering Cooperation?" *Penn State International Law Review* 13 (2): 297–328.

Chanh, Tam. 2015. "Vài Nét Về Công Tác Tuyên Truyền Trong Kháng Chiến Chống Mỹ" [Some Highlights of Tuyen Truyen Work in the Resistance War Against the United States]. *Báo Đồng Tháp* [Dong Thap Newspaper]. April 17. https://baodongthap.vn/chinh-tri/vai-net-ve-cong-tac-tuyen-truyen-trong-khang-chien-chong-my-48281.aspx.

Chapman, Jessica M. 2013. *Cauldron of Resistance: Ngo Dinh Diem, the United States, and 1950s Southern Vietnam*. Ithaca, NY: Cornell University Press.

Chapman, Jessica M. 2014. "Vietnam and the Global Cold War." In *The Routledge Handbook of the Cold War*, edited by Artemy M. Kalinovsky and Craig Daigle, 105–17. London: Routledge.

Chen, Kai. 2014. *Comparative Study of Child Soldiering on Myanmar-China Border: Evolutions, Challenges and Countermeasures*. Singapore: Springer.

Cheng, Stephen K. K. 1990. "Understanding the Culture and Behaviour of East Asians—a Confucian Perspective." *Australian & New Zealand Journal of Psychiatry* 24 (4): 510–15. https://doi.org/10.3109/00048679009062907.

Clodfelter, Micheal. 1995. *Vietnam in Military Statistics: A History of the Indochina Wars, 1772-1991*. Jefferson, NC: McFarland.

Conley, Michael Charles. 1968. "Communist Thought and Viet Cong Tactics." *Asian Survey* 8 (3): 206–22. https://doi.org/10.2307/2642568.

Convention on the Rights of the Child. November 20, 1989, United Nations Treaty Series, Document A/RES/44/25. http://wunrn.org/reference/pdf/Convention_Rights_Child.PDF.

Corfield, Justin. 2008. *The History of Vietnam*. Westport, CT: Greenwood.

Cortes, Liliana, and Marla J. Buchanan. 2007. "The Experience of Columbian Child Soldiers from a Resilience Perspective." *International Journal for the Advancement of Counselling* 29: 43–55. https://doi.org/10.1007/s10447-006-9027-0.

Coulter, Chris. 2008. "Female Fighters in the Sierra Leone War: Challenging the Assumptions?" *Feminist Review* 88: 54–73. https://doi.org/10.1057/palgrave.fr.9400385.

Council of Ministers. 1974. "Quyết Định Về Sắp Xếp Việc Làm Cho Những Người Có Khả Năng Làm Việc" [Decision About Employment Arrangements for People Who Are Able to Work]. Accessed March 23, 2022. https://

thuvienphapluat.vn/van-ban/Lao-dong-Tien-luong/Quyet-dinh-201-CP-sap-xep-viec-lam-cho-nhung-nguoi-co-kha-nang-lam-viec-22454.aspx.

Csernatoni, Raluca-Oana. 2012. "The Praxis of Romania's Euro-Atlantic Security Field: A Bourdieu-Inspired Research Agenda." In *Explaining the EU's Common Security and Defence Policy*, edited by Xymena Kurowska and Fabian Breuer, 212–35. London: Palgrave Macmillan.

Daddis, Gregory A. 2015. "The Vietnam War and American Military Strategy, 1965–1973." In *Oxford Research Encyclopedia of American History*. https://doi.org/10.1093/acrefore/9780199329175.013.239.

Dam, Quang. 1999. *Nho Giáo Xưa Và Nay* [Confucianism in Past and Present]. Hanoi: Nhà Xuất Bản Văn Hóa Thông Tin [Cultural Information Publishing House].

Dang, Trung. 2018. *Vietnam's Post-1975 Agrarian Reforms: How Local Politics Derailed Socialist Agriculture in Southern Vietnam*. Acton: Australian National University Press.

Dang, Trung Dinh. 2010. "Post-1975 Land Reform in Southern Vietnam: How Local Actions and Responses Affected National Land Policy." *Journal of Vietnamese Studies* 5: 72–105. https://doi.org/10.1525/vs.2010.5.3.72.

Dant, Tim. 1999. *Material Culture in the Social World*. Buckingham, UK: Open University Press.

Davidson, Walter P. 1968. *Some Observations on Viet Cong Operations in the Villages*. Santa Monica, CA: RAND.

Davidson, Walter P., and Joseph J. Zasloff. 1966. *A Profile of Viet Cong Cadres*. Santa Monica, CA: RAND.

Davies, Nick. 2015. "Vietnam 40 Years On: How a Communist Victory Gave Way to Capitalist Corruption." *The Guardian*, April 22. www.theguardian.com/news/2015/apr/22/vietnam-40-years-on-how-communist-victory-gave-way-to-capitalist-corruption.

Davis, Jahnine, and Nicholas Marsh. 2022. "The Myth of the Universal Child." In *Safeguarding Young People: Risk, Rights, Resilience and Relationships*, edited by Dez Holmes, 111–29. London: Jessica Kingsley.

D'Costa, Bina, Kim Huynh, and Katrina Lee-Koo. 2015. "Introduction." In *Children and Global Conflict*, edited by Bina D'Costa, Kim Huynh, and Katrina Lee-Koo, 1–32. Cambridge: Cambridge University Press.

Denov, Myriam. 2011. "Social Navigation and Power in Post-Conflict Sierra Leone: Reflections from a Former Child Soldier Turned Bike Rider." In *Child Soldiers: From Recruitment to Reintegration*, edited by Alpaslan Özerdem and Sukanya Podder, 191–213. London: Palgrave Macmillan.

Denov, Myriam. 2012. "Child Soldiers and Iconography: Portrayals and (Mis) Representations." *Children & Society* 26 (4): 280–92. https://doi.org/10.1111/j.1099-0860.2010.00347.x.

Denov, Myriam, and Andi Buccitelli. 2013. "Navigating Crisis and Chronicity in the Everyday: Former Child Soldiers in Urban Sierra Leone." *Stability: International Journal of Security and Development* 2 (2): 1–18. http://dx.doi.org/10.5334/sta.ce.

Denov, Myriam, and Ines Marchand. 2014. "'One Cannot Take Away the Stain': Rejection and Stigma Among Former Child Soldiers in Colombia." *Peace* and Conflict: Journal of Peace Psychology 20: 227–40. https://doi.org/10.1037/pac0000039.

Denov, Myriam, and Richard Maclure. 2007. "Turnings and Epiphanies: Militarization, Life Histories, and the Making and Unmaking of Two Child Soldiers in Sierra Leone." Journal of Youth Studies 10 (2): 243–61. https://doi.org/10.1080/13676260601120187.

Denton, Frank H. 1968. Volunteers for the Viet Cong. Santa Monica, CA: RAND.

Doan, Giang L. 2009. Nho Giáo Nhật Bản Và Nho Giáo Việt Nam [Confucianism in Japan and Vietnam]. VNU Faculty of Literature, Hanoi, April 28. http://khoavanhoc-ngonngu.edu.vn/home/index.php?option=com_content&view=article&id=352:nho-giao-nht-bn-va-nho-giao-vit-nam&catid=72:hi-ngh-khoa-hc-han-nom&Itemid=146.

Donnell, John C. 1967. Viet Cong Recruitment: Why and How Men Join. Santa Monica, CA: RAND.

Donnell, John C., Guy J. Pauker, and Joseph J. Zasloff. 1965. Viet Cong Motivation and Morale in 1964: Preliminary Report. Santa Monica, CA: RAND.

Dror, Olga. 2018. Making Two Vietnams: War and Youth Identities, 1965-1975. Cambridge: Cambridge University Press.

Drumbl, Mark A. 2012. Reimagining Child Soldiers in International Law and Policy. Oxford: Oxford University Press.

Duiker, William J. 2018. The Communist Road to Power in Vietnam. 2nd ed. New York: Westview.

Elliott, David W. P., and Mai Elliott. 1969. Documents of an Elite Viet Cong Delta Unit: The Demolition Platoon of the 514th Battalion—Part Four: Political Indoctrination and Military Training. Santa Monica, CA: RAND.

Emerson, Stephen. 2018. Air War over North Vietnam: Operation Rolling Thunder, 1965-1968. Barnsley, UK: Pen and Sword.

Emirbayer, Mustafa. 1997. "Manifesto for a Relational Sociology." American Journal of Sociology 103 (2): 281–317. https://doi.org/10.1086/231209.

Farrar-Hockley, Anthony. 1984. "A Reminiscence of the Chinese People's Volunteers in the Korean War." China Quarterly 98: 287–304. https://doi.org/10.1017/S0305741000016830.

Frey, R. Scott. 2013. "Agent Orange and America at War in Vietnam and Southeast Asia." Human Ecology Review 20 (1): 1–10. http://www.jstor.org/stable/24707567.

Fung, Heidi, and Thi Thu Mai. 2019. "Cultivating Affection-Laden Hierarchy: Embodied Moral Socialization of Vòng Tay (Khoanh Tay) with Children in Southern Vietnam." Ethos 47: 281–306. https://doi.org/10.1111/etho.12247.

Gabriner, Alice, and Lily Rothman. "'Who Is the Enemy Here?' The Vietnam War Pictures That Moved Them Most." TIME. https://time.com/vietnam-photos.

Gardner, Lloyd C. 2010. "Lyndon Johnson and the Bombing of Vietnam: Politics and Military Choices." In The Columbia History of the Vietnam War, edited by David L. Anderson, 168–90. New York: Columbia University Press.

Garrett, W. Clarke. 1967. "In Search of Grandeur: France and Vietnam 1940–1946." Review of Politics 29 (3): 303–23. https://doi.org/10.1017/S0034670500032733.

REFERENCES

Gates, Scott. 2017. "Membership Matters: Coerced Recruits and Rebel Allegiance." *Journal of Peace Research* 54: 674–86. https://doi.org/10.1177/0022343317722700.

Ghosh, S. K. 1975. "Relations Between North Vietnam, China and the Soviet Union." *India Quarterly* 31(2):136–58.https://doi.org/10.1177/097492847503100203.

Girling, John L. S. 1967. "Vietnam and the Domino Theory." *Australian Outlook* 21 (1): 61–70. https://doi.org/10.1080/10357716708444262.

Gleason, Mona. 2016. "Avoiding the Agency Trap: Caveats for Historians of Children, Youth, and Education." *History of Education* 45 (4): 446–59. https://doi.org/10.1080/0046760X.2016.1177121.

Goscha, Christopher. 2010. " 'Hell in a Very Small Place': Cold War and Decolonisation in the Assault on the Vietnamese Body at Dien Bien Phu." *European Journal of East Asian Studies* 9: 201–23. https://doi.org/10.1163/156805810X548748.

Goscha, Christopher E. 2012. "A 'Total War' of Decolonization? Social Mobilization and State-Building in Communist Vietnam (1949–54)." *War & Society* 31: 136–62. https://doi.org/10.1179/0729247312Z.0000000007.

Goscha, Christopher E. 2013. "Colonial Hanoi and Saigon at War: Social Dynamics of the Viet Minh's 'Underground City', 1945–1954." *War in History* 20 (2): 222–50. https://doi.org/10.1177/0968344512471125.

Goscha, Christopher E. 2022. *The Road to Dien Bien Phu: A History of the First War for Vietnam*. Princeton, NJ: Princeton University Press.

Goscha, Christopher E. 2024 "The Battle of Điện Biên Phủ." In *The Cambridge History of the Vietnam War*, edited by Edward Miller and Lien-Hang T. Nguyen, 238–58. Cambridge: Cambridge University Press.

Government. 1975. "Thông Tư Hướng Dẫn Hoàn Thành Việc Khen Thưởng Gia Đình Quân Nhân Chống Mỹ, Cứu Nước" [Circulars Guiding Rewarding Families of Military Members Who Participated in Stopping America, Liberating the Country]. Accessed March 23, 2022. https://thuvienphapluat.vn/van-ban/Van-hoa-Xa-hoi/Thong-tu-297-TTg-huong-dan-hoan-thanh-khen-thuong-gia-dinh-quan-nhan-chong-My-cuu-nuoc-23377.aspx.

Grosse, Ingrid. 2015. "Gender Values in Vietnam—Between Confucianism, Communism, and Modernization." *Asian Journal of Peacebuilding* 3: 253–72. https://doi.org/10.18588/201511.000045.

Guillemot, François. 2009. "Death and Suffering at First Hand: Youth Shock Brigades During the Vietnam War (1950–1975)." *Journal of Vietnamese Studies* 4: 17–60. https://doi.org/10.1525/vs.2009.4.3.17.

Halberstam, David. 2007. *Ho*. New York: Roman & Littlefield.

Han, Kuei-Hsiang. 2016. " 'The Feeling of 'Face' in Confucian Society: From a Perspective of Psychosocial Equilibrium." *Frontiers in Psychology* 7: 1–9. https://doi.org/10.3389/fpsyg.2016.01055.

Han, Le Mau, Ba De Tran, and Van Thu Nguyen. 2005. *Đại Cương Lịch Sử Việt Nam* [Overview of Vietnamese History]. Hanoi: Nhà Xuất Bản Giáo Dục [Education Publishing House].

Harrison, James P. 1993. "History's Heaviest Bombing." In *The Vietnam War: Vietnamese and American Perspectives*, edited by Jayne S. Werner and Luu Doan Huynh, 130–39. New York: M. E. Sharpe.

Hart, Jason. 2006. "The Politics of 'Child Soldiers.'" *Brown Journal of World Affairs* 13 (1): 217–26. http://www.jstor.org/stable/24590655.

Harvie, Charles, and Van Hoa Tran. 1997. *Vietnam's Reforms and Economic Growth*. London: Palgrave Macmillan.

Hegghammer, Thomas. 2017. "Non-Military Practices in Jihadi Groups." In *Jihadi Culture*, edited by Thomas Hegghammer, 171–202. Cambridge: Cambridge University Press.

Herring, George C. 2004. "The Cold War and Vietnam." *OAH Magazine of History* 18 (5): 18–21. https://doi.org/10.1093/maghis/18.5.18.

Hess, Gary R. 2015. *Vietnam: Explaining America's Lost War*. Chichester, UK: Wiley.

Hirschman, Charles, and Vu Manh Loi. 1996. "Family and Household Structure in Vietnam: Some Glimpses from a Recent Survey." *Pacific Affairs* 69: 229–49. https://doi.org/10.2307/2760726.

Hoang, Thu Trang, and Thi Kim Oanh Hoang. 2020. "Vietnam Confucianism—Some General Specialties." *World Journal of Social Sciences and Humanities* 6: 45–50. https://doi.org/10.12691/wjssh-6-2-3.

Hoang, Thuc Lan. 2014. "Đạo Hiếu Trong Gia Đình Việt Nam Hiện Nay" [Filial Piety in Vietnamese Modern Families]. *Tạp Chí Khoa Học Xã Hội Việt Nam* [Journal of Vietnamese Science and Society] 10 (83): 70–76.

Hoang, Trang T. 2017. "Ảnh Hưởng Của Quan Niệm Đạo Đức Nho Giáo Đến Đời Sống Đạo Đức Ở Việt Nam Hiện Nay" [Influence of Confucian Ethics on the Moral Life in Vietnam Today]. *Khoa Hoc Xã Hôi Việt Nam* [Science and Society in Vietnam] 7: 9–17.

Hoffer, Thomas W. 1974. "Nguyen Van Be as Propaganda Hero of the North and South Vietnamese Governments: A Case Study of Mass Media Conflict." *Southern Speech Communication Journal* 40 (1): 63–80. https://doi.org/10.1080/10417947409372254.

Hoffman, Kasper. 2015. "Myths Set in Motion: The Moral Economy of Mai Mai Governance." In *Rebel Governance in Civil War*, edited by Ana Arjona, Nelson Kasfir, and Zachariah C. Mampilly, 158–79. Cambridge: Cambridge University Press.

Honwana, Alcinda. 2009. "Children in War: Reintegrating Child Soldiers." *IDS Bulletin* 40: 63–68. https://doi.org/10.1111/j.1759-5436.2009.00010.x.

Hopkins, Lucy, and Arathi Sriprakash. 2015. "Unsettling the Global Child: Rethinking Child Subjectivity in Education and International Development." In *The "Poor Child": The Cultural Politics of Education, Development and Childhood*, edited by Lucy Hopkins and Arathi Sriprakash, 3–19. Abingdon, UK: Routledge.

Howell, Allison. 2015. "Making War Work: Resilience, Emotional Fitness, and Affective Economies in Western Militaries." In *Emotions, Politics and War*, edited by Linda Åhäll and Thomas Gregory, 163–75. Oxon, UK: Routledge.

Huijsmans, Roy. 2008. "Children Working Beyond Their Localities: Lao Children Working in Thailand." *Childhood* 15 (3): 331–53. https://doi.org/10.1177/0907568208091667.

Hunt, David. 2008. *Vietnam's Southern Revolution: From Peasant Insurrection to Total War*. Amherst: University of Massachusetts Press.

Hurle, Rob. 2014. "Hồ Chí Minh and the Role of Symbolism in Mobilising People in the Việt bắc-Tuyên truyền in the Prelude to Điện Biên Phủ." Academia. https://www.academia.edu/10022407/H%E1%BB%93_Ch%C3%AD_Minh_and_the_Role_of_Symbolism_in_Mobilising_People_in_the_Vi%E1%BB%87t_b%E1%BA%AFc_Tuy%C3%AAn_truy%E1%BB%81n_in_the_Prelude_to_%C4%90i%E1%BB%87n_Bi%C3%AAn_Ph%E1%BB%A7?source=swp_share.

Huynh, Kim Khanh. 1971. "The Vietnamese August Revolution Reinterpreted." *Journal of Asian Studies* 30 (4): 761–82. https://doi.org/10.2307/2052986.

Huynh, Kim Khanh. 1976. "The Vietnamese Communist Movement Revisited." In *Southeast Asian Affairs*, edited by Institute of Southeast Asian Studies, 445–66. Singapore: Institute of Southeast Asian Studies Publishing.

Huynh, Kim. 2015. "Child Soldiers: Causes, Solutions and Cultures." In *Children and Global Conflict*, edited by Kim Huynh, Bina D'Costa, and Katrina Lee-Koo, 123–57. Cambridge: Cambridge University Press.

Hwang, Kwang-Kuo, and Kuei-Hsiang Han. 2012. "Face and Morality in Confucian Society." In *The Oxford Handbook of Chinese Psychology*, edited by Michael H. Bond, 479–98. Oxford: Oxford University Press.

Hynd, Stacey. 2020. "Small Warriors? Children and Youth in Colonial Insurgencies and Counterinsurgency, ca. 1945–1960." *Comparative Studies in Society and History* 62 (4): 684–713. https://doi.org/10.1017/S0010417520000250.

Immerman, Richard H. 2010. " 'Dealing with a Government of Madmen': Eisenhower, Kennedy, and Ngo Dinh Diem." In *The Columbia History of the Vietnam War*, edited by David Anderson, 120–42. New York: Columbia University Press.

Jamieson, Neil L. 1995. *Understanding Vietnam*. Los Angeles: University of California Press.

Jeffrey, Craig. 2011. "Geographies of Children and Youth II: Global Youth Agency." *Progress in Human Geography* 36: 245–53. https://doi.org/10.1177/0309132510393316.

Jenkins, Rob. 2014. *Pierre Bourdieu*. London: Routledge.

Jennings, Eric T. 2024. "Indochina During World War II." In *The Cambridge History of the Vietnam War*, edited by Edward Miller and Lien-Hang T. Nguyen, 84–105. Cambridge: Cambridge University Press.

Joes, Anthony J. 2001. *The War for South Viet Nam, 1954–1975*. London: Greenwood.

Jordans, Mark J., Ivan H. Komproe, Wietse A. Tol, Aline Ndayisaba, Theodora Nisabwe, and Brandon Kohrt. 2012. "Reintegration of Child Soldiers in Burundi: A Tracer Study." *Biomed Central Public Health* 12: 1–12. https://doi.org/10.1186/1471-2458-12-905.

Kahin, George McTurnan. 1986. *Intervention: How America Became Involved in Vietnam*. New York: Knopf.

Kar, Srestha. 2020. "An Obituary for Innocence: Revisiting the Trauma During the Khmer Rouge Years in Cambodia Through Children's Narratives." *Rupkatha Journal on Interdisciplinary Studies in Humanities* 12 (1): 1–9.

Karnow, Stanley. 1994. *Vietnam: A History*. London: Random House.

Katz, Mark N. 1980. "The Origins of the Vietnam War 1945–1948." *Review of Politics* 42 (2): 131–51. https://doi.org/10.1017/S0034670500031417.

Kelley, Liam. 2006. " 'Confucianism' in Vietnam: A State of the Field Essay." *Journal of Vietnamese Studies* 1: 314–70. https://doi.org/10.1525/vs.2006.1.1-2.314.

Kerkvliet, Benedict J. T. 2005. *The Power of Everyday Politics: How Vietnamese Peasants Transformed National Policy*. Ithaca, NY: Cornell University Press.

Khanh, Ngoc. 2020. "Hội Cựu Thanh Niên Xung Phong Phát Huy Vai Trò, Hiệu Quả Hoạt Động" [The Association of Youth Shock Brigades Promotes Its Role and Effectiveness]. *Phu Tho*, August 7. http://baophutho.vn/xa-hoi/202008/hoi-cuu-thanh-nien-xung-phong-phat-huy-vai-tro-hieu-qua-hoat-dong-172351.

Khuat, Thu Hong. 2009. "Stem Family in Vietnam." In *The Stem Family in Eurasian Perspective: Revisiting House Societies, 17th-20th Centuries*, edited by Antoinette Fauve-Chamoux and Emiko Ochiai. Bern, Switzerland: Peter Lang.

King, Ambrose Y. C., and Michael H. Bond. 1985. "The Confucian Paradigm of Man: A Sociological View." In *Chinese Culture and Mental Health*, edited by Wen-Shing Tseng and David Y. H. Wu, 29–45. London: Academic Press.

Kleinen, John. 1999. *Facing the Future, Reviving the Past: A Study of Social Change in a Northern Vietnamese Village*. Singapore: Institute of Southeast Asian Studies.

Kocher, Matthew Adam, Thomas B. Pepinsky, and Stathis N. Kalyvas. 2011. "Aerial Bombing and Counterinsurgency in the Vietnam War." *American Journal of Political Science* 55 (2): 201–18. https://doi.org/10.1111/j.1540-5907.2010.00498.x.

Kolko, Gabriel. 1995. "Vietnam Since 1975: Winning a War and Losing the Peace." *Journal of Contemporary Asia* 25: 3–49. https://doi.org/10.1080/00472339580000021.

Kryger, Louise, and Cille Lindgren. 2011. "Fighting for a Future: The Potential for Posttraumatic Growth Among Youths Formerly Associated with Armed Forces in Northern Uganda." *Intervention* 9 (1): 6–20: https://doi.org/10.1097/WTF.0b013e32834544c8.

Kucherenko, Olga. 2011. *Little Soldiers: How Soviet Children Went to War, 1941–1945*. Oxford: Oxford University Press.

Lacouture, Jean, and Joseph E. Cunneen. 1965. "The 'Viet Cong.' " *CrossCurrents* 15 (3): 355–62.

Lai, Hoa. 2019. "Chủ Nghĩa Cá Nhân Làm Con Người Ta Xuống Dốc Không Phanh" [Individualism Makes People Go Downhill]. *Voice of Vietnam*, February 11. https://vov.vn/chinh-tri/dang/chu-nghia-ca-nhan-lam-con-nguoi-ta-xuong-doc-khong-phanh-874100.vov.

Landon, Kenneth P. 1966. "The 1954 Geneva Agreements." *Current History* 50 (294): 79–84. https://doi.org/10.1525/curh.1966.50.294.79.

Lanning, Michael L., and Dan Cragg. 2008. *Inside the VC and the NVA: The Real Story of North Vietnam's Armed Forces*. College Station: Texas A&M University Press.

Lau, Raymond W. K. 2004. "Habitus and the Practical Logic of Practice." *Sociology* 38: 369–87. https://doi.org/10.1177/0038038504040870.

Lawrence, Mark A. 2010. *The Vietnam War: A Concise International History*. Oxford: Oxford University Press.

Le, Chan Phuong. 2005. "Phong Trào Phụ Nữ 'Ba Đảm Đang,' Một Mốc Son Lịch Sử Chói Lọi" [Women's Movement "Three Responsibilities," a Shining Milestone]. *Nhan Dan*, February 27. https://nhandan.vn/phong-trao-phu-nu-ba-dam-dang-mot-moc-son-lich-su-choi-loi-post513992.html.

Le, Manh. 2015. "Thanh Niên Xung Phong Quên Mình Vì Tổ Quốc" [Youth Volunteers Forget Themselves for the Motherland]. *Nhan Dan*, April 25. https://nhandan.com.vn/chinhtri/thanh-nien-xung-phong-quen-minh-vi-to-quoc-230928/.

Le, Thi Bich Thuy. 2018. "Vietnamese Family Culture in the Context of International Integration." *World Journal of Social Sciences and Humanities* 4: 170–76. https://doi.org/10.12691/wjssh-4-3-5.

Le, Thi Quy. 2013. Những Giá Trị Truyền Thống Và Hiện Đại Cần Phát Huy Trong Gia Đình Việt Nam Hiện Nay. [The Traditional and Modern Values Worthy of Promoting in the Vietnamese Family Today]. *Tap Chi Cong San*, June 3. http://tapchicongsan.org.vn/web/guest/nghien-cu-/-/2018/21833/nhung-gia-tri-truyen-thong-va-hien-dai-can-phat-huy-trong-gia-dinh-viet-nam-hien-nay.aspx.

Lee, Ah-Jung. 2009. "Understanding and Addressing the Phenomenon of 'Child Soldiers': The Gap Between the Global Humanitarian Discourse and the Local Understandings and Experiences of Young People's Military Recruitment." *Refugee Studies Centre* Working Paper no. 52. Oxford: Refugee Studies Centre. https://www.rsc.ox.ac.uk/files/publications/working-paper-series/wp52-understanding-addressing-child-soldiers-2009.pdf.

Lee-Koo, Katrina. 2011. "Horror and Hope: (Re)Presenting Militarised Children in Global North–South Relations." *Third World Quarterly* 32 (4): 725–42. https://doi.org/10.1080/01436597.2011.567005.

Leichty, Mary M. 1963. "Family Attitudes and Self-Concept in Vietnamese and U.S. Children." *American Journal of Orthopsychiatry* 33: 38–50. https://doi.org/10.1111/j.1939-0025.1963.tb00357.x.

Leites, Nathan. 1969. *The Viet Cong Style of Politics*. Santa Monica, CA: RAND.

Lentz, Christian C. 2017. "Cultivating Subjects: Opium and Rule in Post-Colonial Vietnam." *Modern Asian Studies* 51 (4): 879–918. https://doi.org/10.1017/S0026749X15000402.

Lewy, Guenter. 1980. *America in Vietnam*. Oxford: Oxford University Press.

Li, Xiaobing. 2020. *The Dragon in the Jungle: The Chinese Army in the Vietnam War*. Oxford: Oxford University Press.

Luong, Van Hy. 1988. "Discursive Practices and Power Structure: Person-Referring Forms and Sociopolitical Struggles in Colonial Vietnam." *American Ethnologist* 15: 239–53.

Luong, Van Hy. 2003. "Wealth, Power, and Inequality: Global Market, the State, and Local Sociocultural Dynamics." In *Postwar Vietnam: Dynamics of a Transforming Society*, edited by Van Hy Luong, 81–106. Oxford: Rowman and Littlefield.

Luong, Van Hy. 2007. "The Restructuring of Vietnamese Nationalism, 1954–2006." *Pacific Affairs* 80 (3): 439–53. https://www.jstor.org/stable/40023392.

Mach, Quang Thang. 2019. "President Ho Chi Minh's 'Mass Mobilization': Theoretical and Practical Value." *National Defense Journal*, October 15.

REFERENCES

http://tapchiqptd.vn/en/events-and-comments/president-ho-chi-minhs-mass-mobilisation-theoretical-and-practical-value/14507.html.

Macmillan, Lorraine. 2009. "The Child Soldier in North-South Relations." *International Political Sociology* 3 (1): 36–52. https://doi.org/10.1111/j.1749-5687.2008.00062.x.

Madsen, Richard. 2012. "Confucian Conceptions of Civil Society." In *Alternate Conceptions of Civil Society*, edited by Simone Chambers and Will Kymlicka, 191–206. Princeton, NJ: Princeton University Press.

Mai, Van Hai. 2009. "Gia Đình, Dòng Họ Và Thôn Làng Với Tư Cách Là Các Giá Trị Cơ Bản Của Văn Hoá Người Việt" [Families, Lineages and Villages as Fundamental Values of Vietnamese Culture]. *Xã hội học* [Sociology] 1: 36–40.

Malarney, Shaun K. 2002a. *Culture, Ritual and Revolution in Vietnam*. Honolulu: University of Hawaii Press.

Malarney, Shaun K. 2002b. "The Realities and Consequences of War in a Northern Vietnamese Commune." In *A Companion to the Vietnam War*, edited by Marilyn B. Young and Robert Buzzanco, 65–78. Malden, MA: Blackwell.

Malešević, Siniša. 2008. "The Sociology of New Wars? Assessing the Causes and Objectives of Contemporary Violent Conflicts." *International Political Sociology* 2 (2): 97–112. https://doi.org/10.1111/j.1749-5687.2008.00038.x.

Man, Simeon. 2018. *Soldiering Through Empire: Race and the Making of the Decolonizing Pacific*. Oakland: University of California Press.

Maranto, Robert, and Paula A. Tuchman. 1992. "Knowing the Rational Peasant: The Creation of Rival Incentive Structures in Vietnam." *Journal of Peace Research* 29: 249–64. https://doi.org/10.1177/0022343392029003002.

Marr, David. 2000. "Concepts of 'Individual' and 'Self' in Twentieth-Century Vietnam." *Modern Asian Studies* 34: 769–96. https://doi.org/10.1017/S0026749X00003851.

Marr, David G. 2004. "A Brief History of Local Government in Vietnam." In *Beyond Hanoi: Local Government in Vietnam*, edited by Benedict J. Tria Kerkvliet and David G. Marr, 28–53. Singapore: ISEAS Publishing.

Marr, David. 2013. *Vietnam: State, War, and Revolution (1945–1946)*. Berkeley: University of California Press.

McHale, F. Shawn. 2002. "Mapping a Vietnamese Confucian Past and Its Transition to Modernity." In *Rethinking Confucianism: Past and Present in China, Japan, Korea, and Vietnam*, edited by Benjamin Elman, John Duncan, and Herman Ooms, 397–430. Los Angeles: University of California.

McHale, F. Shawn. 2004. *Print and Power: Confucianism, Communism, and Buddhism in the Making of Modern Vietnam*. Honolulu: University of Hawaii Press.

McLeod, Mark W., and Thi Dieu Nguyen. 2001. *Culture and Customs of Vietnam*. Westport, CT: Greenwood.

McMullin, Jaremey. 2011. "Reintegrating Young Combatants: Do Child-Centred Approaches Leave Children—and Adults—Behind?" *Third World Quarterly* 32 (4): 743–64. https://doi.org/10.1080/01436597.2011.567006.

Mekonnen, Daniel R., and Mirjam van Reisen. 2012. "The EU Lisbon Treaty and EU Development Cooperation: Considerations for a Revised EU Strategy on Development Cooperation in Eritrea." *Verfassung und Recht in Übersee/Law and Politics in Africa, Asia and Latin America* 45: 324–43. https://doi.org/10.5771/0506-7286-2012-3-324.

Merridale, Catherine. 2012. "Masculinity at War: Did Gender Matter in the Soviet Army?" *Journal of War & Culture Studies* 5 (3): 307–20. https://doi.org/10.1386/jwcs.5.3.307_1.

Miguel, Edward, and Roland Gerard. 2011. "The Long-Run Impact of Bombing Vietnam." *Journal of Development Economics* 96 (1): 1–15. https://doi.org/10.1016/j.jdeveco.2010.07.004.

Miller, Edward. 2013. *Misalliance: Ngo Dinh Diem, the United States, and the Fate of South Vietnam*. Cambridge, MA: Harvard University Press.

Miller, Edward. 2024. "Introduction: Points of Departure: – The Global and Local Origins of the Vietnam War." In *The Cambridge History of the Vietnam War*, edited by Edward Miller and Lien-Hang T. Nguyen, 8–24. Cambridge: Cambridge University Press.

Miller, Edward, and Tuong Vu. 2009. "The Vietnam War as a Vietnamese War: Agency and Society in the Study of the Second Indochina War." *Journal of Vietnamese Studies* 4 (3): 1–16. https://doi.org/10.1525/vs.2009.4.3.1.

Milne, David. 2007. " 'Our Equivalent of Guerrilla Warfare': Walt Rostow and the Bombing of North Vietnam, 1961–1968." *Journal of Military History* 71 (1): 169–203. https://doi.org/10.1353/jmh.2007.0056.

Ministry of Education. 1964. "Chỉ Thị Về Việc Phấn Đấu Đẩy Mạnh Phong Trào Thi Đua '2 Tốt', Củng Cố, Phát Triển Các Tổ Lao Động Xã Hội Chủ Nghĩa Trong Toàn Ngành Giáo Dục" [Directive on Striving to Promote the "2 Goods" Emulation Movement, Consolidate and Develop Socialist Labor Groups in the Entire Education Sector]. Accessed September 25, 2024. https://thuvienphapluat.vn/van-ban/Lao-dong-Tien-luong/Chi-thi-03-CT-LT-phan-dau-day-manh-phong-trao-thi-dua-2-tot-cung-co-phat-trien-to-lao-dong-XHCN-nganh-giao-duc-60619.aspx.

Ministry of Education. 1966. "V/V Giải Quyết Số Học Sinh Miền Nam Bỏ Học, Không Học Được Và Đau Yếu Năm 1966" [Regarding the Problem of Southern Students Dropping Out, Not Being Able to Study or Being Ill in 1966]. File number 2060; Archival Centre 3: Hanoi.

Ministry of Finance. 1976. "Thông Tư Hướng Dẫn Việc Tiếp Nhận, Trả Lương, Sinh Hoạt Phí Hoặc Trợ Cấp Cho Cán Bộ, Học Sinh, Quân Nhân Chuyển Ngành Được Chuyển Từ Miền Nam Ra Miền Bắc" [Circulars Guiding the Receipt, Payment of Salaries, Living Expenses or Allowances for Cadres, Students and Military Personnel Transferred from the South to the North]. Accessed March 23, 2022. https://thuvienphapluat.vn/van-ban/Lao-dong-Tien-luong/Thong-Tu-12-TC_HCVX-Huong-dan-tiep-nhan-tra-luong-sinh-hoat-phi-hoac-tro-cap-can-bo-hoc-sinh-quan-nhan-chuyen-nganh-tu-mien-Nam-ra-Bac-53901.aspx.

Ministry of Labor. 1972. "Thông tư Giải thích và hướng dẫn thi hành điều lệnh về nghĩa vụ lao động trong thời chiến ban hành kèm theo Nghị định số 117-cp ngày 13-6-1972 của Hội đồng Chính phủ" [Circulars explaining and guiding on the implementation of the War Order of Labor Obligation, issued together with Decree No. 117-cp, dated June 13, 1972, of the Cabinet of Ministers]. Accessed March 23, 2022. https://thuvienphapluat.vn/van-ban/Lao-dong-Tien-luong/Thong-tu-10-LD-TT-Dieu-lenh-nghia-vu-lao-dong-thoi-chien-huong-dan-Nghi-dinh-117-CP-18975.aspx.

Ministry of Public Security–Ministry of Labor. 1974. "Thông tư liên bộ lao động—công an số 12/ttlb ngày 24 tháng 3 năm 1975 hướng dẫn thi hành chế độ bắt buộc lao động theo quyết định số 201/cp ngày 30-8-1974 của Hội đồng Chính phủ" [Circulars: The Ministry of Labor—public security no.12/ttlb March 24, 1975, guiding the implementation of compulsory labor regime under Decision No. 201/cp, dated August 30, 1974, of the Cabinet of Ministers]. Accessed March 23, 2022. https://thuvienphapluat.vn/van-ban/Lao-dong-Tien-luong/Thong-tu-12-TTLB-huong-dan-che-do-bat-buoc-lao-dong-Quyet-dinh-201-Cp-44674.aspx>.

Ministry of Unification. 1971. "Báo cáo của Ủy ban Thống nhất về một số nét của học sinh miền Nam nội trú năm 1971" [Ministry of Unification Report About Some Features of Boarding Students from the South in 1971]. File number 2140; Archival Centre 3: Hanoi.

Moyar, Maureen. 2006. *Triumph Forsaken: The Vietnam War, 1954-1965*. New York: Cambridge University Press.

Moynagh, Maureen. 2013. "Political Futurity and the Child-Soldier Figure: A Romance of Globalization." *Interventions* 16 (5): 655–74. https://doi.org/10.1080/1369801X.2013.858969.

Mugadza, Hilda T., Budayi Mujeyi, Brian Stout, Nidhi Wali, and Andre M. N. Renzaho. 2019. "Childrearing Practices Among Sub-Saharan African Migrants in Australia: A Systematic Review." *Journal of Child and Family Studies* 28: 2927–41. https://doi.org/10.1007/s10826-019-01463-z.

Nakamura, Hajime. 1964. *The Ways of Thinking of Eastern Peoples: India-China-Tibet-Japan*. Honolulu: University of Hawaii Press.

The New York Times. 1964. "Close-up of the Vietcong in Their Jungle; A French Reporter Held Captive by Guerrillas in South Vietnam Here Reports on What he Saw of the Vietcong—The Men, Their Morale, Their Methods." *The New York Times*, September 13.

Ngo, Thi Lan Anh, and Thu Thuy Hoang. 2018. "Ý Nghĩa Của Đạo Hiếu Đối Với Quan Hệ Gia Đình Ở Việt Nam Hiện Nay" [The Significance of Filial Piety for Family Relations in Vietnam Today]. *Tạp Chí Khoa Học & Công Nghệ* [Journal of Science and Technology] 191 (5): 9–13.

Ngo, Vinh Long. 1989. "Vietnam: The Real Enemy." *Bulletin of Concerned Asian Scholars* 21 (2–4): 6–34. https://doi.org/10.1080/14672715.1989.10404454.

Nguyen, Anh Cuong. 2014. "Vài Nét Về Nghệ Thuật Chiến Dịch Trong Chiến Tranh Nhân Dân Việt Nam" [A Few Highlights About the Campaigns During Vietnam People's War]. *Ho Chi Minh University Journal of Science* 5 (38): 112–15.

Nguyen, Huong. 2012. "When Development Means Political Maturation: Adolescents as Miniature Communists in Post-War and Pre-Reform Vietnam, 1975–1986." *History of the Family* 17 (2): 256–78. https://doi.org/10.1080/1081602X.2012.715244.

Nguyen, Lien-Hang T. 2012. *Hanoi's War: An International History of the War for Peace in Vietnam*. Chapel Hill, NC: University of North Carolina Press.

Nguyen, Lien-Hang T. 2024. "General Introduction." In *The Cambridge History of the Vietnam War*, edited by Edward Miller and Lien-Hang T. Nguyen, 1–7. Cambridge: Cambridge University Press.

Nguyen, Mai Anh. 2022. "'Little People Do Little Things': The Motivation and Recruitment of Viet Cong Child Soldiers." *Critical Studies on Security* 10 (1): 30–42. https://doi.org/10.1080/21624887.2022.2073740.

Nguyen, Mai Anh. 2023. "Parenting Patriots: Filial Piety, Family Socialization, and Insurgency in the Vietnam War." *Journal of Vietnamese Studies* 18 (4): 1–29. https://doi.org/10.1525/vs.2023.18.4.1.

Nguyen, Nam. 2018. "The Noble Person and the Revolutionary: Living with Confucian Values in Contemporary Vietnam." In *Confucianisms for a Changing World Cultural Order*, edited by Roger T. Ames and Peter D. Hershock, 128–63. Honolulu: University of Hawaii Press.

Nguyen, Ngoc Huy. 1998. "The Confucian Incursion into Vietnam." In *Confucianism and the Family: A Study of Indo-Tibetan Scholasticism*, edited by Walter H. Slote and George A. De Vos, 91–105. New York: State University of New York Press.

Nguyen, Ngoc Tho. 2016. "Confucianism and Humane Education in Contemporary Vietnam." *International Communication of Chinese Culture* 3 (4): 645–71. https://doi.org/10.1007/s40636-016-0076-8.

Nguyen, Phong. 2023. "Lời Bác Năm Xưa: 5 Điều Bác Hồ Dạy Thiếu Niên, Nhi Đồng" [Uncle Ho's Words from the Past: 5 Things Uncle Ho Taught Teenagers and Children]. *Báo Thanh Hoá* [Thanh Hoa Newspaper], June 1. https://baothanhhoa.vn/theo-guong-bac/loi-bac-nam-xua-5-dieu-bac-ho-day-thieu-nien-nhi-dong/187387.htm.

Nguyen, Quang Tuan. 2009. "Tư Tưởng Hồ Chí Minh Về Đạo Đức Cách Mạng, Cần, Kiệm, Liêm, Chính, Chí Công Vô Tư" [Ho Chi Minh's Thoughts on Revolutionary Ethics, Need, Thrifty, Integrity, Righteousness, and Impartiality]. Accessed March 22, 2022. http://dl.ueb.vnu.edu.vn/handle/1247/15743.

Nguyen, Thi Nhung. 2020. "Người Lính Trở Về Sau Chiến Tranh" [A Soldier Returning from the War]. Accessed September 19, 2023. https://vannghe.hagiang.gov.vn/tin-tuc-chi-tiet?newsId=176400.

Nguyen, Thi Tho, and Thanh Binh Nguyen. 2012. "Filial Piety and the Implementation of Taking Care of Elderly People in Vietnamese Families at Present Time." *Journal of Educational and Social Research* 2: 227–34. https://www.richtmann.org/journal/index.php/jesr/article/view/11885.

Nguyen, Trung Kien. 2016. "Daily Deference Rituals and Social Hierarchy in Vietnam." *Asian Social Science* 12 (1): 34–46. https://doi.org/10.5539/ass.v12n5p33.

Nguyen, Van Chinh. 2000. *Work Without Name: Changing Patterns of Children's Work in a Northern Vietnamese Village*. PhD diss., University of Amsterdam.

Nguyen, Van Duoc. 2021. "Đẩy Mạnh Phong Trào "Cựu Chiến Binh Giúp Nhau Giảm Nghèo, Làm Kinh Tế Giỏi" [Pushing Forward the Movement of Veterans Helping Each Other to Escape Poverty and Excel in Business]. *Quốc Phòng Toàn Dân* [Journal of National Defense], December 6. http://tapchiqptd.vn/vi/bao-ve-to-quoc/day-manh-phong-trao-cuu-chien-binh-giup-nhau-giam-ngheo-lam-kinh-te-gioi/18014.html.

Nguyen, Van Huy, and Laurel Kendall. 2003. *Vietnam: Journeys of Body, Mind, and Spirit*. Berkeley: University of California Press.

Nguyen-Marshall, Van. 2024. "Nation-Building in South Vietnam After Geneva." In *The Cambridge History of the Vietnam War*, edited by Edward Miller and Lien-Hang T. Nguyen, 326–46. Cambridge: Cambridge University Press.

REFERENCES

Niemi, Maria, Huong T. Thanh, Tuan Tran, and Torkel Falkenberg. 2010. "Mental Health Priorities in Vietnam: A Mixed-Methods Analysis." *BMC Health Services Research* 10: 1–10. https://doi.org/10.1186/1472-6963-10-257.

Nolas, Sevasti-Melissa, Christos Varvantakis, and Vinnarasan Aruldoss. 2017. "Talking Politics in Everyday Family Lives." *Contemporary Social Science* 12: 68–83. https://doi.org/10.1080/21582041.2017.1330965.

Ó Briain, Lonán. 2021. *Voices of Vietnam: A Century of Radio, Red Music, and Revolution*. Oxford: Oxford University Press.

Olson, James S., and Randy W. Roberts. 2011. *Where the Domino Fell: America and Vietnam 1945-1995*. Malden, MA: Wiley.

Opper, Marc. 2019. *People's Wars in China, Malaya, and Vietnam*. Ann Arbor: University of Michigan Press.

Özerdem, Alpaslan, and Sukanya Podder. 2011. "Mapping Child Soldier Reintegration Outcomes: Exploring the Linkages." In *Child Soldiers: From Recruitment to Reintegration*, edited by Alpaslan Özerdem and Sukanya Podder, 309–23. Basingstoke, UK: Palgrave Macmillan.

Özerdem, Alpaslan, Sukanya Podder, and Eddie L. Quitoriano. 2010. "Identity, Ideology and Child Soldiering: Community and Youth Participation in Civil Conflict—A Study on the Moro Islamic Liberation Front in Mindanao, Philippines." *Civil Wars* 12 (3): 304–25. https://doi.org/10.1080/13698249.2010.509566.

Pape, Robert A. 1990. "Coercive Air Power in the Vietnam War." *International Security* 15 (2): 103–46. https://doi.org/10.2307/2538867.

Park, Mijung, and Catherine Chesla. 2007. "Revisiting Confucianism as a Conceptual Framework for Asian Family Study." *Journal of Family Nursing* 13 (3): 293–311. https://doi.org/10.1177/1074840707304400.

Parker, Evelyn L. 2001. "Hungry for Honor: Children in Violent Youth Gangs." *Interpretation* 55 (2): 148–60. https://doi.org/10.1177/002096430005500204.

Pauletto, Elettra, and Preeti Patel. 2010. "Challenging Child Soldier DDR Processes and Policies in the Eastern Democratic Republic of Congo." *Journal of Peace, Conflict and Development* 16: 35–57. https://www.icc-cpi.int/sites/default/files/RelatedRecords/CR2017_04717.PDF.

Pelzer, Kristin. 2015. "Love, War, and Revolution: Reflections on the Memoirs of Nguyen Thi Dinh." In *The Vietnam War: Vietnamese and American Perspectives*, edited by Jayne Werner and Luu Doan Huynh, 95–112. Oxon, UK: Routledge.

Peters, Krijn, and Paul Richards. 1998. "'Why We Fight': Voices of Youth Combatants in Sierra Leone." *Africa* 68 (2): 183–210. https://doi.org/10.2307/1161278.

Pham, Duy Nghia. 2005. "Confucianism and the Conception of the Law in Vietnam." In *Asian Socialism & Legal Change: The Dynamics of Vietnamese and Chinese Reform*, edited by John Gillespie and Pip Nicholson, 76–91. Canberra: ANU Press.

Pham, Mai. 2020. "Kháng Chiến Chống Mỹ Và "Mặt Trận" Đặc Biệt Của Ngành Giáo Dục" [The Resistance Against America and the Special "Battlefield" of the Education Sector]. Accessed September 17, 2023. https://thanhtra

.com.vn/xa-hoi/giao-duc/khang-chien-chong-my-va-mat-tran-dac-biet-cua-nganh-giao-duc-170569.html.

Pham, Quynh Phuong, and Chris Eipper. 2009. "Mothering and Fathering the Vietnamese: Religion, Gender, and National Identity." *Journal of Vietnamese Studies* 4: 49–83. https://doi.org/10.1525/vs.2009.4.1.49.

Pham, Thi Nhung. 2017. "Tình Cảm Của Bác Hồ Dành Cho Thiếu Niên, Nhi Đồng" [Uncle Ho's Love for Teenagers and Children]. Accessed September 17, 2023. https://www.xaydungdang.org.vn/tu-tuong-ho-chi-minh/tinh-cam-cua-bac-ho-danh-cho-thieu-nien-nhi-dong-10444.

Pham, Thi Thuy An. 2018. "Khắc Ghi Lời Bác Dạy Về Đoàn Kết, Thống Nhất Trong Quân Đội" [Remember the Teaching Uncle Ho Taught About Solidarity and Unity in the Army]. *UBND Phuong Hoa Thanh*, December 12. http://hoathanh.tanphu.hochiminhcity.gov.vn/hoc-tap-va-lam-theo-tu-tuong-dao-duc-phong-cach-ho-chi-minh/khac-ghi-loi-bac-day-ve-doan-ket-thong-nhat-trong-quan-doi-cmobile312-2671.aspx.

Pham, Thuan Duc, and Tran Minh Thuan. 2024. "The First Indochina War (1946–1954) and the Geneva Agreement (1954)." *Cogent Arts & Humanities* 11 (1): 1–10. https://doi.org/10.1080/2331.

Pham, T. Lan. 2021. "The Role of Confucianism in Sociopolitics of the Nguyen Dynasty in the First Half of the 19th Century." *Linguistics and Culture Review* 5: 2403–2412. https://doi.org/10.21744/lingcure.v5nS4.2003.

Pham, Van Bich. 1999. *The Vietnamese Family in Change: The Case of the Red River Delta*. Surrey, UK: Curzon.

Phan, Dai Doan. 2006. *Làng Việt Nam Đa Nguyên Và Chặt* [Villages in Vietnam: Plurality and Closeness]. Hanoi: Nhà Xuất Bản Đại Học Quốc Gia Hà Nội [Hanoi National University Publishing House].

Phan, Dang Thanh. 2008. "Trị "Kẻ Bất Hiếu" Ra Sao?" [How to Deal with Unfilial People?] *Nguoi Lao Dong*, November 26. tps://plo.vn/ban-doc/tri-ke-bat-hieu-ra-sao-255875.html.

Phan, Loan T. K. 2017. *The Impact of Vietnamese National Culture on the Effectiveness of Quality Management in Higher Education Institutions*. International Conference VNSEAMEO.

Phan, Ngoc. 2015. *Bản Sắc Văn Hóa Việt Nam* [Cultural Identity of Vietnam]. Ho Chi Minh City: Nhà Xuất Bản Văn Học [Literature Publishing House].

Phung, Quan. 2018 (1988). *Tuổi Thơ Dữ Dội* [Violent Childhood]. 19th ed. Hanoi: Kim Dong Publishing House.

Phuong, Phuong. 2021. "Tết Trung Thu—Đọc Lại Những Vần Thơ Của Bác Viết Cho Thiếu Nhi" [Mid-Autumn Festival—Rereading Uncle Ho's Poems Written for Children]. *Tạp Chí Mặt Trận* [Mat Tran Magazine], September 21. https://tapchimattran.vn/nhan-vat-su-kien/tet-trung-thu-doc-lai-nhung-van-tho-cua-bac-viet-cho-thieu-nhi-40962.html.

Phuong, Thanh. 2019. "Người Không Hát Tình Ca" Và Những Câu Chuyện Cảm Động Về Chiến Sĩ Trường Sơn" ["A Person Who Did Not Sing" and Touching Stories About Truong Son Soldiers]. Accessed March 23, 2022. http://www.thiduakhenthuongvn.org.vn/dien-hinh-tien-tien/nguoi-khong-hat-tinh-ca-va-nhung-cau-chuyen-cam-dong-ve-chien-si-truong-son.

Pike, Douglas. 1966. *Viet Cong: The Organization and Techniques of the National Liberation Front of South Vietnam*. Cambridge, MA: MIT Press.

Podder, Sukanya. 2011. "Neither Child nor Soldier: Contested Terrains in Identity, Victimcy, and Survival." In *Child Soldiers: From Recruitment to Reintegration*, edited by Alpaslan Özerdem and Sukanya Podder, 141–59. Basingstoke, UK: Palgrave Macmillan.

Podder, Sukanya. 2017. "Understanding the Legitimacy of Armed Groups: A Relational Perspective." *Small Wars & Insurgencies* 28: 686–708. https://doi.org/10.1080/09592318.2017.1322333.

Pokalova, Elena. 2019. *Returning Islamist Foreign Fighters: Threats and Challenges to the West*. London: Palgrave Macmillan.

Popkin, Samuel L. 1963. "The Myth of the Village: Revolution and Reaction in Viet Nam." PhD diss., Massachusetts Institute of Technology.

Power, Elaine M. 2004. "Toward Understanding in Postmodern Interview Analysis: Interpreting the Contradictory Remarks of a Research Participant." *Qualitative Health Research* 14 (6): 858–65. https://doi.org/10.1177/1049732304265935.

Prime Minister. 1978a. "Chỉ Thị Về Việc Tổ Chức Lực Lượng Thanh Niên Xung Phong Xây Dựng Kinh Tế Ở Các Tỉnh Và Thành Phố Miền Nam" [Directive on the Organization of the Youth Volunteers for the Economic Construction in the Southern Provinces and Cities]. Accessed March 23, 2022. https://thuvienphapluat.vn/van-ban/Van-hoa-Xa-hoi/Chi-thi-460-TTg-to-chuc-luc-luong-thanh-nien-xung-phong-xay-dung-kinh-te-tinh-thanh-pho-mien-Nam-17228.aspx.

Prime Minister. 1978b. "Thông Tư Về Việc Khen Thưởng Những Gia Đình Có Người Thân Thoát Ly Tham Gia Vào Hàng Ngũ Cách Mạng" [Circular About Rewarding Family with Emancipated Family Members Who Joined the Revolutionary Ranks]. Accessed March 23, 2022. https://thuvienphapluat.vn/van-ban/Van-hoa-Xa-hoi/Thong-tu-177-BT-khen-thuong-gia-dinh-co-nguoi-than-thoat-ly-tham-gia-hang-ngu-cach-mang-55137.aspx.

Prime Minister. 1980. "Chỉ Thị Về Việc Sắp Xếp Và Sử Dụng Quân Nhân Xuất Ngũ" [Directive About the Arrangement and Use of Discharged Military Personnel]. Accessed September 13, 2024. https://thuvienphapluat.vn/van-ban/Lao-dong-Tien-luong/Chi-thi-276-TTg-sap-xep-su-dung-quan-nhan-xuat-ngu-44260.aspx.

Pugel, James B. 2009. "Dissaggregating the Causal Factors Unique to Child Soldiering in Liberia." In *Child Soldiers in the Age of Fractured States*, edited by Scott Gates and Simon Reich, 160–82. Pittsburgh: University of Pittsburgh Press.

Quinn-Judge, Sophie. 2001. "Women in the Early Vietnamese Communist Movement: Sex, Lies, and Liberation." *South East Asia Research* 9: 245–69. https://doi.org/10.5367/000000001101297405.

Quynh, Uyen. 2019. "Trẻ Em Việt Nam Trong Khói Lửa Chiến Tranh" [Vietnamese Children in the Fire of War]. *Báo Lâm Đồng* [Lam Dong Newspaper], December 5. http://baolamdong.vn/hosotulieu/201912/tre-em-viet-nam-trong-khoi-lua-chien-tranh-2977204/index.htm.

REFERENCES

Race, Jeffrey. 2010. *War Comes to Long An: Revolutionary Conflict in a Vietnamese Province*. Berkeley: University of California Press.
Ralph, Hammond. 1967. "Quotations and Documents: Viet Cong Documents on the War (II)." *Communist Affairs* 5: 22–34. https://doi.org/10.1016/0588-8174(67)90043-5.
Ratelle, Jean-François. 2013. "Making Sense of Violence in Civil War: Challenging Academic Narratives Through Political Ethnography." *Critical Studies on Security* 1 (2): 159–73. https://doi.org/10.1080/21624887.2013.824654.
Reay, Diane. 2004. "'It's All Becoming a Habitus': Beyond the Habitual Use of Habitus in Educational Research." *British Journal of Sociology of Education* 25 (4): 431–44. https://doi.org/10.1080/0142569042000236934.
Reay, Diane, Gill Crozier, and John Clayton. 2009. "'Strangers in Paradise'? Working-Class Students in Elite Universities." *Sociology* 43 (6): 1103–21. https://doi.org/10.1177/0038038509345700.
Rosen, David M. 2005. *Armies of the Young: Child Soldiers in War and Terrorism*. New Brunswick, NJ: Rutgers University Press.
Rosen, David M. 2007. "Child Soldiers, International Humanitarian Law, and the Globalization of Childhood." *American Anthropologist* 109 (2): 296–306. https://doi.org/10.1525/aa.2007.109.2.296.
Rosenoff, Lara. 2010. "A Habitus of War and Displacement? Bourdieu's 'Third Way' and Rural Youth in Northern Uganda After Two Decades of War." *Nokoko* 1: 49–64. https://carleton.ca/africanstudies/wp-content/uploads/2010-Nokoko-1.pdf#page=57.
Rottman, Gordon L. 2007. *Viet Cong Fighter*. Oxford: Osprey.
Ruane, Kevin. 1998. *War and Revolution in Vietnam*. London: UCL Press.
Rydstrom, Helle. 2002. "Sexed Bodies, Gendered Bodies: Children and the Body in Vietnam." *Women's Studies International Forum* 25: 359–72. https://doi.org/10.1016/S0277-5395(02)00261-3.
Rydstrom, Helle. 2003. *Embodying Morality: Growing up in Rural Northern Vietnam*. Honolulu: University of Hawaii Press.
Rydstrom, Helle. 2006. "Masculinity and Punishment: Men's Upbringing of Boys in Rural Vietnam." *Childhood* 13: 329–48. https://doi.org/10.1177/0907568206066355.
Rydstrom, Helle. 2015. "Politics of Colonial Violence: Gendered Atrocities in French Occupied Vietnam." *European Journal of Women's Studies* 22 (2): 191–207. https://doi.org/10.1177/1350506814538860.
Sanín, Francisco Gutiérrez, and Elisabeth Jean Wood. 2014. "Ideology in Civil War: Instrumental Adoption and Beyond." *Journal of Peace Research* 51 (2): 213–26. https://doi.org/10.1177/0022343313514073.
SarDesai, Damodar R. 2019. *Vietnam: Past and Present*. New York: Routledge.
Schafer, John C. 2000. "The Collective and the Individual in Two Post-War Vietnamese Novels." *Crossroads: An Interdisciplinary Journal of Southeast Asian Studies* 14: 13–48. https://www.jstor.org/stable/pdf/40860735.pdf.
Schlichte, Klaus. 2014. "When 'the Facts' Become a Text: Reinterpreting War with Serbian War Veterans." *Revue de Synthèse* 135: 361–84. https://doi.org/10.1007/s11873-014-0262-y.

Schulzinger, Robert D. 1997. *A Time for War: The United States and Vietnam, 1941-1975*. Oxford: Oxford University Press.
Scott, James C. 1985. *Weapons of the Weak: Everyday Forms of Peasant Resistance*. New Haven, CT: Yale University Press.
Sewell, William H. 2004. "The Concept(s) of Culture." In *Practicing History*, edited by Gabrielle M. Spiegel, 76-95. London: Routledge.
Shah, Alpa. 2013. "The Intimacy of Insurgency: Beyond Coercion, Greed or Grievance in Maoist India." *Economy and Society* 42 (3): 480-506. https://doi.org/10.1080/03085147.2013.783662.
Shaplen, Robert. 1965. *The Lost Revolution: Vietnam 1945-1965*. London: Andre Deutsch.
Sheehan, Neil. 1971. "Should We Have War Crime Trials?" *New York Times*, March 28. https://www.nytimes.com/1971/03/28/archives/should-we-have-war-crime-trials-war-crime-trials.html.
Shepler, Susan. 2014. *Childhood Deployed: Remaking Child Soldiers in Sierra Leone*. New York: New York University Press.
Shohet, Merav. 2021. *Silence and Sacrifice: Family Stories of Care and the Limits of Love in Vietnam*. Oakland: University of California Press.
Short, Anthony. 2013. *The Origins of the Vietnam War*. Oxon, UK: Routledge.
Singer, Peter W. 2006. *Children at War*. Berkeley: University of California Press.
Slote, Walter H. 1998. "Destiny and Determination." In *Confucianism and the Family: A Study of Indo-Tibetan Scholasticism*, edited by Walter H. Slote and George A. De Vos, 311-29. New York: State University of New York Press.
Smith, David. 2012. "Congo Warlord Thomas Lubanga Convicted of Using Child Soldiers." *The Guardian*, March 14. https://www.theguardian.com/world/2012/mar/14/congo-thomas-lubanga-child-soldiers.
Smith, Ralph. 1971. *Viet Nam and the West*. Ithaca, NY: Cornell University Press.
Srichampa, Sophana. 2007. "Vietnamese Propaganda Reflections from 1945-2000." *Mon-Khmer Studies Journal* 37: 87-116.
Starry, Donn A. 2002. *Mounted Combat in Vietnam*. Washington, DC: Department of the Army.
Stur, Heather M. 2011. *Beyond Combat: Women and Gender in the Vietnam War Era*. Cambridge: Cambridge University Press.
Sturken, Marita. 1997. *Tangled Memories: The Vietnam War, the AIDS Epidemic, and the Politics of Remembering*. Berkeley: University of California Press.
Sutherland, Lee-Ann, and Ika Darnhofer. 2012. "Of Organic Farmers and 'Good Farmers': Changing Habitus in Rural England." *Journal of Rural Studies* 28: 232-40. https://doi.org/10.1016/j.jrurstud.2012.03.003.
Tabak, Jana. 2020. *The Child and the World: Child-Soldiers and the Claim for Progress*. Athens: University of Georgia Press.
Tam, Trang. 2020. "Những Bức Thư Cảm Động Bác Hồ Gửi Thiếu Niên, Nhi Đồng" [Touching Letters from Uncle Ho to Children and Youth]. Accessed September 11, 2024. https://www.bqllang.gov.vn/tin-tuc/tin-tong-hop/9561-nhung-buc-thu-cam-dong-bac-ho-gui-thieu-nien-nhi-dong.html.
Tanham, George K. 2006. *Communist Revolutionary Warfare: From the Vietminh to the Viet Cong*. Westport, CT: Greenwood.

Taylor, Keith W. 2010. "The Vietnamese Civil War of 1955–1975 in Historical Perspective." In *Triumph Revisited: Historians Battle for the Vietnam War*, edited by Andrew Wiest and Michael J. Doidge, 17–28. New York: Routledge.

Taylor, Keith W. 2013. *A History of the Vietnamese*. Cambridge: Cambridge University Press.

Taylor, Milton C. 1961. "South Viet-Nam: Lavish Aid, Limited Progress." *Pacific Affairs* 34 (3): 242–56. https://www.jstor.org/stable/2753362.

Taylor, Sandra C. 1999. *Vietnamese Women at War: Fighting for Ho Chi Minh and the Revolution*. Lawrence: University Press of Kansas.

Thai, Bao. 2020. "Công Tác Tư Tưởng Góp Phần Làm Nên Đại Thắng Mùa Xuân 1975" [Ideological Work Which Contributed to the Great Victory of Spring 1975]. Accessed September 23, 2023. https://tuyengiao.vn/nghien-cuu/cong-tac-tu-tuong-gop-phan-lam-nen-dai-thang-mua-xuan-1975-127776.

Than, Thanh Cong, and Chi Trung Bui. 2022. "The Aftermath of Toxic Chemicals from the Vietnam War." In *Overcoming Legacies of War in Vietnam*, 87–105. Hanoi: Thanh Nien Publishing House.

Thanh, Huyen. 2013. "Phong Trào Thi Đua Ái Quốc: Những Lời Bác Hồ Căn Dặn Thiếu Niên, Nhi Đồng" [Movement of Patriotism: Uncle Ho's Teachings to Children and Youth]. Accessed September 11, 2024. https://www.bqllang.gov.vn/tin-tuc/tin-tu-ban-quan-ly-lang/1314-phong-trao-thi-dua-ai-qu-c-nh-ng-l-i-bac-h-can-d-n-thi-u-nien-nhi-d-ng.html.

Thanh, Long. 2021. "Cựu Chiến Binh Gương Mẫu Đi Đầu" [Model Veterans Take the Lead]. *Báo Hải Dương* [Hai Duong Newspaper], September 1. http://baohaiduong.vn/lam-theo-guong-bac/cuu-chien-binh-guong-mau-di-dau-178329.

Thanh Nien. 2006. "Việc Gì Lợi Cho Dân Ta Phải Hết Sức Làm. Việc Gì Hại Đến Dân Ta Phải Hết Sức Tránh" [Whatever Is Beneficial for Our People Must Be Done with All Our Might. Anything That Harms Our People Must Be Avoided as Much as Possible]. *Thanh Nien*, May 18. https://thanhnien.vn/viec-gi-loi-cho-dan-ta-phai-het-suc-lam-viec-gi-hai-den-dan-ta-phai-het-suc-tranh-185209647.htm.

"Thơ Bác Hồ chúc Tết xuân Tân Sửu—1961" [Uncle Ho's Poem Wishing the New Year of the Ox—1961]. 2022. *Báo Điện Tử - Đảng Cộng Sản Việt Nam* [Vietnam Communist Party Newspaper], January 25. https://dangcongsan.vn/mung-dat-nuoc-doi-moi-mung-dang-quang-vinh-mung-xuan-nham-dan-2022/tho-xuan-cau-doi-tet/tho-bac-ho-chuc-tet-xuan-tan-suu-1961-602577.html.

Thomas, Lynn M. 2016. "Historicising Agency." *Gender and History* 28 (2): 324–39. https://doi.org/10.1111/1468-0424.12210.

Thomson, Andrew. 2020. "The Credible Commitment Problem and Multiple Armed Groups: FARC Perceptions of Insecurity During Disarmament in the Colombian Peace Process." *Conflict, Security & Development* 20 (4): 497–517. https://doi.org/10.1080/14678802.2020.1794139.

Thrift, Nigel. 1987. " 'Difficult Years': Ideology and Urbanization in South Vietnam, 1975–1986." *Urban Geography* 8: 420–39. https://doi.org/10.2747/0272-3638.8.5.420.

Thu, Hoai. 2021. "Tổng Kết Hội Liên Hiệp Phụ Nữ—Hội Cựu Chiến Binh Thị Trấn Chợ Chu Năm 2020" [Summary Cho Chu's Women's Association—Veteran's Association's

Activities in 2020]. Accessed March 23, 2022. http://dinhhoa.thainguyen
.gov.vn/tin-moi/-/asset_publisher/qae6RUchMAqw/content/tong-ket
-hoi-lien-hiep-phu-nu-hoi-cuu-chien-binh-thi-tran-cho-chu-nam-2020
/pop_up?_101_INSTANCE_qae6RUchMAqw_viewMode=print&_101
_INSTANCE_qae6RUchMAqw_languageId=vi_VN.

Tonnesson, Stein. 1993. "From Confucianism to Communism, and Back?" Paper presented in the working group The Political Uses of Culture and Religion at the Conference of the Norwegian Association of Development Studies, June 18–20.

Tønnesson, Stein. 2024. "The August Revolution of 1945." In *The Cambridge History of the Vietnam War*, edited by Edward Miller and Lien-Hang T. Nguyen, 106–24. Cambridge: Cambridge University Press.

Tovy, Tal. 2010. "Peasants and Revolutionary Movements: The Viet Cong as a Case Study." *War in History* 17 (2): 217–30. https://doi.org/10.1177/0968344509357125.

Trager, Frank N. 1966. "France and the Guerrilla War in Vietnam, 1945–1954." In *Isolating the Guerrilla: Classic and Basic Case Studies (Volume II)*, 47–91. Washington, DC: Historical Evaluation and Research Organization.

Tran, Van Chanh. 2012. "Những Bài Học Thuộc Lòng, Một Thứ Văn Chương Tiểu Học Của Miền Nam Trước Đây" [Texts for Learning by Heart, a Type of Literature for Primary Education in the South Before 1975]. *Tạp Chí Nghiên Cứu Và Phát Triển* [Journal of Research and Development] 6 (95): 105–25.

Tran, Van Doan. 2003. "Confucianism: Vietnam." In *Encyclopedia of Chinese Philosophy*, edited by Antonia S. Cua, 173–77. New York: Routledge.

Tran, Van Hai, Hong Chuong Pham, Viet Quang Ly, Thi Hang Le, Minh Truong Tran, and Van Tich Le. 2011. *Hồ Chí Minh Toàn tập - Tập 15* [Ho Chi Minh Complete Works—Volume 15]. Hanoi: Chính Trị Quốc Gia—Sự Thật [National Political Publishing House].

Tre Em Thoi Chien [Children at War]. 2017. 3rd ed. Hanoi: Kim Dong Publishing House.

Tucker-Jones, Anthony. 2014. *The Vietnam War: The Tet Offensive, 1968*. Barnsley, UK: Casemate.

Turner, Karen G. 2002. "'Vietnam' as a Women's War." In *A Companion to the Vietnam War*, edited by Marilyn B. Young and Robert Buzzanco, 93–113. Oxford: Blackwell.

Turse, Nick. 2013. *Kill Anything That Moves: The Real American War in Vietnam*. New York: Macmillan.

Tynes, Robert. 2018. *Tools of War, Tools of State: When Children Become Soldiers*. Albany: State University of New York Press.

Ugarriza, Juan E., and Matthew J. Craig. 2013. "The Relevance of Ideology to Contemporary Armed Conflicts: A Quantitative Analysis of Former Combatants in Colombia." *Journal of Conflict Resolution* 57 (3): 445–77. https://doi.org/10.1177/0022002712446131.

United Nations. 1973. *Agreement on Ending the War and Restoring Peace in Viet-Nam*. Signed June 13, 1973. United Nations Treaty Series, registration I. Nos. 13295–13302. https://treaties.un.org/doc/Publication/UNTS/Volume%20935/volume-935-I-13295-English.pdf.

Utas, Mats. 2011. "Victimcy as Social Navigation: From the Toolbox of Liberian Child Soldiers." In *Child Soldiers: From Recruitment to Reintegration*, edited by Alpaslan Özerdem and Sukanya Podder, 213–30. London: Palgrave Macmillan.

Van Eijck, Koen. 1999. "Socialization, Education, and Lifestyle: How Social Mobility Increases the Cultural Heterogeneity of Status Groups." *Poetics* 26 (5–6): 309–28. https://doi.org/10.1016/S0304-422X(99)00008-X.

Van, Thi Thanh Mai. 2019. "Di Huấn Hồ Chí Minh Về "Cần Kiệm Liêm Chính, Chí Công Vô Tư" [Ho Chi Minh Testament on "Need of Integrity, Fairness, and Impartiality"] Accessed September 23, 2024. https://tulieuvankien.dangcongsan.vn/c-mac-angghen-lenin-ho-chi-minh/ho-chi-minh/nghien-cuu-hoc-tap-tu-tuong/di-huan-ho-chi-minh-ve-can-kiem-liem-chinh-chi-cong-vo-tu-3485.

Van, Thi Thanh Mai. 2023. "Bản Tuyên Ngôn Của Tinh Thần Và Ý Chí Độc Lập, Tự Do" [Declaration of the Spirit and Will of Independence and Freedom]. *Báo Điện Tử Đảng Cộng Sản Việt Nam* [Communist Party of Vietnam Electronic Newspaper], August 21. https://dangcongsan.vn/tieu-diem/ban-tuyen-ngon-cua-tinh-than-va-y-chi-doc-lap-tu-do-645425.html.

Veale, Angela, and Aki Stavrou. 2007. "Former Lord's Resistance Army Child Soldier Abductees: Explorations of Identity in Reintegration and Reconciliation." *Peace and Conflict: Journal of Peace Psychology* 13 (3): 273–92. https://doi.org/10.1080/10781910701471306.

Velitchkova, Ana. 2021. "Institutionalized Behavior, Morality, and Domination: A Habitus in Action Model of Political Violence." *Journal for the Theory of Social Behaviour* 51 (1): 1–20. https://doi.org/10.1111/jtsb.12292.

Veterans' Association of Vietnam [Hội Cựu Chiến Binh Việt Nam], n.d. *Biên Niên Sự Kiện Hội Cựu Chiến Binh Việt Nam* [Chronicle of Events Vietnam Veterans Association]. Accessed January 26, 2025. https://hoiccbvietnam.vn/lich-su-truyen-thong-pa15.html.

Vo, Nguyen Giap. 2015. *People's War, People's Army: The Viet Cong Insurrection Manual for Underdeveloped Countries*. Potomac, MD: Pickle Partners.

Vo, Thi Cam Van. 2016. "Sự Du Nhập Và Ảnh Hưởng Của Nho Giáo Đến Giá Trị Truyền Thống Văn Hóa Việt Nam" [The Introduction and Influence of Confucianism on Vietnamese Cultural Traditional Values]. Accessed September 23, 2024. http://vanhoanghean.com.vn/component/k2/30-nhung-goc-nhin-van-hoa/11261-su-du-nhap-va-anh-huong-cua-nho-giao-den-gia-tri-truyen-thong-van-hoa-viet-nam.

Voicu, Malina, and Bogdan Voicu. 2009. "Volunteers and Volunteering in Central and Eastern Europe." *Sociologia* 41: 539–63.

Vu, Hong Lien, and Sharrock, Peter. 2014. *Descending Dragon, Rising Tiger: A History of Vietnam*. London: Reaktion.

Vu, Khieu. 2009. "Về Giá Trị Đương Đại Của Nho Giáo Việt Nam" [About Contemporary Values of Vietnamese Confucianism]. *Tạp Chí Triết Học* [Journal of Philosophy] 8 (219). http://philosophy.vass.gov.vn/triet-hoc-vietnam/Ve-gia-tri-duong-dai-cua-Nho-giao-Viet-Nam-70.0.html.

Vu, Tuong. 2009. "'To Be Patriotic Is to Build Socialism': Communist Ideology in Vietnam's Civil War." In *Dynamics of the Cold War in Asia: Ideology, Identity, and Culture*, edited by Tuong Vy and Wasana Wongsurawat, 33–52. New York: Palgrave Macmillan.

Vu, Tuong. 2017. *Vietnam's Communist Revolution: The Power and Limits of Ideology*. New York: Cambridge University Press.

Watson, Alison M. S. 2006. "Children and International Relations: A New Site of Knowledge?" *Review of International Studies* 32 (2): 237–50. https://doi.org/10.1017/S0260210506007005.

Watson, Alison M. S. 2008. "Can There Be a 'Kindered' Peace?" *Ethics & International Affairs* 22 (1): 35–42. https://doi.org/10.1111/j.1747-7093.2008.00128.x.

Watson, Alison M. S. 2015. "Resilience Is Its Own Resistance: The Place of Children in Post-Conflict Settlement." *Critical Studies on Security* 3 (1): 47–61. https://doi:10.1080/21624887.2015.1014687.

Weaver, Gina M. 2010. *Ideologies of Forgetting: Rape in the Vietnam War*. New York: State University of New York Press.

Wedeen, Lisa. 2002. "Conceptualizing Culture: Possibilities for Political Science." *American Political Science Review* 96 (4): 713–28. https://doi.org/10.1017/S0003055402000400.

Weiner, Bernard. 1967. "Review of Viet Cong: The Organization and Techniques of the National Liberation Front of South Vietnam, by D. Pike." *Western Political Quarterly* 20 (2): 505–7. https://doi.org/10.2307/445459.

Weinstein, Jeremy M. 2007. *Inside Rebellion: The Politics of Insurgent Violence*. Cambridge: Cambridge University Press.

Wessells, Michael G. 2019. "Do No Harm: How Reintegration Programmes for Former Child Soldiers Can Cause Unintended Harm." In *Research Handbook on Child Soldiers*, edited by Mark A. Drumbl and Jastine C. Barrett, 471–92. Cheltenham, UK: Edward Elgar.

Westheider, James. 2011. *Fighting in Vietnam: The Experiences of the US Soldier*. Mechanicsburg, PA: Stackpole.

Whitmore, John K. 1977. "Chiao-Chih and Neo-Confucianism: The Ming Attempt to Transform Vietnam." *Ming Studies* (1): 51–92. https://doi.org/10.1179/014703777788765553.

Wiest, Andrew. 2009. *The Vietnam War 1956–1975*. New York: Routledge.

Wiest, Andrew, and Chris McNab. 2016. *The Vietnam War*. New York: Cavendish Square Publishing.

Winther-Lindqvist, Ditte. 2009. "Game Playing: Negotiating Rules and Identities." *American Journal of Play* 2 (1): 60–84.

Wong, Martin R., and David Cook. 1992. "Shame and Its Contribution to PTSD." *Journal of Traumatic Stress* 5 (4): 557–62. https://doi.org/10.1002/jts.2490050405.

Wood, Reed M., and Jakana L. Thomas. 2017. "Women on the Frontline: Rebel Group Ideology and Women's Participation in Violent Rebellion." *Journal of Peace Research* 54: 31–46. https://doi.org/10.1177/0022343316675025.

Woodside, Alexander. 1984. "Medieval Vietnam and Cambodia: A Comparative Comment." *Journal of Southeast Asian Studies* 15: 315–19. https://doi.org/10.1017/S0022463400012558.

Wu, Zhongsheng, Rong Zhao, Xiulan Zhang, and Fengqin Liu. 2018. "The Impact of Social Capital on Volunteering and Giving: Evidence from Urban China." *Nonprofit and Voluntary Sector Quarterly* 47: 1201–22. https://doi.org/10.1177/0899764018784761.

Wyness, Michael. 2006. *Children and Society: An Introduction to the Sociology of Childhood*. Houndsmills, UK: Palgrave Macmillan.

Xuan, Sach. 2012 (1966). *Đội Thiếu Niên Du Kích Đình Bảng* [Children's Guerrilla Team of Dinh Bang]. 12th ed. Hanoi: Kim Dong Publishing House.

Yao, Xinzhong. 2000. *An Introduction to Confucianism*. Cambridge: Cambridge University Press.

Yinusa, Mohammed, Joseph Oluyemi, Salawu Bashiru, Raji Abdulateef, Emmanuel Atolagbe, and Joseph Adejoke. 2018. "The Family and National Development: How Can the Family Forestall Future Insurgency Activities in the Nigerian Society?" *Anthropological Researches and Studies* 1 (8): 232–44. https://www.ceeol.com/search/article-detail?id=666862.

Yu, In-Son. 1994. *Luật Và Xã Hội Việt Nam Thế Kỷ XVII—XVIII* [Law and Society in Seventeenth- and Eighteenth-Century Vietnam]. Hanoi: Nhà xuất bản Khoa Học Xã Hội [Sociology Publishing House].

Zack-Williams, Alfred B. 2001. "Child Soldiers in the Civil War in Sierra Leone." *Review of African Political Economy* 28 (87): 73–82. http://www.jstor.org/stable/4006694.

Zasloff, Joseph J. 1968. *Political Motivation of the Viet Cong: The Viet Minh Regroupees*. Santa Monica, CA: RAND.

Zheng, Haolan. 2021. "Childhood, Education, and Everyday Militarism in China Before and After 1949." In *Childhoods in Peace and Conflict*, edited by Marshall J. Beier and Jana Tabak, 103–23. Cham, Switzerland: Palgrave Macmillan.

Zyck, Stephen. 2011. " 'But I'm a Man': The Imposition of Childhood on and Denial of Identity and Economic Opportunity to Afghanistan's Child Soldiers." In *Child Soldiers: From Recruitment to Reintegration*, edited by Alpaslan Özerdem and Sukanya Podder, 159–72. Basingstoke, UK: Palgrave Macmillan.

Index

agency
  of children, 9, 10, 93–96, 97
  in Confucian society, 96
  as relational and contextual, 11, 167–70
  See also autonomy
Agent Orange, 34, 130
anticolonial movement, 23–24, 28, 161, 164, 172
autonomy
  of young recruits, 108–9, 111, 157–58, 162–64
  See also agency

Bao Dai, 26
Battle of Dien Bien Phu (1954), 27–28
benevolence, 45, 47, 50, 55
Ben Tre uprising (1960), 30–31
bombing raids, 106, 124
Bourdieu, Pierre
  defines field, 139
  on habitus, 11–12, 41, 68, 118–19
  on internalized ways of understanding and common sense, 42
  on language, 110
  on reasonableness of actors, 11, 43
  and reconceptualization of agency, 167–70
  on relationships, 81
  research framework of, 17
  on socialization, 68, 92, 110
Buddhism, 44–45

camaraderie, 116–17, 142–43, 150–53
chemical warfare, 33–34, 130
childhood
  assumptions regarding, 4
  in context of Vietnamese military struggle, 118
  cultural specificity of notion of, 6–7
  flexibility of Vietnamese terms for, 5–6
  militarization of, 64–66, 168–69

politicization of, 76–80, 84, 157, 171
  strategic navigation of stereotypes of, 124–27
  during Vietnam War, 61–66
  See also children and youth
children and youth
  agency of, 9, 10, 93–96, 97
  as political/social actors, 7–10, 170–71
  See also childhood; military service; recruitment
civilian life, return to. *See* postwar life
Cold War, 28–29
collectivism, 47–49, 59, 90–91, 137. *See also* community; individualism
colonization of Vietnam, 23–24, 25–28
communes, 133–34
communism
  and Cold War, 28–29
  convergence of Confucianism and, 57
community
  and youth mobilization, 96–97
  See also collectivism; villagers
Confucianism
  and agency, 96
  and childhood during Vietnam War, 61–62
  and duty as recruitment motivation, 80, 159–60
  as dynamic doctrine, 42–43
  history of, in Vietnam, 43–47
  manifestations of, in Vietnamese social practices, 47–52
co-ops, 131, 133, 147
criticism sessions, 100, 102, 112
Cu Chi, 71–72, 89–90
cultural systems, 42–43. *See also* Vietnam War, historical and social context of

danger, as recruitment motivation, 72–73
decolonization, 28. *See also* anticolonial movement

203

INDEX

domino theory, 28–29
duty, 49–50, 62–63, 80. *See also*
    righteousness

economy, postwar, 130–32, 139–40, 147, 158
education, political, 77, 86–87, 100–101, 157–58
Emirbayer, Mustafa, 11
employment, following war, 134–35, 141, 144, 145, 148–49, 153
equality/equal treatment, 109–10, 117, 163–64, 170
exploitation
    of peasants, 89–90
    and recruitment motivation, 78, 79–80

face-saving, 48–49, 57, 100, 102, 112, 161–62
family
    as factor influencing mobilization, 82–83, 157, 159
    postwar honors for, 136
    and socialization of recruits, 101, 102–3, 150
    young revolutionaries welcomed back into, 138–39
    See also filial piety
famine, 26
field
    habitus and, 12, 146
    navigating new, 139
    and reconceptualization of agency, 167–68
filial piety, 50–52, 56–59, 62–63, 159–61, 165–66. *See also* family
First Indochina War (1946–1954), 26–27, 49
France, and colonization of Vietnam, 23–24, 25–28
freedom, in Confucian society, 52

gender
    and hierarchy, 112–17
    See also women
Geneva Accords, 28, 30, 36
Government of Vietnam (GVN), 35, 59–60, 71, 73–74, 122–23
Gulf of Tonkin incident (1964), 32

habitus, 11–12, 68, 118–19, 145–53, 155, 166, 167–68
hamlet program, 31–32
hardships
    faced in military service, 105–7
    of postwar life, 139–43
hierarchies, 110–12, 117–18, 163–64. *See also* power relations
Ho Chi Minh
    and establishment of Viet Minh, 25
    letters to children and youth, 85–86
    on mass mobilization, 39–40
    as "national father," 57
    teachings of, 64
honor, 48–49, 57, 100, 112, 161–62
hunger, 105–6

ideology
    loyalty to, 146–47
    See also communism; political ideology
individualism, 49, 62, 142–43. *See also* collectivism
Islamic State of Iraq and Syria (ISIS), 9–10

joking, 123–24

labor, 106–7
language, and reinforcement of hierarchy, 110–11, 163
Le dynasty, 45–46, 51, 62
local guerrilla units (*du kich dia phuong*), 103–4
loss
    exposure to, 107
    trauma from, 152–53
"loss of face," 48–49, 57, 100, 102, 112, 161–62
loyalty
    to ideological goals, 146–47
    to village, 54
    See also filial piety

Maoist groups, 110
Marxism, 39
mass mobilization, 39–40
memory, 16–17
menstruation, 115
militarization of everyday life, 83–84
military service, 98, 127–28
    hierarchies and power relations in, 108–27
    training and work, 99–108
    See also recruitment
military training, 99–108, 157–58

mischief, 123–24
mobilization. *See* recruitment
morale, 102, 113, 124, 164–65
My Lai massacre, 34

National Liberation Front (NLF)
  in context of anticolonial struggle, 23–24
  establishment and structure of, 35–38
  ideology of, 38–40
  recruits' perspectives on Vietnam War, 24
  sheltering and first encounters with, 138
  and transformation of societal practices in mid-twentieth-century, 54–55, 60–61
Ngo Dinh Diem, 30, 32
Nguyen dynasty, 46, 51
Nguyen Thi Dinh, 113–14

Operation Rolling Thunder, 32–33

peasants
  and Confucianism, 45, 54
  and co-ops, 133
  economic hardship of, 25
  exploitation of, 89–90
  and recruitment processes, 69, 87–88
  revolutionaries as integrated with, 154
  and strategic hamlet program, 31–32
  See also villagers
physical labor, 106–7
political education, 77, 100–101, 157–58
political ideology
  interaction of social practices and, 164–67
  of National Liberation Front (NLF), 38–40
  of Viet Minh, 38
  See also communism
politicization of childhood, 76–80, 84, 157, 171
postwar life, 129–30, 153–55, 158
  coping in, 143–45
  hardships of, 139–43, 145–53
  perception of young revolutionaries, 136–39
  privilege of former revolutionaries, 132–35, 140–41, 143–45, 158, 170
  transition to, 132
poverty, 8, 25, 39, 132

power relations, 108–27
  and bypassing rules, 123–24
  and children's and youth's navigation of social context, 118–23
  and complex navigation of equality and hierarchy, 117–18
  and gendered structural constraints, 112–17
privilege, of former revolutionaries, 132–35, 140–41, 143–45, 158, 170
problem-solving, 122–23
pronouns, 110–11, 163

rear support, 104–5
recruitment, 68–69, 96–97
  and children's and youth's appropriation and negotiation of social norms, 92–96
  factors influencing decisions regarding, 81–92, 158, 159–67
  motivations for, 72–76
  and politicization of childhood, 76–80
  processes for, 69–72
  selectivity in, 175n2
  as voluntary, 80–81, 157
  of women, 91–92
  See also military service
reputation, 48–49, 57, 100, 102, 112, 161–62
resilience, 8, 145, 149, 154, 155
righteousness, 49–50, 55. *See also* duty
rules, bypassing, 123–24

salt, lack of, 106
sexual violence, 34, 113, 114, 115
sheltering guerillas, 39, 85, 89–90, 92–93, 122, 136, 138
socialization, 101–3, 150, 155
social justice, 78, 79–80
social networks, 142–43, 150–53, 158
social norms
  children's and youth's navigation of, 118–19
  Confucianism and maintenance of, 48
  interaction of political ideology with, 164–67
  recruitment and negotiation of, 92–96, 161–62
  reinforcement of, 119–23
songs, and raising morale and cultivating patriotism, 102, 103, 120, 124

INDEX

Soviet Union, 10, 29, 166
strategic hamlet program, 31-32

teachers, and politicization of education, 87
Tet Offensive, 34
"Three Responsibilities" campaign, 91
thriftiness, 56
tradition, as factor influencing mobilization, 82-83
training, 99-108, 157-58
tuyen truyen, 74-76, 81, 84, 120, 160

United States
  and Cold War, 28-29
  and First Indochina War, 26-27
  impact on struggles between guerillas and, on villages, 59-60
  involvement in Vietnam, 23, 31-32
  and surveillance and oppression of Ngo Dinh Diem's opponents, 30
  use of chemical warfare, 33-34
  and Vietnamization of conflict, 34-35
  young revolutionaries' interactions with American soldiers, 124-27

Veterans' Association, 150-51
victimization, refusal of, 129, 143-45, 154-55
Viet Minh, 23-24, 25-28, 38, 55-61, 65, 85
Vietnamization, 34-35
Vietnam War
  impact of, 130
  postwar context of, 130-39
  timeline of, 30-35
Vietnam War, historical and social context of, 41-43, 66-67
  childhood in Vietnam, 61-66
  history of Confucianism in Vietnam, 43-47
  manifestations of Confucianism in Vietnamese social practices, 47-52
  postwar context, 130-39
  transformation of societal practices in mid-twentieth-century, 54-61
  villages as units of society, 52-54
villagers
  give support to guerillas, 39-40, 85, 89-90, 92-93, 122, 136, 138
  NLF operations' reliance on, 39-40
  relationship between resistance forces and, 137-38
  See also peasants
villages
  and childhood during Vietnam War, 62
  and historical and social context of Vietnam War, 52-54
  and transformation of societal practices in mid-twentieth-century, 59
violence
  exposure to, 107-8
  as factor influencing mobilization, 72-74, 83-84
  structural, against women, 115
  trauma from, 152-53
  See also sexual violence
Vo, Nguyen Giap, 55, 103
voluntarism, 80-81, 90-91, 97, 157.
  See also recruitment

wartime skills and experience, transferred to everyday postwar life, 148-50
water, lack of, 115, 116
women
  camaraderie among, 116-17
  recruitment of, 91-92
  structural violence against, 115
  See also gender
Women's Association, 65, 151

Youth Shock Brigades (Thanh Nien Xung Phong), 6, 14, 104-9, 134-35, 140-41, 151

www.ingramcontent.com/pod-product-compliance
Lightning Source LLC
Chambersburg PA
CBHW031401230426
43670CB00006B/605